DEATH MARCH THROUGH RUSSIA

This book is dedicated to all those prisoners of war who suffered the agonies of sickness, hunger, exhaustion and freezing temperatures in Stalin's empire.

Contents

Translator's Note

It was a delicate task to translate *Death March*, written in the first person and as the personal memoir of Lothar Herrmann, a German prisoner of war of the Russians during and after World War II. The original German-language edition was in fact ghost-written by a journalist, Klaus Willmann, who interviewed Herrmann over a series of meetings half a century after Herrmann had returned from the *gulag*. From this perspective it is a memoir once-removed, but it very much demanded Lothar's own voice to resonate as principal narrator.

Thankfully, Klaus Willmann is a sensitive, honest and sharp listener who approached this undertaking with enormous integrity and thus provided a text which allowed me as translator to hear the protagonist's own account, to establish an immediate rapport with him and in turn to offer the reader what I hope is the feeling of a direct and authentic narrative.

Invariably, through the passage of time, memories become obscured, pain is dulled and anger mitigated, with survivors of trauma thus often leaving us with little more than silence. Whilst the deprivations and cruelty suffered in the Russian camps can surely never be adequately expressed, neither in the original language nor in translation, the challenge remains: how to convey these experiences to the readership? How to allow an emotional bond to develop between the younger generation and the past, a past which begs to be understood? How is one to impart something for which no vocabulary exists? While trying my absolute best to allow the suffering of Herrmann and his fellow men to echo in the account, I was frequently reduced to using a phrase such as 'indescribable stench'.

Herrmann did not grow up in a milieu that appreciated profound discussion or deeper political thought. Hence, he offers many short sentences and logbook-like accounts; and whilst the reader might wish for more, it would invalidate Herrmann's testimony had either the author or myself moved beyond the language he used.

Though not 'men of letters', Herrmann and his friends coped with their life experiences with a sense of wry, deprecating humour and irony, rather typical of the young men who grew up in those parts of Germany and Austria, but perhaps somewhat foreign-sounding to British people, who would instead have shown the traditional 'stiff upper lip', unwilling or unable to turn those difficult emotions into words when faced with adversity.

I have referred to towns and cities by their usual names in German before 1945 but to avoid confusion have included the modern equivalents in notes whenever possible. Military and similar ranks (including those created by the Nazi regime for the SS and so on) are translated from the German to their nearest equivalent in the British services. A few well-known German terms like *Führer* (for Hitler) have been retained.

Eva Burke

Foreword

Around 3 million German soldiers became prisoners of the Soviet Union during and after the Second World War. As *woina pleni* (prisoners of war), they were paraded, abused and forced to work in Stalin's vast network of camps, payback for the horrors that they had unleashed upon the Soviet people during Hitler's war. By the time that the last of these prisoners were repatriated – in 1956, more than a decade after the end of the war – as many as a third of them, some 1 million individuals, are estimated to have perished; victims of maltreatment, malnutrition and disease.

Yet, despite their numbers, German former prisoners of war were scarcely commemorated, let alone written about. They were largely ignored, as embarrassing, painful reminders of the lost war, of the Nazi regime, and of all those soldiers who did not return from the front. Moreover, Germany's post-war narrative quickly developed into one dominated by an overwhelming sense of its own guilt: of shame for the Holocaust, for its military aggressions and transgressions, and for its own brutal treatment of enemy prisoners and civilians.

There was little room in that dark world for an objective treatment of the fate of Germany's former prisoners, or indeed for anything that portrayed the Germans themselves in any way as victims.

All of which should serve to explain why Lothar Herrmann's memoir is so necessary. Born in humble circumstances in Breslau (now Wrocław in Poland) and apprenticed as a painter, he lived an uneventful and largely unpolitical youth before being conscripted into a Wehrmacht mountain division in 1940. He then participated in the invasion of the USSR in the summer of 1941, alongside

Germany's Romanian allies, ending the operation at Odessa on the Black Sea coast.

Though interesting in its own right, Herrmann's military career is passed over swiftly, and most of the book covers the period after his capture, itself a wildly dramatic episode in the autumn of 1944, when his unit was left stranded after the Romanian troops alongside whom he was conducting a fighting retreat switched sides with the fall of the Romanian leader General Antonescu. After a desperate race to reach the safety of German lines, with the advancing Red Army hard on their heels, he and his fellows became prisoners, initially of the Romanians, and then of the Soviets, and – almost inevitably – were packed into cattle trucks for the long journey eastward to an unknown fate.

Herrmann's experiences as a POW in the Soviet Union were searing, characterised by casual brutality, maltreatment and the ever-present threat of disease. The contempt of his Soviet guards was palpable. As Hermann lamented, 'We were no longer human beings. We were nothings.'

Already by the end of the war, Herrmann reckoned, less than a year after his capture, only a third of his original cohort of prisoners were still alive. The remainder had fallen victim to dysentery and malnutrition.

But Herrmann was fortunate. Put to work in a succession of *kholkhoz* collective farms and then in a car factory, a bread factory and in the kitchen of a *gulag* camp, he was determined throughout to survive his ordeal, and benefited from being able to use his skills as a painter and decorator to good effect, thereby often avoiding the most onerous – and deadly – work details.

The Soviet Union that Herrmann describes is one that will be familiar to many. It was a world, he wrote, where 'melancholia and indifference, empathy and cruelty' lived side by side. A world of occasional individual kindnesses, perhaps, but also one of pettifogging bureaucracy, of stultifying paranoia and – for the prisoners, at least – an all-pervading fear of being sent to 'Siberia', code for a forgotten death in distant parts.

Notwithstanding his own comparative good fortune, Herrmann even attempted to escape, absconding from a decorating job in eastern Ukraine and enjoying a few brief days of freedom before being recaptured by Soviet militiamen. Though he avoided Siberia, he nonetheless found himself sent to central Kazakhstan – 1,000 miles further east than the high-water mark reached during the war by his compatriots – in a camp amongst Latvians, Lithuanians, Japanese, Koreans, even Spaniards of the former 'Blue Division': the assorted human detritus of war and occupation.

For men such as Herrmann, freedom, when it came, was bitter-sweet. Of course, the relief of being released from Soviet hard labour was overwhelming, but for many of the prisoners, it was tinged with a fear of what would greet them back home. For some, their former homes – in Pomerania, East Prussia, Silesia or the Sudetenland – were no longer German territory, and they would return to one of the new Germanies as refugees. For others, release meant finally confronting the horrors, bitterness and destruction that the war had unleashed. Herrmann recalled, for instance, how their train was pelted with stones by a hostile crowd, as they passed westward through Poland.

It is experiences such as these that make Herrmann's memoir such a remarkable document, yet – pleasingly – it is a story that is as well-written as it is eventful. Penned by Klaus Willmann, following interviews with Herrmann himself, it is lively, engaging and full of vignettes and episodes – such as Herrmann's capture by the Soviets – that are so well-drawn as to be almost cinematic in nature.

As such, it is a powerful reminder of a chapter of modern history that rarely receives the attention it deserves. For drama and human interest alone, the fate of the countless thousands of German prisoners of war, who were shipped into the wild expanses of the Soviet Union to atone through their labour for their country's brutal invasion, would rank as one of the most important episodes of the war and its aftermath. Yet, beyond a narrow circle of specialists, it is routinely ignored. It remains to be seen whether this narrative is one that will develop, or find an echo and a favourable audience, but Lothar Herrmann's story is certainly remarkable and fully deserves to be read.

Roger Moorhouse
2019

Preface

An article in the *Münchner Merkur* of 22 June 2016 entitled 'Suddenly our world collapsed' led me to Lothar Herrmann in Garmisch-Partenkirchen.

Already at our first meeting he wanted to impress on me how comforted he felt by the thought that the youth of today were able to live in peace.

> They should never have to experience the school of hard knocks which I and so many of my contemporaries had to experience. But let me also point out that those who don't have any idea about the past or what it entailed will certainly be unable to understand the present. Whilst neither our politicians of today nor our younger generation have themselves experienced war, we can only hope that we can rely on them to safeguard the prosperity which our society is able to enjoy now, and which we've fought so hard to achieve after the war. Seeing as I am probably one of the last witnesses of that era, it is yet another reason why I'm so keen to try and preserve the memory of my wartime experiences for posterity.

Having been credited as author of *U-188: A German Submariner's Account of the War at Sea, 1941–1945,*[*] I decided to follow the same route with *Death March Through Russia* and thus assumed authorship for this book as well. So, whilst this book also appears under my name and is narrated in the first person, the

---

[*] Klaus Willmann/Anton Staller, *U-188: A German Submariner's Account of the War at Sea, 1941–1945*, Pen & Sword, 2015.

story and memories are those of Lothar Herrmann, as he described them to me in our many meetings. Why did I go down that route? After giving the issue much thought, I remain convinced that this is most certainly the better way of transmitting to our readers the message of how the dictators of all the states involved in that war condemned their young people to misery and death, without a care in the world, ruthlessly and without ever offering any definition of what they considered just or unjust.

Klaus Willmann

CHAPTER 1

Apprentice and Journeyman

I came into this world on 24 September 1920 in Breslau.* At that time the city was considered to be the Venice of the German east, and I enjoyed a modest, but carefree childhood. My father was a master decorator who also pursued a sideline career painting ornamental features of churches and, on top of that, and together with my mother, he managed a bar in the Old City of Breslau. Seeing as I was an only child, I was on my own at home. But outside, in the narrow lanes around the Dominikaner Platz where there wasn't yet as much traffic as there is today, it was a different story. There, I would run around with other children of my neighbourhood and have a lot of fun playing cops and robbers, or screaming and yelling whilst pretending we were in the Wild West.

The primary school I attended was on Taschenstrasse in the so-called Kanonenhof, and my first day was 1 April 1926. Just a year later, my childhood, which had until then been a happy and untroubled one, was overshadowed by a dark cloud: my parents decided to divorce and this was a deep shock for me, especially since there were so few divorces at the time. This was the reason I was put into the care of my grandmother who, as a strict Catholic, was insistent I attend church services regularly. When my father got custody of me later on, I was much relieved to be able to return to my old school. Sadly, my father was never able to find a suitable partner to marry, someone who could have become a warm stepmother to me.

---

* Now Wrocław, in Poland.

During the following years, my school holidays were spent in the countryside with farmers my father knew. For me it was an ideal opportunity to get to know all that nature had to offer, along with the animals, large and small, and I grew to love them. After I had successfully finished my schooling on 7 May 1934, I managed to find a permanent home for myself. My father knew of a master decorator in Waldtal, a small village some twenty-five kilometres outside the city, who was happy to take me into his home and take me on as his apprentice. Even today I thank my lucky stars for this fortunate turn in my life.

It was a day like any other when, during my second year of this apprenticeship, I was approached by the *Fähnleinführer* (local leader) of the Hitler Youth, who introduced himself as Fritz: 'Look here, Lothar! Even though you've got to work during the day, why don't you join us in the evenings? Surely you've heard about us. We organise exciting cross-country games and our social events are great fun . . .' He was trying to convince me that I was the ideal member and had obviously done his homework.

He continued: 'Why, isn't it true that you're learning how to do decorative painting? You could help us when we do our craft sessions and put together our aeroplane, tank and ship models! Surely this kind of stuff interests you as well. Why on earth would you want to spend all your time with those Kolping brothers* or that kind of silly stuff? Such nonsense isn't of any use to our *Führer*. Quite honestly, such associations shouldn't even exist any more!'

'Sure, Fritz, but oftentimes I have to work longer hours. But if I should get off early one of these days, you can certainly count me in,' I responded.

When I came home to Master Reinhold Schindler, his wife happened to be in the corridor and I immediately broached the subject: 'Frau Schindler, if I have the time to spare, I would very

---

* A reference to the *Gesellenvereine* or 'Journeymen's Unions', Roman Catholic organisations for young working men.

much like to spend my free evenings with the Hitler Youth. They asked me whether I would like to join as a new member!'

Up until then, the mistress of the house had always been friendly towards me, constantly looking after my physical well-being. But on hearing what I intended to sign up for, she became quite angry and, as she was by nature a no-nonsense and resolute woman, she did not hold back.

'What's this I'm hearing? Now listen to me – I want you to forget about this at once. Do you really want to spend the whole evening shouting your lungs out, or getting into fistfights, or hanging about somewhere with mates you think are like-minded? Lothar, you've got another think coming, you have! No, Lothar, absolutely not! What you will be doing when you've finished work is going to bed in the evening at a reasonable time so that the next day you'll get up fresh and alert. Have I made myself clear?'

What could I do but nod in agreement. Indeed, the law forcing all young Germans to become members of the Hitler Youth or League of German Girls only came into force later on, in 1939. That was the reason I had to go back to Fritz, somewhat with my tail between my legs, and meekly withdraw my earlier agreement to join. Deep down I felt regret, but then decided to turn my disappointment around and put in more effort and commitment to my further professional development.

During the course of that year I was sadly to experience yet a further blow when my father died unexpectedly. Since my mother no longer wished (or perhaps wasn't able to have) any contact with me, I was thus left to my own devices; Master Schindler gradually became something of a substitute parent for me and the small village of Waldtal my new home. My master was invariably friendly towards me, even paternal on some level, but at the same time he was uncompromising and demanding in his approach and quite strict.

I was a fast learner and quickly perfected the task of repainting old farmhouse kitchens and refurbishing rooms in nearby castles and mansions, and became proficient in the decoration of wall ornaments. In the run-up to the annual Christmas celebrations, one of my main duties was to give rocking chairs or other toys a new coat of paint or lacquer, something, as it turned out, that would hold me in good stead in the following years when I was asked to design signs and placards. I developed quite a talent and artistic eye, which came in handy when I had to choose the right fonts and colours.

Such was our reputation for these kinds of jobs that during my apprenticeship there wasn't a dance hall in town that wouldn't accept our offer to have us paint their walls. Even then my master's workshop could only cope with the number of orders he received by employing two drivers, as our customers would often be located at quite a distance from Waldtal

It so happened that my birthday fell on the same day as my master's, and, having become friendly with one another, we usually had a celebratory drink together at the local bar. In truth, it wasn't by any means the only evening that we went for a beer or two after work. Much to the chagrin of his staunch wife, who kept her husband on a short leash, such pit stops were frequent, and she also worried about his safety. The master would therefore ask me to take the steering wheel of his Opel P4 on our way home. He trusted me, though I was only his apprentice and didn't have a licence, and nothing untoward ever happened.

Even though I was occupied from morning to night and felt quite content, and whilst for me that period was linked with many unforgettable and lovely memories, I always planned to go travelling after I had completed my apprenticeship. The wish to learn new things and get to see different places grew steadily, and for that reason I eventually decided to continue my journeyman years somewhere else.

I left the town I had become so very fond of on 4 January 1939. Only a few days later, fate, or rather the weather – we suffered a bitterly cold winter that year – played a trick on me, and it wasn't a pleasant one in the slightest. A doctor diagnosed bronchial asthma and sent me off to recuperate in a spa in Oberschreiberhau,* up in the Giant Mountains. It was the first occasion when I spent any length of time in a mountainous region, and whilst resting and recovering I started reading a lot about the forthcoming Winter Olympics, which were due to take place in 1940 in Garmisch-Partenkirchen. A strong desire to be part of this world-renowned event took hold of me. Lothar, I said to myself, just as soon as you're feeling better, you have to find employment in your line of work in Garmisch-Partenkirchen for when the Winter Olympics are on.

It has never been in my nature to just sit back and rest, so even during my time in Oberschreiberhau and whilst trying to recuperate I did everything I could to find some work. I didn't set myself unreasonable goals and was quite prepared to get even a short-term job in the village, to make a bit of money which would help me towards realising my dreams. But all my efforts were in vain, and so I ended up having to move elsewhere with more job opportunities.

Eventually I found some work at the Dömitz Fortress, situated along the Elbe. At the time the place was known for its construction of underground armament and ammunition plants, employing so many people that several workers' housing estates† had to be built. Frankly, the work there was all monotonous and didn't excite me in the least, and seeing as I was an adventurous chap who was thirsty to master new skills and to travel, I quickly switched jobs and found employment in Arnsdorf in Saxony. I was able to get a short-term assignment helping refurbish the psychiatric clinic.

On a Sunday, visiting nearby Dresden, I met a young and energetic master decorator who, without much fuss and checking on my past experience, offered me some work and lodging. His name was Willi Lutter, and I didn't hesitate to accept his terms. From day one, we both felt that this would turn into an enduring and honest friendship, and it helped that he himself had been a

---

* Now Szklarska Poręba, in Poland.
† After the war began these developed into forced labour camps.

travelling journeyman in his apprenticeship only a few years beforehand.

Together with my employer I got to know the Vogelwiese festival in Dresden. We went on bicycle tours together and explored the Elbe valley which, extending for some 20 kilometres, reached as far as the Sudetenland.

All this only made me more determined in my desire to see the world and never will I forget my master's words which supported me throughout my life: 'Lothar, those who don't make it their mission to get to know as many places and workshops as possible, will never amount to anything, least of all an experienced master. If you feel that the day has come that you have learnt from me all I have to teach and show you, then all you need to do is move on to the next place. If you want, I'm happy to refer you and put in a good word on your behalf with my own previous master who lives at the Timmendorfer Strand, way up there on the Baltic. Now that's a workshop where I was able to really improve my skills and build up my experience. Why, you can always go to Garmisch at a later point – but then, when you do, you'll have more professional know-how under your belt than you have now.'

Willi Lutter was right. After hesitating for a while, I decided to follow his suggestion, even though I never quite gave up on my original idea to be part of the forthcoming Winter Olympic Games.

It thus came to pass that I packed my rucksack on the last day of July 1939, grateful that my then employer was walking with me to the outskirts of the town. He had obviously been very pleased with my work, as demonstrated in his wonderful recommendation letter which I added to my folder of papers. He took his leave at the last bus stop right at the edge of town, shook my hand vigorously and wished me godspeed for the rest of my journey. His previous vague and rather allusive comments concerning his worries about peace in Europe being in danger went in one ear and out the other, what with me being a young and carefree lad who could only think about himself.

Whilst Willi Lutter immediately boarded the bus to return to his town, I had only walked on foot for a few kilometres when I hitched a ride with a gentleman from Berlin, who was travelling on his own and seemed friendly enough. I reached Potsdam quite early on that same evening and got a place to stay overnight in the local youth hostel. Just before drifting off to sleep, abandoning myself to the world of dreams, I still remember thinking: 'Well, that was a breeze. If things continue to go this smoothly, I'll reach my goal well before Willi Lutter or I would have expected.'

I got up the next morning and decided that a visit to Frederick the Great's Sanssouci Palace would by no means be considered a waste of my time. During the guided tour I got into a discussion with a young biker and he voluntarily offered to take me as a pillion passenger all the way to Flensburg. This was an opportunity to get a glimpse of Travemünde, the so-called 'Holstein-Switzerland' area, Kiel and Eckernförde, if only fleetingly and in passing. At the end of our trip, somewhat stiff from the ride, I dismounted from the bike in Flensburg, thanked the driver, whom I barely knew, for his kind offer to help me out, and once again had to make some decisions.

Seeing as I was now in Flensburg, I naturally wanted to explore the city with its picturesque harbour front. But, of course, I knew full well that I had an appointment with my new employer and master at the Timmensdorfer Strand, which I still had to get to somehow. Standing at the roadside, on the lookout for a free ride to reach my destination, I finally got lucky and managed to get myself to Schleswig that very evening and, once again, was fortunate that the youth hostel had a vacancy.

Anyone familiar with one of those useful overnight places for young travellers knows the routine: you take your shoes off, store them away, and go to your assigned quarters. You must observe all the rules, and leave your bed the same way as you would have wished it to be upon your arrival. Nothing in this hostel was new or unexpected as far as I was concerned, but there was one thing that did surprise me, and that was the splendid view from the open bedroom window at sunrise. What a marvellous sight greeted me that early morning, looking across the riverbank of the Schlei. That was a novelty.

'I thank you Herr Lutter, you really gave me good advice,' I thought to myself.

Immediately after breakfast I packed my belongings and headed down to the riverbank, once again needing to hitch a ride. It seemed that other travellers in that region could also recognise the look of a journeyman, and obviously considered me trustworthy, as I never had to wait long for a driver to let me hop into his car. When I was only a few kilometres away from my destination, a Tempo three-wheeler stopped and offered me a lift. It only took me a few minutes to find out that he was the master stove builder of the Timmendorfer Strand. Obviously up here, like everywhere, all master craftsmen knew each other, and so the dear old man drove me right up to the door of my future boss.

When I entered his office, Master Steger was very welcoming. 'Well, if that isn't the highly recommended man from Silesia' he said, whilst measuring me up. When he realised that I had pulled out my documents in order to hand these to him, he waved his hand to decline my intentions. 'No need to bother, Herr Hermann. Up until now I've only had the best experiences with apprentices from Silesia, and I wouldn't expect it to be any different with your good self.'

Of course he noticed that I blushed in embarrassment, but I couldn't help but feel a joy and pride surging up inside me on hearing his words. He then returned to his desk to sit down again and all I could hear was a gurgling laugh rising from his large chest. All of a sudden he turned serious.

'Herr Herrmann, you will take your lodgings right here, one floor up from the workshop, and this means free accommodation plus meals for you. The boarding house is managed by the Missus. You'll be living and working together with two other apprentices, one chap from the Vogtland, another one from Denmark and two chaps from Upper Silesia. I am, of course, hoping that you'll all get along. Now get yourself going, see yourself to the reception which is . . . my wife. She'll show you to your quarters. Naturally, you'll not live as comfortably as our other paying guests, but I haven't had any complaints yet.'

I was already about to close the door behind me when I heard him shout, 'Oh, and make sure not to let the others convince you to go out too much. You all have turn up to work on time, that goes without saying, even if you've spent the night enjoying lots of wine and pretty girls in some dance hall until the early hours of the morning. But bear in mind, your agreed hourly pay is 91 *Pfennig* and not a single *Pfennig* more. I'm not one to pay for missed hours. The cheapest entertainments here are the municipal concerts. So, keep this in mind and off you go!'

Quite honestly, I felt that this last piece of advice wasn't necessary, and I just nodded and smiled. To me, everything pointed to the real possibility that I would stay put and that Garmisch simply had to wait.

It didn't take more than a few days for me to get used to everything. My new lodgings, the jobs, my schedule and work conditions, but above all the exceptionally good atmosphere all made it a very pleasant experience. The many possibilities to spend entertaining evenings certainly played a big part. In plain language, I felt as happy as a pig in muck, up there in the far north.

Some four weeks on, my master dispatched me along with the two chaps from Silesia (their names were Bernhard Bauer and Martin Schendel) to a place called Malente-Gremsmühlen. Considering the sorry state of our wallets, that particular contract came in very handy. All three of us were the same age – born in 1920 – and our commission involved the renovation of a mothers' sanatorium owned by the Nazi Party, which fortunately for us would also provide us with free housing and food for the duration of the restoration.

None of us could, however, ignore the rumbling noises on the political horizon. On a near daily basis it was drummed into us what an ignominious defeat we had suffered in the Versailles

Treaty after 1918 and that it was high time that we finally set it right. Thus, none of us three was even the tiniest bit surprised when we were called away from Malente and ordered to report to Bad Schwartau for a medical inspection. What did surprise me, though, was that I became aware of feelings I had never sensed before: a mixture of longing and fear. Was life finally beginning in earnest for me?

The medical examiners didn't spot that I was prone to asthma attacks, and because I didn't want to run away from the call of duty, a call made by my homeland, I didn't mention anything about my previous illness. In any event, apart from that, I felt totally healthy and it would never have occurred to me to hide behind my sickness in order to avoid being drafted. When I left the gym where the medical exams had taken place, I, like the numerous other young men who shared this experience with me, held within my hands the piece of paper with the letters KV stamped on it,* declaring me fit for regular service, and didn't much worry about it.

Together the three of us celebrated our joy that each one of us had been passed fit for military duty and, along with some other chaps who passed the test as well, we went to a nearby bar. The date to sign up for the then compulsory period in the Reich Labour Service (Reichsarbeitsdienst, RAD) had certainly moved closer, and it became clear to me that I would soon after be a soldier. The only branch of the military I really feared was the navy, and I couldn't even explain why that was. I just didn't want to go to sea.

'Lothar,' I quietly said to myself, 'I think it's high time to get yourself up to the mountains. You would do much better serving in the *Gebirgsjäger* [mountain infantry] and you will be much happier there rather than being locked away somewhere on a warship. You just would rot away in such confined quarters.'

During that October, I continued working at the Timmen-dorfer Strand for another two weeks. The sky over the Baltic and its coastline tended to be overcast or covered by heavy clouds

---

* KV = *Kriegsverwendungsfähig* = fit for ordinary service.

with outbursts of rain pelting down onto deserted beaches. In the meantime our mistress and landlady had been left to fend for herself, as her husband had been drafted. The invasion of Poland had been successful, and people seemed to speak with a fair amount of pride about the *Blitzkrieg* and our victorious armed forces. The general euphoria certainly was infectious, and it felt good to be amongst my mates, but I packed my few belongings in order finally to make the step of moving to Garmisch in the Alps, all the while, it has to be said, feeling deeply sad and pained to leave the Baltic coast which had become so dear to me in the meantime.

Heinrich Holler, my colleague who came from the Saxon part of the Vogtland, had previously spent some time in Upper Bavaria. He had given me the address of one Konrad Wolf, and I immediately contacted him. It didn't take long for him to get back to me and offer to take me on. Because the Winter Olympic Games, which had been due to take place in Garmisch, had been cancelled on account of the war, I certainly didn't want to take any chances, such as moving to a new place without being assured of solid employment with a piece of paper in my hands. I had also calculated that once I moved to a new location far inland I could be fairly certain that I wouldn't be drafted to the navy.

Once again I thought to myself: 'Lothar, if you have to go the army, then make sure to choose a branch you feel comfortable with, like the *Gebirgsjäger*.'

So that's how I found myself on a train on the night of 15 October on my way to Garmisch. During a stopover in Hamburg I was quite shocked by what I saw: a city shrouded in darkness in response to bombing alerts. With my rucksack on my back and trying to find a café, I didn't meet a single person walking on the pavements, let alone driving a car. But it didn't really hold me back or make me feel intimidated, as I still had the words of our Reichs-marschall Göring ringing in my ears, assuring us all in his recent speech that if even a single enemy plane dared cross over our Reich, his name would no longer be Göring and we could call him

Meier. Little did these poor citizens of Hamburg know, nor indeed those of any other major German city, what would transpire. Even country folk would learn their lesson some years later, when Herr Meier was sentenced to death at Nuremberg.

This was certainly something I couldn't even so much as suspect that evening when I wandered through this ghostlike town, and thus I boarded the train to Munich the next day confident and full of hope and anticipation.

The soft murmurings of the fellow passengers in my train compartment soon lulled me into a deep and peaceful sleep and when I woke up, there I was in Munich's train station, refreshed and curious about the 'capital of the movement'. Three hours later, on another train, this time heading towards Garmisch, I peered through the windows and gazed in wonderment as we sped up the Loisach Valley.

The view of the surrounding mountains, with their peaks already covered in snow, truly surpassed my already high expectations. So that's what people were always on about, I thought to myself: these then were the much spoken about Alps! The landscape gleamed in the rays of the autumn sun, filling me to the core with warmth and a love for my homeland. It felt as if the beauty of the landscape enfolded me with a welcoming embrace. Still glued to the window panes and eager for the train finally to come to a halt at Garmisch station, I asked myself why I hadn't visited this beautiful area much sooner. But regret made way for excitement of the moment.

On the day I arrived in the market-town of Garmisch-Partenkirchen it was a church festival Sunday, and I was amazed at how vibrant the atmosphere around the market place was, and how jolly the people who had gathered there were as they went about their business and celebrations. Here, peace seemed to reign supreme, unperturbed by the outside world. The girls and women wore their best festive *dirndl* outfits and chatted in a dialect, which at the time I couldn't understand at all and would only much later on in my life manage to get to grips with.

The only tiny reminder of the war being waged was the fact that most of the young men milling around from one market stall to the next and trying to pick up one of the *dirndl* girls were dressed not in their customary embroidered *Lederhosen* and white shirts of the traditional costume, but were instead garbed in the uniforms of the *Gebirgsjäger*. In their midst and carrying my rucksack, I all of a sudden felt slightly foolish, like a foreigner who was being gaped or gawked at in wonderment. Meanwhile, however, the people showed me nothing but kindness, and some even bothered to inquire where I was from and where I was headed to.

Konrad Wolf, my new employer, a master painter who was versed in several different types of painting technique and decoration work, had arranged some lodgings for me in a one-family home which was small but very warm, neat and inviting, situated in Danielstrasse. The family's name was Maier and the warm manner in which *Mutter* Maier and her daughter Kathi greeted me and right from the start addressed me with the familiar '*Du*', as if there was nothing to it, was a pleasant surprise for me. Kathi was a year older than me, and at the beginning seemed somewhat reserved. *Mutter* Maier, however, definitely took an immediate shine to me and said to me not long after my arrival that, 'Lothar, we seem to be a really good fit and if this continues to be the case, you can stay with us as long as you want.' There was perhaps a faint air of regret in the words which followed: 'Surely, you'll soon be drafted. Just be careful and make sure to survive our victories. My husband has already been called up.'

For me, living with a family, and ideas such as every member sticking up for one another or looking out for the other one's welfare had been concepts foreign to me until then. This was just another reason that right from the start I felt so at home with those people and so embraced and secure right from the beginning of my stay with the Maier family. Indeed, Frau Maier and her daughter would turn out to become like a mother and a sister to me.

The days and weeks that followed were filled with work, but the Sundays at least belonged to me. I had purchased some new skis and taught myself how to ski on the nearby slopes and, much to my surprise, I improved quite quickly from one Sunday to the next, managing downhill with ease. In March 1940, I thought I was good enough to challenge myself a bit further, so I buckled climbing skins onto my two wooden boards and ascended the mountain towards its peak. Down in the valley spring had already sprung and the fresh green of the meadows in the lower region stood in a curious and stark contrast to the white snow area above glistening in the sunshine. Full of expectation I left the valley behind, climbing up towards the snow. Once I decided that the snow was sufficiently deep, I strapped on the skins and began the strenuous ascent, step by step, following an existing trail.

For me this climb, albeit difficult, was actually exhilarating, what with being enveloped by a peaceful silence and the snow gleaming under the bright blue sky. Not to mention that with each further metre I put behind me and thus steadily gaining in height, I benefited from an increasingly better view of the surrounding region. Though heartened by my skiing progress, I still didn't feel sufficiently confident that I could manage the entire run from the top down, so I stopped at the shoulder of the mountain. I unbuckled the leather straps from the boards (no stick-on skins were available at the time), rested my skis upside down in the snow for me to sit on and gobbled down my packed snack which I had carried along in my rucksack. I was just taking a bite out of my bread, spread with artificial honey, when a young man and his girlfriend joined me. They had obviously followed me and they too didn't want to climb any higher but preferred to chat with me, using the 'Du' form which was a familiar way of conversing up in the mountains.

Each one of us was deeply impressed, even moved, by the beauty that surrounded us. It was 1940 and, as yet, the region was undisturbed by the ski circus we have today, and on that particular morning it was only the three of us up there on the slopes, making us feel at one with nature.

Much as we would have wanted to remain in this idyllic spot and enjoy the warm rays of the sun, the descent still had to be overcome. At the start we skied through delightful powder snow but as we crossed the Hochalm it quickly turned harder and became heavier and then turned into an unpleasant slush straight before the Kreuzeck, so I had to abandon any kind of fancy work with my skis and instead resort to using my behind, as my skis wouldn't do it. I ended up face down in the snow and having a good laugh along with the others about how clumsy a skier I actually still was. It took me quite a while to get myself up and onto my boards again.

'Anybody can ski in good snow,' Konrad shouted up to me from where he was standing slightly further below, 'This certainly will happen to you many times over.'

'Never mind, I'm still having fun! Let's get on with it, let's move, even if the going gets tougher from now on.'

Once safely down at the bottom and carrying our skis on our shoulders, we passed some gorgeous meadows already strewn with crocuses. Then, upon reaching Danielstrasse, I exclaimed: 'If I could yodel, I would yodel a song of joy in celebration of this day and my first ski trek, which I'll never forget.'

Konrad's girlfriend commented with a grin: 'Well, look here everyone, our friend from North Germany now wants to learn how to yodel? Lothar, if you keep going you'll turn into a real Garmisch guy!'

Though rather exhausted on that evening, I nevertheless felt like going out for a dance. I had promised my girlfriend Kathi, who was quite a bit younger than me, to go to the Ettaler Mandl inn. I felt by then that I had put down roots and that this place was now my home, despite my having come here to the Loisach valley merely as a journeyman.

But then, of course, the inevitable and unavoidable happened. The Tuesday after my skiing excursion the postman delivered my call-up letter with for the Reich Labour Service. I was to report on 15 May 1940 at the RAD Hochbrück labour camp near

Schleissheim, which was close to Munich. It so happened that my firm was scheduled to get started on quite a large refurbishment project on that same day in an army barracks in Mittenwald,* which my boss had managed to secure, and so I had to inform him gently of this change of plans.

He was actually quite incensed and, turning towards me, he angrily said: 'Lothar, this simply can't continue. Just as soon as I've finished teaching a young fellow everything I know, they come along and just snatch him away from under my nose. After all, isn't our work in those barracks also important for our war? Doesn't it count for anything? I just won't be able to cope with a workforce which only consists of old men. Why isn't it clear to them that you can accomplish far more for our people by working for me here than by joining the RAD? Surely the RAD and the military call-up can do without you for a long while yet to come? But me, stuck here with a bunch of tired assistants – it's unacceptable! I'll definitely be able to have you declared as exempt seeing as you are such a hard and solid worker.

'I have friends in high places and I'll call on them as they will certainly support my application. That's definitely doable!'

But I was a young and adventurous lad, and thus declined his offer. I also felt duty-bound to heed the call of my country. I didn't mind being called names generally, but for sure I didn't want to have a finger pointed at me as a draft-dodger. Anyway, as it stood, we had racked up one victory after another, good news from the front came pouring in and I wanted to be part of the Wehrmacht's glorious history. Never could I have suspected that such glory would be a passing phenomenon, and never could I have imagined what gruesome horror lay ahead of me.

---

* Lothar would undergo his initial military training at the Mittenwald mountain warfare establishment in 1940 (*see* Chapter 3). In late April 1945 several thousand Jewish prisoners from the Dachau concentration camp were brought to the Mittwenwald area. Many died before the survivors were liberated by US forces in early May.

CHAPTER 2

At the Reich Labour Camp

On 15 May 1940 Anton Siess, Ernst Wölpl and I travelled from Garmisch. At the time I didn't know them very well, but after a brief chat each one of us felt that we all shared the same goal, the same ambitions. After we changed to the train which would get us to Oberschleissheim, another fellow from the Oberammergau joined and the four of us carried on conversing in our carriage, musing about what lay in wait for us at our destination, and what we could expect to happen there. What with being quite anxious, our voices were raised and attracted the attention of fellow passengers, but we didn't let this bother us. While curious about what our future held, we were also quite enthralled by the military successes our Wehrmacht had already achieved, and thus eager to be part of them.

'Who amongst you has ever doubted that we would succeed?' exclaimed Anton Siess in a raucous voice.

'None of us, never!' we all shouted at once, one of us adding, 'We sure won't accept rubbish from that lot of foreigners! Don't worry for even a minute, we'll put this bit of RAD behind us in no time.'

'Exactly, I couldn't agree more,' I chimed in, 'We'll be wearing army grey before we know it and we'll throw ourselves into the job.'

Ernst Wölpl wasn't so confident: 'If our guys perform the way they've done up to now over there in France, there won't be a lot left for us to do,' he said with obvious disappointment.

Ernst's words gave Anton immediate cause to contradict him: 'Ernst, what on earth are you thinking?' he blustered, 'Where do you think we are, are you dreaming that we've already taken England? Just you wait and see, there'll be plenty for us to do yet, and we'll still have to crack that hard nut – England is not in the bag!'

Once we had arrived at Oberschleissheim station, our squad had grown to sixteen men. We recognised each other by the small suitcases each one of us was carrying. Bursting with curiosity, but at the same time exceedingly tense on the inside, we walked towards the RAD camp, previously a training camp for the Waffen-SS, and located at the far end of the town.

Once inside the orderly room of the barracks, which also housed our officer's quarters, we didn't exactly receive the most effusive of welcomes.

'You lot are all two weeks late. But I can't really blame you, as the fault lies with another bunch of lazy men. You will be kitted out today. Himmelstoss and Roidl, the two overseers, will show you around and make sure that you catch up in all aspects of the training. That's by order of our boss, Lieutenant Brutscher.'*

Nodding vigorously, the orderly in charge of the registration room reinforced these words by smirking maliciously with each movement of his head.

The camp was spotless, reminding me of the saying that one could truly eat from the floors of German barracks. Our quarters consisted of low huts arranged around a square where the drills took place. Looking through the gaps in between, I could make out some fields and meadows in the background, sparse shrubbery and some single farms dotted around.

It only took an hour until we were all wearing our new uniforms and, probably in response to the general grumbling which had erupted, the guy in charge of clothing, invariably a bully, yelled some traditional insults across the barrack:

'The tunic of your uniform isn't too tight, it's your belly that's too big!'

---

* Brutscher held the rank of *Oberfeldmeister* in the RAD.

'Why don't you switch boots with your neighbour – he's complaining that his are too small.'

'This field jacket looks as if it's been specially made for you. Wear it with pride! It's perfect for hard labour!'

On our return to the barracks, accompanied by the two assistant instructors, Himmelstoss and Roidl, my comrade Ernst Wölpl whispered into my ear: 'I hear Himmelstoss is an okay guy but apparently Roidl isn't . . . I heard he tends to big himself up more than he ought to.'

Arranged along the side walls of our room were bunk beds made of rough spruce timber; the mattresses, duvets and pillows were covered in blue and white chequered bedding and it of course had to be Roidl, eyes bulging, who immediately hollered: 'Just beware fellows, anyone who dares leave his bed in a state different from how he found it today will not know what's hit him. So, now I will demonstrate to you how the rule book orders you to arrange your lockers', and, moving to one of the lockers (there was one for each of us standing between the bunk beds), he embarked on the tedious routine of how we were supposed to organise them.

Night was falling and Roidl was still busy instructing us how to fold clothes and put each garment on top of the other in the opposite sequence of how we would require them the following morning. The white footwraps were at the very bottom. Roidl gave us a whole performance of how to wrap them around our feet before slipping our boots on. We called them *Knobelbecher* ('dice cups'). I can still hear his gruff voice in my ears today: 'The one who's sloppy,' he predicted maliciously, 'will have only himself to blame if he gets blisters and wounds on his feet.' His warning, that slovenliness would turn every march, every cross-country run into sheer hell, would be proven right.

'In our vocabulary there will be no such thing as calling it quits!' he droned on. 'Saturday', he gleefully informed us, 'is a work day like any other. But you'll have plenty of time to wash your stuff in the evenings or on Sundays. Mummy isn't looking after you any more!'

Switching subjects he moved to our footwear: 'And now, here is something totally different. You men have all been issued brand new boots and some of you had a hard time squeezing your feet in. That can be changed. Here is some grease – all you have to do is knead it into the boot with your fingers and you'll turn them into the softest leather! Take my word for it, they'll feel like slippers in no time.'

We got straight to work, kneading the stuff into the leather, and no sooner had we finished than we heard the next order: 'Everybody out – get your grub!'

Truppführer Kiessl was standing at the door barking further orders: 'Show me your hands! What the hell? You're telling me that you want to eat with those filthy paws? That's not going to happen around here. It's hand washing first!'

The impression these first days spent at the RAD left on us didn't really take me by surprise as, of course, I was aware that it was a sort of training for the military. Then, on the fourth night after our arrival at the camp, just before we were allowed to go to sleep, or rather collapse into our beds, tired and worn out, Anton Siess, who was the son of a baker in Garmisch, murmured into my ear: 'Believe me, I'm totally dedicated to our fatherland – but I'm absolutely fed up with all that silly thumping around with our spades, "left turn" and "right turn" . . . having to stand still and all that nonsense. Can't they think of anything better for us to do? I thought that fellows at the RAD did some proper work!'

However, the following morning things began to change. The order came to report to the Oberwiesenfeld airfield and with that we hoped that finally some action was ahead of us. Singing at the top of our voices some of the marching songs we had been taught the evenings before, we advanced in perfectly straight columns towards the airfield, carrying our kitbags on our backs, packed as per instructions, and clasping in our hands the polished spades straight up and leaning against our shoulders. Our task was to fix some minor damage to the airfield as well as carry out a bit of light digging. Approaching, we could only make out two machines belonging to the Luftwaffe which were standing idly in the hangar. Judging by their three radial engines, my guess was that these were Ju 52 freight haulers, the so-called 'Aunt Jus'.

While it only took us two hours to get the job done, what with the marching back and forth it ultimately amounted to quite a few hours' work, and I was mightily relieved that I had taken great pains to wind the footwraps around my feet properly. Some of my comrades hadn't been so mindful and had had quite a rude awakening. Franz Bauzer, a comrade from my cabin, was forced to pierce his blisters with a needle before sticking a whole bunch of plasters on his wounded feet. Ferdinand Weber, standing close by and observing the procedure, couldn't hide his bemusement and laughingly exclaimed: 'Gosh, you lazybones, us lot wrapped the foot cloths around our feet exactly as the big bully had drummed it into us. Were you asleep? Just look at us: none of our dogs are barking! Count yourself lucky that one of us had enough plasters, otherwise you would look pretty damn stupid!' Several comrades joined in the fun and admittedly the poor fellow didn't get a lot of sympathy, certainly not seeing as he was stuck with us lot.

The tell-tale sign that this so called labour service was in reality nothing but a cover-up for preparing us for war was borne out by what followed: the instructions in arms. Relentless and uncompromising, Staff Sergeant Gaul put us through our paces until we nearly threw up. After only a few days each one of us, blindfolded, knew how to disassemble, clean and oil the Karabiner 98k.

I wasn't the only one who found this whole instruction business boring. You wouldn't have found a single youngster amongst us who didn't feverishly wish for the day to come when we would finally see some real action. And what did we do instead? Drain some lousy swamps in the neighbourhood.

We all, of course, listened excitedly to the reports coming in from the front and would then discuss amongst ourselves what we thought about how the war was developing. Eagerly we tuned in to the news broadcast on the Reich Broadcasting Service and read the *Völkischer Beobachter.** Every day a different fellow from our cabin would volunteer to walk over to the army kiosk and fetch the most recent edition of that NSDAP paper, knowing full well that doing so would earn him extra approval from our superiors.

After the invasion of Poland on 1 September 1939, France and Britain had declared war on us which, mind you, didn't do much for them if their intention was to help Poland launch a counterattack. Nothing new in the West up to that point then. The so-called *Sitzkrieg*† set in over on that side and lasted until Hitler put an end to it on 10 May 1940 by outflanking what our enemy falsely believed to be the impregnable Maginot Line.

The day I started my service in Hochbrück, 15 May 1940, the Netherlands capitulated, followed by Belgium a few days later, and on 20 May German tanks reached the Channel coast. How we cheered when on 22 June our General Wilhelm Keitel and the French Charles Huntziger signed the armistice agreement in the Compiègne forest.

With that, the 'humiliation suffered at Versailles' had at long last been wiped out. At least that's how the propaganda would have it, and so that the signing be performed with maximum symbolism, the same railway carriage in which Germany had surrendered back in 1918 was retrieved from a French museum and taken to the forest north-east of Paris.

Two days later the picture of Hitler in front of the Eiffel Tower in Paris stared out at us from the front pages. We were filled with admiration. Some of my group made no secret of their impatience to be real soldiers, rifle in hand and a squad to belong to. Each wanted that day to arrive sooner rather than later. Whilst I myself didn't actually voice my opinion out loud, I had to admit that I too was swept up by the general hysteria and carried away by the frenzy of victory.

It was towards the end of June, a boiling hot day, when we were ordered to embark on a so-called *Gewaltmarsch* (route march) with

---

* The official newspaper of the Nazi Party.
† The German term used for the Phoney War.

our kit bags on our backs and our spades in hand. No destination had been disclosed.

'Who the hell had this crazy idea of sending us on this trek?' grumbled Ernst Wölpl, who lined up next to me. In that same second we heard the sergeant bellow out the order: 'Forward, march!' Our column moved out. Every now and again we were instructed to sing a song, and we belted out one of the traditional soldier tunes, but our throats were usually too parched for us to sound even vaguely melodious.

After marching for some two and a half hours, whirling up the dust on the country roads, we reached the centre of a village, where Lieutenant Brutscher and our captain were already expecting us, both standing next to the village well, with their bikes leaning against the fountain. We could hear the soft bubbling of the water flowing from the bent steel pipe into the well and longed to have a drink. Although our throats were totally dried up, we had received strict orders back at the camp that drinking during the march was absolutely prohibited. Did the order apply to this brief reprieve here at the fountain?

'Before we turn you over to the army, we will make damn sure to transform you from a bunch of mummy's boys into a slick company of hardened German men!' Those were the words of our sergeant.

'Squad, halt!' came the order and then: 'Right turn!' Standing to attention, in dead straight lines, we faced our superiors. 'First man, one step forward, third man three steps back!'

Taking his time, Lieutenant Brutscher strutted up and down between the lines and told each one of us to pull out his water bottle for inspection to ascertain whether the water level had remained intact. Only two of us had disobeyed the strict instruction not to drink.

Brutscher jotted down their names and then yelled for everyone to hear: 'Each of these fellows with no self-control is confined to barracks for the next two weekends!'

The next day we proudly marched to the shooting grounds in Freimann, this time with rifles on our shoulders, leaving the spades behind.

Finally, it looked like we were going to get to do some live shooting. Every one of us had feverishly longed for that moment to arrive. When my name was called up and I approached the shooting stand, my eyes fell on our overseer Kiessl, who was supervisor of my stand. Just when I was about to aim and fire my first shot, I could hear him mumbling under his breath: 'Not much to get too excited about here, we won't be seeing great shakes from this Prussian fellow.'

Once our group had shot their rounds at the target placed some hundred metres away – two shots standing, two kneeling and two flat on our stomachs – I turned out to be the third best marksman of the lot, and much to my delight was rewarded with one day's extra leave. Gloating inside, I couldn't help but shout over to Kiessl even though he only stood a few metres away from me: 'What are you staring at me for! That's how we shoot in Silesia!'

Because he abruptly turned his back on me, I couldn't catch the expression on his face. Back in the camp, before entering our quarters, my comrade Manfred Schur went into great detail about the sad figure Kiessl had cut at the shooting range. 'You won't believe it, Lothar, this guy just turned red like a tomato when you showed him up like that in front of everybody!' The story eventually did the rounds and gave rise to a great deal of laughter.

Together with the other two prize winners I left the camp that following Sunday at 6 p.m. It was a glorious, balmy day and the sun was shining as we walked until we reached the Danziger Freiheit from where we boarded a tram that took us to the main train station in Munich.

It turned out that each of us had planned to take a different onward journey from Munich: Werner Hall wanted to go to Weilheim, Karl Reith to Oberammergau and I wanted to get to Garmisch. In spite of our brown uniforms, none of us attracted any attention as the crowds of people rushing around at the station seemed preoccupied with other worries. And besides, in those days uniforms of all colours and styles were part of normal everyday life.

Late that same morning I arrived at Garmisch. The Maiers, my host family, warmly welcomed and embraced me, and I thoroughly enjoyed the short time I had with them. After but a few hours, I once again had to take my leave and catch the train to return to camp. Then, as before, I became acutely aware of how the simple yet so cosy lounge of these modest people had become home to me.

Kathi accompanied me to the train station, and only when I was about to board the train did it suddenly dawn on me how throughout that afternoon she had been very quiet, hardly saying anything. She then told me with a trembling voice that her fiancé had been killed in France. 'I can only hope that very soon this whole sorry business comes to an end,' she whispered softly, and then wished me Godspeed.

At six o'clock sharp we reported back to the guard in charge of the orderly room.

On 16 July we got on a train in Munich that was headed towards nobody knew where, as the destination wasn't revealed to us, but in any case we didn't actually much care. It was one of those Reichsbahn passenger trains with wooden running boards installed along the length of the carriage. Each of us was carrying his kit bag and spade. The day before, a military lorry had been sent to a depot to pick up the Karabiner 98s, but nobody knew when they would be handed out or what exactly the cargo of three freight wagons at the end of the train consisted of.

Whilst being ordered to move further down into the carriage, I could hear Manfred Schur's high-pitched voice commenting: 'Probably they don't have any more work for us around here!'

Soon after the train departed we burst into song, mindful not to miss out 'Oh du schöner Westerwald'.* Karl Ritter from

---

* 'In the Wondrous Westerwald'.

Mittenwald had managed to dig up an old accordion in Hoch-brück, and once en route every member of our ten-men squad took turns carrying it, in addition to his own bags of course. Stein, our squad leader, had a broad grin on his face, because Karl really was an accomplished accordion player and it certainly lifted our morale. We turned into quite an attraction with more and more guys surrounding us.

My friend Ernst Wölpl was one who always had his eyes everywhere and must have been observing the officers in the front carriage through the window whilst the long train turned round the bends. He reported back to us that he had seen how the senior sergeant glanced back at our wagon, obviously wishing he was sitting with us. 'It must be dead boring up there in the front!' Ernst concluded, convinced that our superiors were missing out.

In Ulm the train came to a screeching stop and we had a short wait. Rumours started spreading from one carriage to the other. One version spoke of us being on our way to France where we were supposed to repair an airfield. Others whispered something about our destination being Alsace, with Strasbourg close by.

A few stops before Kehl we were told to switch from the train to buses. Driving through totally deserted villages, we realised that the inhabitants must have been evacuated and resettled somewhere else for their own safety. We were quite incensed that such precautions had been deemed necessary in the assumption that our enemy would come this far. 'These pathetic French guys would never in their wildest dreams have managed to get this far!' one of my mates snarled, clearly dismissive of any war techniques other than our own.

At Kehl, the bridge over the Rhine had been blown up, and while crossing by bus one of the makeshift bridges erected by our pioneers,* we saw some large pieces of debris from the bridge in the water, with others lodged between stones on the bank.

---

* An alternative term for military engineers.

In the early evening, we arrived in Hagenau,* where we were being put up for the night in a school building. Along the length of the hall, underneath the windows, they had covered the floor with a two-metre-wide layer of straw while spruce pillars, some thirty centimetres high and screwed down into the floorboards, demarcated the individual sleeping areas.

We realised that we weren't the first to spend the night in this place. 'The *Landsers*† were here first,' said someone standing behind me. There must have been thirty of us put up in that hall, and seeing as we were exhausted from travelling we were keen to call it a day. Dumping our coats onto the straw, we then spread blankets over it and some canvas over our kit bags – that was our bed. From that moment on, these 'monkeys', as we called our kit bags, would serve as pillows. Pleased with how our night camp had turned out, and looking forward to sinking down for some rest, we weren't too happy when instead we were ordered out of the room. 'Grab your food,' yelled Senior Troop Leader Breitsamer, standing legs apart in front of the exit.

Piling out of the now converted school into the courtyard holding our crockery in our hands, we realised that our stomachs were grumbling. This *Essgeschirr*‡ consisted of a kidney-shaped one-litre tin container which could be fastened to the back of the waist belt, next to the bread bag. The collapsible spoon, fork and knife were loosely riveted together by a metal pin. The cover of the billy had a swivelling handle and could be used as a soup bowl. Once outside we saw the welcome sight of our cook waiting next to his *Gulaschkanone*. This referred to a mobile kitchen unit which had a chimney consisting of a tin pipe. One by one we lined up in front of him. 'I have for you today on the menu, goulash, roasted potatoes and fresh green salad,' he announced, pleased with himself and his offering. 'Not even your mummy at home

---

* Hagenau is the German spelling used during 1940–5; Haguenau is the French name.
† Army privates.
‡ Mess kit.

cooks for you like that!' Chef Hannes liked to make these menu announcements from a slightly higher pedestal, and never failed to add that he didn't want any pushing and shoving, and that nobody need worry as he had sufficient food for seconds. In truth, he always did and we were indeed well fed at the time, something I would longingly remember later on.

The next morning we set off in our white overalls, wearing our freshly polished boots and belts and carrying our spades over our left shoulders. We were to report to the senior sergeant at the airfield, located some three kilometres away from the village. We had been divided into several groups with three being ordered to begin work by refilling several shell craters right next to the grass-covered runway, which had obviously never been concreted like regular tarmac. It looked like the previous job had needed to be done in haste for some reason, and the soil had neither settled nor been pressed down to a totally flat surface as it should have been.

'It's quite possible that we'll have to relocate the runway, depending on the weather,' warned the senior sergeant, and added, shouting at the top of his voice: 'You'll then need to change the red and white markers along the sides of the route. In any event, the runway needs to be rock hard and mustn't sink even a centimetre into the mud! Make sure that the craters look and feel as if they've never been there in the first place. Everything has to be done with utmost precision and to total perfection. What I want is a fully operational airfield!'

The work group I was assigned to was ordered to ram heavy wooden poles some twenty centimetres into the ground. Reams of barbed wire had already been delivered and we were to use these to connect the poles to each other. To get the airfield up and running, it was to be secured by walls of barbed wire reaching nearly two metres high. Remainders of the old damaged fence lay cast away in the field at the edge of the nearby forest.

Toiling away at the far end of the field, our chests bare, we dug and pounded the soil without so much as looking up. Some men carted the wood cuttings from the other end of the airfield to where we were doing the excavation, and I had just finished scooping out a one metre deep circle with only a hand rammer when Rudi Heller screamed over to me that I must, without delay, get myself to Gaul, the staff sergeant, who was waiting for me at the administration building. Rudi was emphatic that I shouldn't waste another second.

Whilst struggling to get my jacket back on and adjust my brown cap properly, I kept wondering what Gaul could possibly want from me. Five minutes later, out of breath and before I could even properly salute Gaul as prescribed, I could hear him shouting: 'Herrmann! I told my Luftwaffe comrade here that you've got particularly nice handwriting.' With that he pointed to Sergeant-Major Heiner, a tall slim man dressed in the blue Luftwaffe uniform standing next to him. 'Your talents are requested by the Luftwaffe,' he added and, looking me straight into the eyes, he warned: 'Make us proud!'

Standing erect in front of them, I snapped my boots together and stretched out my right hand in the Hitler salute as we were ordered to do, but Sergeant-Major Heiner wasn't one for etiquette and he waved my greeting away: 'Come with me, Workman Hermann. I'm taking you to our depot manager who'll give you some items which you should label nicely – apparently you are a genius when it comes to such matters.'

Without another word, he turned on his heels and marched in front of me toward a large tent next to what once was a farmhouse, and where at that time the headquarters and the radio station were housed. I noticed some of our men climbing around on top of the roof. Under supervision of a sergeant they were busy mending a damaged radio aerial which had been badly twisted, and fixing some holes in the roof. We had experts from every single profession on our team.

A light drizzle fell during the following days and it gave me good reason to take my sweet time with the paint work. Nobody actually pressured me either, so I leisurely labelled drawers and cupboards with large ornate lettering indicating what they contained. For the most part they were filled with small spare parts meant for aircraft engines, but I had no clue what precisely they were used for.

Every evening the line-up in front of our *Gulaschkanone*, over which Hannes in the meantime had erected a roof made out of planks, was encircled by children who clasped milk canisters or similar containers in their hands. The first night Hölzl and I stood a bit further away in the entrance to the courtyard and overheard Hannes explaining to Lieutenant Brutscher that it would be a terrible pity simply to throw away the left-overs, seeing as the children were clearly hungry. 'Nearly all of them speak German,' he added, to justify his decision. The lieutenant didn't reply and simply walked away.*

There was one day when a small army lorry brought a load of French rifles into our camp along with the proper ammunition. These rifles were similar to their German counterparts, but just a few centimetres longer. We spent the following few days practising with them. Bellowing his orders incessantly across what once served as the schoolyard, Lieutenant Brutscher drilled us to the point of near collapse.

Long into the night, when we had already fallen into a sleep of total exhaustion, the voice of Brutscher still rang in our ears: 'Attention', 'Ready, front', 'Eyes right', 'Eyes left', 'Jump', 'Slow march', 'Quick march' – alternating with insults: 'Can't you do it, or are you refusing to do it?' 'Do you need a dressing down?' 'Look here, don't hold your rifle with such disdain, it's precisely because the French have so kindly offered them to us that you now have to operate them properly, otherwise we'll look like real fools . . .!' And on and on it went: 'Don't even think about embarking on your service before you know this inside out because not a single barracks of the Wehrmacht will have you!' Of course, it also turned personal, with the sergeant's pride and reputation being at risk of getting a beating were we to show him up. 'I will certainly

---

* The population of Alsace was of mixed French and German heritage and the territory had been part of France between the two world wars. It was annexed by the Nazis following their victory in 1940.

not be embarrassed in front of the RAD by the likes of you lot!' Punishments such as thirty knee-bends with the rifle held up with both hands above our heads was the minimum we received for even the slightest incorrect move.

Two amongst my group even started talking loudly in their sleep, which naturally resulted in them being bullied. Well, this was understandable, as nobody in our barrack room wished to re-live the entire drill they had to endure during the day whilst trying to catch some sleep. Others suffered diarrhoea caused by the heat, and the latrines at the end of the schoolyard – at the time entirely redesigned for our purposes – were visited more often than usual. This place was no more than a shit-house, as we called it, as it only consisted of a trench of some eight metres in length over which rested a beam for sitting down on. We had built around it a shed-like structure, leaving the front open. Some of us didn't mind the disgusting state of the loo and we'd often even chose to sit there having a smoke and skiving off.

On Saturday evenings and Sundays we did our laundry and, whilst at it, usually managed to down several bottles of beer. Even though we needed to be mindful not to lose any of the under-collars, we enjoyed every minute of our short breaks. On one of these Sundays we were even able to make an excursion to Strasbourg and its famous cathedral, its tower looming high above all the buildings. Somehow, the view we had from standing up on the minster meant more to us than just a change of scenery.

Thanks to our efforts, the airfield had become operational once again and the Luftwaffe could make use of it, though none of us knew which unit would be stationed there.

The group of officers in charge of this assignment were fortunately satisfied with the results and it didn't go unrecognised. It was a sunny day in July when our sergeant ordered us to report for duty, and proudly announced that in appreciation of our commendable efforts we would be permitted to take a two-day tour of the Maginot Line. We were to set off within the hour and would be sleeping in tents that night.

Some of us started grumbling at the thought of what was most certainly going to turn out to be a tedious outing rather than a pleasure trip, but the sergeant raised his hand ordering silence. Seemingly oblivious to our obvious annoyance he said: 'I know that the prospect of actually finding out more about this line fills you with joy, seeing as our *Führer* was a true genius in devising a brilliant strategy to circumvent it!' And with that he dismissed us.

Throughout the war this was the only time I truly enjoyed one of these route marches, as I, for one, genuinely *was* interested to see for myself what this famous defence line built by our western neighbour was all about. That afternoon, no sooner had we finished pitching our square four-man tents on a meadow, building each out of four canvas tarpaulins, the tour of the famous line started.

We got to inspect the massive concrete fortifications which had been dug into a densely wooded slope alongside a road, and which looked to be totally impregnable. At close examination we could detect traces of where shell fire had hit them, but obviously the bullets must have merely grazed the surface as we didn't see any real damage. Whilst we were discussing what had and hadn't happened, Hans Meissner concluded that the German attack couldn't have been anything more than a military deception. 'The tanks', he said dismissively, 'had by then already advanced far into the French hinterlands.'

Another guy, Heiner Manz, begged to differ, declaring that what we should be focusing on was how cleverly the bunkers had been laid out, but his opinion didn't much impress a third chap in our group who ridiculed Heiner: 'Frankly, you don't have a clue about strategy. Why, don't you realise how precious little this so-called strategy did to help the French?'

That evening our squad sat in front of our tent, surrounding a flickering fire, singing marching songs but also adding some sentimental songs about our homeland. In the course of the night more and more fellows joined us, with even our sergeant-major and Lieutenant Brutscher eventually sitting with us cross-legged on the ground, reminiscing on good old times and long-lost loves.

The following day we marched to the other side of the hill, to the camouflaged rear entrance of the bunker complex, and whilst we could only briefly survey the situation and but imagine what might have been the military hopes of our enemy, it still left an indelible mark on us all. A few moments before we departed, my friend Franz Burg quietly remarked: 'Lothar, by golly, these French men must really have been blown away by ours!'

'They should have realised that right from the start!' someone behind us butted in, 'Anybody could have predicted what would happen.' He was swiftly told off by the sergeant and ordered to shut up. 'Forward, march!'

Once back in the schoolyard we were told by the sergeant-major that our next location was to be Versailles, that we would leave in the morning by train and would be given further details on arrival. Invariably, we debated this next move amongst ourselves, analysing it from varying perspectives, weighing up the pros and cons for which we all thought we had the low-down. Whilst some of us looked forward to sightseeing in Paris, perhaps getting a glimpse of the Eiffel Tower, others saw this relocation as an opportunity to have a rest from work.

And of course there were some who relished the thought of the French women. 'Can't wait to get a look at those French chicks!' But none of these musings seemed to interest our superiors in the slightest. 'Silence! Dismiss!'

Triumphantly, the swastika flag flew over Versailles. Our lodgings, quite close to the palace, were accessible by three winding staircases leading up to large set of entrance doors, and were by far the most comfortable dorms we had ever stayed in. Grinning from one ear to the other, our cook now lorded over a properly equipped kitchen on the ground floor right next to a large dining hall. There were six of us to each of the rooms on the upper floor, all radiating warmth and a degree of elegance, with single beds and a wardrobe for each of us. On the far side of the corridor was the bathroom, simple but fit for purpose, and above all with hot water on tap.

Suddenly it dawned on us why the saying 'Living like a god in France' rang true, and we regretted that our RAD stay in Paris would be just a short one. But no sooner had some of us vented our disappointment about the all too brief respite, than Heiner Klotz, a rather cautious guy, issued a fair warning: 'Our superiors are well aware of the promises this sweet life in France holds for us! Mark my words, they'll most definitely make sure that we're not going to have too much of a good time here.'

Franz Struss, a thin sort of a fellow with a high-pitched voice, wondered out loud about who might have occupied these lodgings prior to our arrival, but his question, perhaps alluding to some forceful expulsion of the previous tenants, fell on deaf ears. Nobody really cared or worried. 'Who gives a damn, Franz! It's our turn now and let's enjoy it,' was Heiner Klotz's response.

The next day the officer distributed steel helmets and the French carbines, which we now knew only too well, and we were divided into groups of fifteen. Army sergeants took us to the grounds surrounding the palace and we were given precise instructions as to how to guard them. Our job consisted of providing round the clock double sentry patrol duty and preventing anybody from coming anywhere near the senior staff of the Wehrmacht, whose quarters were either in the palace or in some of its annexes. But above all, we were ordered to ensure that not a single French civilian entered the railway station without being fully inspected beforehand. Furthermore, it was left to us to intercept anybody roaming around the tracks, and nobody except uniformed station staff who had the proper special identification card was permitted in that area. It was practically sealed off.

One of the master sergeants, he was a bit older than the others, made a special point of reinforcing the importance of our role: he impressed upon us that the security of that sector was fully our domain and up to us to control. We were to ensure day and night that no unauthorised person was allowed to cause any damage. 'Should you encounter anybody who doesn't immediately obey your order to stop, you are permitted to use your firearms!' Not in any way meaning to be humorous, he added for good measure: 'And make sure to hit your target – or else!'

Late that same afternoon we were handed the duty roster for the following ten days so each one of us knew where, when and with whom he was on patrol. Anton Siess, taking a mischievous stab at Heiner who had sworn he was right by having predicted that we had nothing but a period of idle tourism lying ahead of us, turned to him and asked if he had anything to say for himself. 'You can kiss my arse!' Klotz growled curtly, but didn't fail to make yet a further prediction: 'Our days at the RAD are numbered, you just wait and see.'

The patrol and guard duty very quickly became routine for us but, once again, luck was on my side, as I was frequently assigned to office tasks and thus spent a fair amount of time doing what I liked best. Just as before, my graphic talents came in handy. And on top of that, the head honcho had found out that I knew shorthand – another reason why I wasn't put down for Sunday guard duty.

During those days Anton Siess, Heiner Klotz, Ernst Wölpl and I would take a bus which had been commandeered by the Wehrmacht to indulge in some sight-seeing in Paris. Everyone not assigned to guard duty was perfectly at liberty to do that. Even *Landsers* joined us and frequently female auxiliaries of the Wehrmacht wearing their pretty uniforms also wanted to take part in these jolly day trips. We certainly welcomed them on board. In the eyes of our comrades we were 'the four inseparable ones' and, in truth, it wasn't just a coincidence that the four of us were off-duty all at the same time. It was actually thanks to the office manager that this came about. He was partially responsible for putting the duty rota together and wanted to do me a good turn.

Naturally, we couldn't take in all the sights of the metropolis in those few days, but first and foremost we got to see the Eiffel Tower with the statue of its architect in front of it. Never in my life will I forget the view we enjoyed after having climbed up. The capital of

France was truly a most beautiful city. Admiring it, I couldn't help but ask myself why people since time immemorial didn't get along and were continuously at war with each other.

In a restaurant, which had been opened up by the Wehrmacht and which was recommended to us due to its reasonably priced menu, we would enjoy meals that didn't break the bank. Once, a cheeky chappy from the infantry came over to engage us in conversation and in his colourful Berlin accent tried charming us, saying how honoured he would be to guide us lads from the Bavarian mountains to a 'house of pleasure'. Assuring us that this particular bordello was reserved especially for Wehrmacht personnel and that it was medically supervised, he beckoned us to follow him.

Naturally, we were all quite curious and we most certainly accepted those kinds of invitations. However, it has to be said that we didn't just leave Paris with a closer inspection of the ladies of the horizontal profession; we also dutifully took in the sights of the Dôme des Invalides, the Arc de Triomphe and, of course, Montmartre.

Our RAD times were almost over. Dismissed on 7 October, I returned home and was startled to realise that the letter calling me up for active duty had already been waiting on my table for several days. I was never to find out why the call-up was dated 2 October 1940, but it didn't matter one way or the other. Without further ado I immediately went to the local recruitment station where my details had been registered ever since my move to Garmisch.

CHAPTER 3

How We Became Soldiers

The official at the army registration office was a man in his forties with hair greying around his temples. His eyes spoke of friendly bemusement mixed with a degree of condescension as he eyed me up and down, and when I started sort of complaining that I didn't understand why I was being called up, seeing as I had only been dismissed the day before, he simply laughed, raised his hands and interrupted me:

'You're not the first one to give me that story, good man, and I'm sure there will be more coming my way.' He then let me know that two of my comrades from Garmisch had also reported at the office that day, with one of them having been assigned to the *Jägers* in Garmisch and the other one to Mittenwald. Briefly glancing at my discharge note from the RAD, he added in a sarcastic tone: 'Well, looks like Herr Lothar Herrmann doesn't seem to be as ideally suited for the mountain infantry as his comrades seemed to be.' This made me feel rather apprehensive, but his next comment allowed me breathe a sigh of relief: 'You were expected to report on the 14th to enlist for the mountain artillery,' he informed me and, requesting I hand him the conscription order so that he could change it, commented that I was one of the very few lucky ones allowed to enlist so close to home. 'Those few extra days of leave will do you good,' he added magnanimously.

October 14th arrived sooner than I expected, of course, and merely coming face to face with the sentry at the barracks in the Maximilianstrasse caused me renewed palpitations. The little wooden sentry box at the entrance was painted in black, white and red stripes. 'Where am I supposed to report?' I asked the guard standing straight, his legs slightly apart and with his rifle slung over his shoulder. With his heavy helmet in place, and without saying a word he nodded his head towards the left where the guardroom was.

What with the mountains looming above the valley where the barracks had been built, my first impression wasn't exactly favourable and didn't do anything to calm my jittery nerves. The large concrete house at the entrance, behind which stood some rather bland-seeming soldiers' quarters all painted in pale colours, was not in the least bit welcoming, yet it would be dishonest of me if I claimed today that I had found the place entirely forbidding.

Even before lunch was served in the dining hall, I had received my full uniform and in exchange had handed in my civilian clothing all packed into a small suitcase on which hung a label with my home address: Danielstrasse 20, Garmisch. The sergeant of my unit was only a few years older than me and, as he showed me to my quarters, he rattled off the instructions of how to arrange my locker according to the HDv rulebook.*

Our artillery battery, he explained carrying on with his tour, was divided into four platoons. He said I was to join the third platoon tasked with communication, clarifying that the two first platoons operated the guns while the fourth one consisted of porters; those were the men who looked after the pack animals. We commonly referred to them as mule drivers and felt slightly superior to them, perhaps because of the sturdy dungarees they had to wear when working in the stables instead of the smart uniforms we had. We also got to handle sophisticated equipment whilst they were stuck with disobedient animals they had to control. Our battery commander was Major Raimund Lang and together with two other batteries we made up a mountain artillery division.

While still lingering at the dorm entrance, the sergeant impressed on me that there hadn't been any trouble whatsoever under his watch and, smiling smugly, he then asked whether

---

* HDv – *Heeresdienstvorschrift*, the Army service and conduct manual.

I liked what I had seen. 'The single bed right next to the window belongs to me, of course,' he didn't fail to point out, just to make sure I knew my place, so to speak.

Perhaps assuming that I ought to give my opinion on what he had shown me, I quickly scanned the small dorm, taking in the wooden bunk beds lined up along the left and right side-walls with the lockers next to them. To me, the entire room seemed dismal. 'As a professional decorator,' I finally blurted out, 'I wouldn't mind fixing up those bare walls.' What I thought was a perfectly reasonable comment was not, however, met with the approval I had hoped for. 'Well, look at this fine gentleman! Somebody fancies himself quite the artist!' The sergeant sniggered and, looking at his wristwatch he curtly told me to follow him into the dining hall where I would be able to meet the others, whilst he, as he specified once again to emphasise his status, would sit with the other sergeants at a separate table. 'Up to now, your seat was empty' were his last words to me, perhaps he meant to be reassuring.

A few minutes later those 'others' gave me a very warm reception and I immediately felt at home. All through supper and whilst enjoying a most delicious meat and vegetable stew I got a further briefing, this time more of the informal type. I was given the insider perspective of all that stood ahead of me, what I would have to learn from the word go, for example how to hold myself correctly, how to salute our superiors (which meant folding my upper arm at a right angle, tilting the lower one at forty-five degrees and placing my hand to my cap), to other more household matters such as how to tidy up, how and where to wash and so forth. It looked like we would be put through our paces, but most of it was more than familiar to us from our RAD days. 'Our instructor is Sergeant Koch,' explained Heiner Munz, moving his head unobtrusively towards the direction of the door where the sergeant was busy talking to someone else. 'He's tough but fair,' Munz mumbled, and with a knowing look he predicted rather ominously: 'You'll meet him soon enough!' He then launched into an overview of the daily schedule and assured me, not that I didn't know it already, that it would be drilled into us night and day. Only once we had a solid handle on things, he sighed, would we be given permission to go on leave, and this wasn't going to happen for four weeks. None of it was news to me.

Our foundation course lasted two months. During its first part we were instructed in how to march properly, we learned the different salutations required for different occasions, we were drilled in to how to operate firearms such as unlocking the bolt, pulling back the receiver, opening the breech, engaging the sear and so forth, lessons we had to repeat over and over again. Crawling on our stomachs in mud with our carbines outstretched was part of the course, as was becoming skilled in how to look after all the equipment and arms entrusted to us. After four weeks had gone by our superiors finally judged us presentable and we were ceremonially sworn in two days before our first period of leave began. Somewhat to my surprise, quite a few civilians whom I didn't know from Adam, nor for that matter did any of my comrades, obviously didn't want to miss the show and were also present.

Organised in precise rows of three, with our hobnailed mountain boots all polished up, our grey top-of-boot gaiters in place and wearing our coats, we were quite the sight. Our steel helmets shone in the pale autumn sun and following a short drum roll, we solemnly swore our oath. There was something eerie, something gruesome about pronouncing the words which reverberated through the courtyard of the barracks: 'I swear to God this sacred oath to the Leader of the German Empire and people, Adolf Hitler, supreme commander of the armed forces . . .'

I myself wasn't particularly impressed by the event, but my comrades may well have felt differently.

Just before being permitted to exit the camp to go on leave, a sergeant who was standing at the gate inspected us from top to bottom, which I found rather demeaning. Insults and admonitions were hurled through the air. We were being told off for just about anything, from dirty finger nails to owning a pocket comb that hadn't been washed. 'Do you call that clean underwear?' he hollered, 'Back to your quarters, immediately, and on your return report for another inspection!'

Once this procedure was over and done with and we were given permission to leave the army grounds, we were finally out on the street and at long last able to vent our anger. 'That guy frisked us as if we were a piece of dirt!' said one of my comrades, 'Wait till I bump into him after the war's over – he won't know what hit him!'

Even before we had taken our oath our squad was allowed to get into the thick of things. We were trained to send and receive radio signals and relocate telephone wires. This we did by criss-crossing the terrain while pulling and pushing the heavy cable rolls mounted on hand barrows and shoving them up steep slopes whilst allowing the cables to uncurl. The Esel, a mountain not far from our barracks, had been picked as a particularly suitable site for these exercises. Even though many of us hated this mountain with a passion, a sort of rivalry developed between the groups, with each one vying to be the fastest and most professional. Comments on how slow or clumsy a particular group was, or whose men originated from which particular geographical region with its particular jargon and lack of natural beauty – as if that had anything to do with our communication skills – abounded after each exercise; but all was forgiven and forgotten when, united in song, we marched back to the barracks.

Though comrades from the other platoons had fun belittling us and derisively referred to our lot as not being the real deal but 'mere radio operators', we underwent the very same munitions training as they did. At my first gun drill, the sergeant explained that this particular Skoda 15, of which there were still quite a few around, had been 'left to us' by the Czechs, and that it was ideal for training purposes. The Austrian mountain corps had, he pointed out, deployed them way back when during the First World War, but he assured us they were still up to the task. 'Use the old auntie the way she deserves it!' he advised. 'Even though her calibre is only 7.5 centimetres, she is a dangerous piece of metal, spewing death and the devil!'

Operating this particular gun required us to follow the exact same procedure as we would for all field guns, he explained and added: 'Ignore any visible differences! They have no significance.' He then ordered us to demonstrate and prove to him that we had polished the barrel to perfection and as he walked up and down the line warned us to be careful not to shift the bore axis whilst pulling the trigger. Karl Mergel, standing next to me completely trashed this idea, whispering something about the sergeant taking us for complete idiots. 'This idea of a bore axis between the breech chamber of the barrel and the target is a total myth. He doesn't seem to have a clue.'

The exercises continued for several days under the strict supervision of our instructors, a hard to please bunch indeed.

Generally, we in the communication platoon didn't seem to warrant special attention when it came to being drilled in firearms, as our superiors had decided that this shouldn't be our top priority. Thus, we were only twice ordered to report to the firing range and, with that and much to my disappointment, the opportunity for me to compete with other more experienced shooters went out the window even though I had previously been such a successful marksman at the RAD. As for actually finding ourselves in a position where we had to fire our guns, this only happened once when we were deployed on an operation. However, in spite of us 'only' being radio operators, we still weren't exempt from the many strenuous army chores, especially the one involving having to run up and down the mountains carrying not only our own cumbersome equipment but loaded carbines as well. During that particular deployment, Sergeant-Major Wurzer appeared on the scene in full field uniform and marching gear and chased us through the icy valley: 'Go, march, fast! The enemy is over there, across the river on the other shore! Off with you!'

Winter had arrived and the Loisach valley was covered in a thick blanket of snow. A rumour that we were soon going to be given orders to move out had begun making the rounds. One evening I overheard a sergeant mumbling something about his fear of us being relocated to Yugoslavia. 'I understand that these Balkan twits have become rebellious,' he said.

On that same evening we had an arms and uniform inspection and because of the draconian rules, many of which seemed to us totally arbitrary and objectionable, a number of our comrades didn't get to sleep that night. They were either not fast enough or hadn't stuck to the guidelines. Even the tiniest misplaced object had aroused the sergeant's wrath.

Shortly thereafter, during the last days of December, our unit set out. While not formally apprised, we had got wind that a new division had been set up at the Heuberg training grounds in Württemberg,* which was to be deployed in Yugoslavia. Many of my comrades had been assigned to join that group, but I was not part of this redeployment. Since I had suffered a sudden bronchial attack, the staff medic relegated me to remain for the foreseeable future in the sick bay. I felt quite sad looking out of the window and seeing my comrades march off, as we had all grown fond of each other and I would have loved to remain part of the team.

After about a week, and tired of feeling useless, I reported to the company sergeant-major and informed him that I was ready for service. An amiable sort of fellow, he greeted me in quite a friendly way and enquired whether I would prefer training the new recruits or working in the office, not before he checked, of course, whether I knew how to type and write shorthand. 'I only learnt shorthand, sergeant, sir,' I responded, but it seemed to suffice. 'It's something, at least,' he said, adding that should I really want to work in the office, I would surely be able to teach myself how to type. 'Certainly sergeant, sir!'

---

* The new division was 4th Mountain Division. The Heuberg facilities had previously been used as a concentration camp and then as a RAD barracks.

I immediately went back to my cabin, sat myself down at a table and, with the help of a training manual and a replica of a keyboard, started to practise. Though I embarked on my office job with great enthusiasm, I was only assigned to do minor errands to start with, but eventually, seeing as I was a fast learner, they trusted me with distributing the mail as well other tasks. Feeling physically much stronger and steadily more able, I was even promoted at one point. So, at the beginning of April, when together with some other fellows I was relocated to the artillery barracks in the northern part of Landshut on the Isar, my position was upgraded to that of second clerk, whilst my buddies, poor chaps, needed to undergo training in the operation of the heavy French guns that had been captured.

As one does, we would often chat amongst ourselves about our comrades and what we thought about the war situation, our own career and so forth. Horst Ulmer, the senior clerk, put into words what was on all our minds: 'What on earth are we to do with these four humungous monsters?' he would ask more than once, then shake his head and mumble something about the uselessness of such railroad guns when one is up in the mountains. He himself had long been harbouring the wish to embark on the sergeant's training course, but because of his cleft lip Captain Rummel, our new battery commander, turned his application down.[*]

Ulmer and I became friendly and got to speaking, with both of us trying to figure out what might be in store for us and what we were to make of the bits of news filtering down to us, especially the rumour about a possible transfer to some army coast artillery division. Neither of us could quite get our heads around the vast contrasts between the camps we had been assigned to throughout the past months, first Garmisch, then Lower Bavaria, and now it looked like we were going to be ferried out to the Atlantic coast! What was the purpose of all this?

---

[*] Nazi ideology regarded people with such problems as defective and degenerate.

As for me, I much preferred my position as a clerk in an office to the daily outdoor drilling on firearms, but when it came to guessing what the future might hold for me, what our next mission was all about, I had no idea what to pin my hopes on. What did trouble me, however, was that we had to hand in our mountain boots in exchange for marching boots. A niggling and foreboding feeling began to take hold of me.

Seeing as I worked in the office, I was one of the first ones to hear about our next operation. Reliable information had it that we were to leave the next day to be transported somewhere to the east.

It was one of the last days in May 1941.

Unravelling one of his foot cloths and giving this his full attention, Horst Ulmer grumbled for only me to hear that this would probably mean we would have to say goodbye to our beloved mountains. 'Romania, as far as I know, is our ally and on one side borders the Black Sea,' he mused and then, sharpening his tone, asked 'but are we really expected to help them out?' Not waiting for an answer, Horst continued his ruminations, making no secret of his belief that it was highly implausible that we would be in a position to provide any support and that, in any case, nobody even knew who the enemy was.

As for me and in spite of my clerk position, I had little intelligence of any value and was thus unable to shed any more light on the issue or on what our next destination might be. Deep down, however, I knew that we would find out soon enough. I said so to Horst, who in return growled something incomprehensible. He was often hard to understand due to his cleft lip.

It took quite a while to organise the transport at the freight depot. Loading those four unbelievably massive French guns onto the freight trains required a huge amount of energy and enormous manpower. Orders and instructions were yelled from one person to another throughout the day: 'All together!' 'At once!' – these words would ring in my ears for years.

With our hands clutching the spokes, we shoved and pushed each gigantic piece of artillery onto the open cargo bed of the train, laboriously and painstakingly, heaving and dragging it, tumbling back and on top of each other and then forced to start afresh. I don't remember how many men slogged away at this enormous task, but it took us hours to get the four gargantuan guns onto the train, where we finally secured them to prevent any accidental and unforeseen collision dislodging them. Then, our two half-tracks had to be loaded onto the wagons in the front, and that was our armament done.

The following day we had to fill up the cargo wagons – these were covered carriages where we stowed away our equipment, our marching gear, carbines, steel helmets and so forth, leaving some room for ourselves to sit down. In our carriage there were only four of us, which meant that we were actually quite comfortable, but in the other ones some ten to fifteen men had to find space – a very tight fit for them.

As we rolled along the Isar River towards Munich, our train seemed endlessly long to me. It was a mild evening in May, but we took little notice of spring or the countryside we passed by, as we were preoccupied and deep in thought. At the Munich Ost-bahnhof we had to wait for about one hour, allowed outside our carriages only a few at a time and purely to relieve ourselves – any lingering was strictly prohibited. The journey continued on via Salzburg and Vienna, and because the train frequently had to come to a prolonged halt, probably due to engineering problems, we made very slow progress.

The train rumbled through Hungary. Once, when we had come to yet another stop in the midst of the Danube plain, our wagon was suddenly encircled by a bunch of dancing gypsies who were unashamedly begging for money. We were cautioned not to let them come up too close. 'These people always steal!' was the warning.

Some of us threw them cigarettes and at the same time waved our hands to keep them well away from our carriage. This, however, didn't prevent one of the fellows, a cheeky young man with curly dark hair, from attempting to climb up the few steps onto the footboard. One of our sergeants felt it necessary to draw his Luger pistol in a clear sign of warning. We had a good laugh watching the gypsy dash back like a weasel to join his folks, but not before picking up his hat which had fallen off, clutching it in front of his breast and performing an inimitably submissive bow towards us.

Later on, when we made a further stop right in the middle of an open field, we found two little girls standing in front of our carriage door. Four of us had been playing cards and looking up from just having finished a round, our eyes fell on two lovely faces, peering up at us from under white kerchiefs. They were dressed in blue blouses and long skirts that reached down to their feet and were covered by gaily embroidered aprons. We were immediately attracted to these beautiful young creatures and our sergeant, perhaps wanting to provide some entertainment for us, laughingly asked them whether they too had come for cigarettes.

But they didn't understand us. The taller of the two curtseyed and then handed us a bunch of flowers they must have picked in the meadow. We graciously accepted these and in return threw them a bar of chocolate. Once the train got moving again, the two girls, still standing near the tracks, waved to us goodbye.

At a small station in the midst of the plain, a more prolonged stop had obviously been scheduled, during which we were ordered to do our laundry at the local village fountain where they had a pump. Our cook was able to heat up the water in his kitchen carriage, and whilst his helper handed out the full buckets, they also distributed our ration of bread, hard sausage, some tinned food and cigarettes. We were in high spirits throughout, though still none the wiser as to where we were heading on this journey.

As we were approaching Budapest we saw that the Danube had burst its banks, flooding the meadows on either side. From the top of the railway embankment we were able to make out the river lying about one kilometre ahead of us, and for a split second my thoughts travelled back to my home town, wondering whether, in the waters of the Danube now soaking the fields around me, a few drops of the Loisach River would be mixed in

Slowly the train took us past Budapest and we got to see the splendid buildings of the parliament, though little else. Another stop followed but we were ordered to remain on the train. This continued for a long time, and once again we were only allowed off the carriage to relieve ourselves, taking turns in pairs to do our business and report back before another couple was let out.

Alternating between playing cards or looking out of the window at the Carpathian mountain passes, we rolled past the villages of Transylvania. I must have fallen asleep as, when Horst shook me awake, we had reached the outskirts of Bucharest, where our train briefly came to a halt. 'Time to rise and shine, my friend!' he said, whilst announcing in a sarcastic tone of voice that though no sight-seeing tour had been arranged, he felt certain that I wanted to be awake whilst travelling through the capital of a country that belonged to our comrades in arms. 'You might as well take a look at them, seeing as we are united together to fight a common enemy,' he said, adding under his breath 'whoever that might be.'

Chiming in, Sergeant Kurz questioned the reason behind Hitler's non-aggression pact with the Russians, seeing as this region seemed at peace. 'Are we perhaps expected to shoot holes into the Black Sea?' he asked nobody in particular.

Towards the end of the third day of our journey we reached Galati on the northern side of the Danube, where we had assumed we would finally be ordered to unload. But it was a false alarm, with our train stopping only for a short while before once again departing from the station and heading north.

Night had fallen and we all looked at each other in puzzlement when the train came to a stop next to some wooden shacks. Hanging from a hut was a sign saying 'Fulgaresti'.

'Night guards on duty report now!' yelled our sergeant, whose voice was unmistakable. In quick succession orders of how we were to organise ourselves followed, with the office, my domain, being located 'in a house next to the station'. I had a sneaking suspicion that when the sergeant pronounced the word 'house' with such obvious disdain in his tone, he himself didn't have high expectations. And indeed, once I and the sergeant-major arrived at the designated house, we understood.

The rest of our unit was ordered to march a further two kilometres to a field at the bottom of some mountain where they would pitch their tents. 'Some exercise will be good for all of us!' commented the sergeant, pre-empting any moaning from the men.

A single shadeless light bulb hanging precariously from the ceiling of our so-called office cast a dim light. Whilst the sergeant-major, quite obviously much displeased with the sparse surroundings, fiddled around with a switch next to the entrance door, our eyes fell on a rat which dashed out into the open from under the duckboard. 'Well, at least we don't have to spend the night on our own!' he remarked sarcastically, and instructed us immediately to hang all edible provisions on a beam at the back of the shed. 'Our hosts have truly thought of all our needs!' he sneered, but indeed that beam was perfect for the job.

We then set up our office, using three old chests we had found to serve as desks, and also spotted some chairs and camp beds. 'Tomorrow,' promised the sergeant 'we'll get a phone connection and hopefully we'll soon also find some better quarters.'

We had already had our evening meal during our train journey and, grateful not to have been given guard duty, we went straight to the beds we had made up earlier. Exhausted, we fell asleep immediately, and even if there had been a rat during that night, we would certainly not have noticed it. 'But', my friend Hans Maul assured us all, 'the next time we set eyes on one of these creatures, it will die a hero's death!' words which amused us greatly.

The following day nobody minded that we took our time to unload. The crew, together with our sergeants, set up home in suitable accommodation in a school building and some private houses in Roscani. This was a small village nearby, situated in the midst of fertile countryside, which, as far as the eye could reach, undulated out to the horizon. We, the office clerks, were assigned a house at the edge of the village, constructed, as must have been the custom, out of clay bricks and a thatched roof. Somewhat surprised at how eagerly the Romanian sergeants tried to make us feel welcome, we started speculating as to what might be the reason behind their enthusiasm. Were we expected to help the farmers? How did these farmers themselves view the situation, and what did they make of our presence, seeing as all seemed peaceful? Surely we would soon be relocated to the Black Sea coast, we thought. Wherever *Landsers* gathered, rumours and guesswork abounded.

We had already spent five days in Roscani when we were ordered to shave our heads right down to the scalp. This, we were told, was for hygiene reasons. Several of the guys had a really hard time saying goodbye to their locks or their carefully arranged parting, and once again there was moaning and groaning amongst the men. When it was us office dragons' turn, we decided to see only the funny side of it and felt it was beneath us to kick up any fuss. On that particular day, it so happened that we were one happy bunch of lads in any event, as one of the lance-corporals from our squad had been promoted to corporal. Occasions such as these gave us good cause to celebrate.

But not everybody felt that way. The advancement of our chum put Horst's nose out of joint as he once again felt that he had been overlooked. A few hours later he lay flat out in the orchard behind our house, drunk as a lord, with beer, wine and liquor bottles littered on the grass round him, completely oblivious to the amorous advances the eighteen- or nineteen-year-old daughter of our hostess had attempted to bestow on him. This young, some-what plump Romanian girl couldn't quite get it into her head why none of us, not even our drunk Horst, had tried to pick her up.

During the second week in June things finally began to move. As office clerk, I was once again among the first to be informed that our artillery battalion had been seconded to the Romanian Army. What could that mean? Was our new master suddenly the Romanian king? We felt insecure and at a loss. Questions, assumptions and predictions started circulating once again.

'Aren't the Romanians our friends in arms? But then again, against whom are these arms directed? Are they preparing to attack the Russians? Surely, Hitler won't allow this. Surely, we are honouring our non-aggression pact!' We tried our very best to come up with convincing arguments to allay our fears. 'Why, surely . . . it couldn't be the Russians – they supply the Reich with all the grain!' Overall, we had no solid information to go by. 'Aren't the Romanians much too weak to take on Russia?' asked Horst. 'Not if they fight alongside our troops,' came the reply from somebody next to him.

Discussing the possibilities of what might be in store for us, a number of us gathered in the village centre of Roscani and debated the likelihood of war, deep down sensing all the while that our restful period was nearing its end but that, nonetheless, we had the upper hand. Thus, when nineteen-year-old gunner Heiner Kunz euphorically exclaimed that we would be victorious even before Ivan[*] had a chance to attack us, nobody contradicted him. 'Look at us,' he blustered, 'Just remember, didn't we punish France for declaring war on us? Just you watch what will happen this time round!' Carrying on in the same cocky tone, he predicted that 'It won't be us helping the Romanians, trust me, it'll be the other way round.' Then, slightly more grim-faced, he concluded: 'One thing is obvious: what with all those guns around us, we're sure here for a reason. It'll kick off any minute, mark my words!'

---

[*] The usual German Army slang term for a Russian or Soviet soldier.

CHAPTER 4

On Sick Leave

Straight ahead of us, right beyond the sluggish River Pruth, lay Bessarabia. We were positioned on the border of Stalin's Soviet Union where we had set up camp a few days earlier, hiding our guns under camouflage as best we could in the slightly undulating terrain, void of any trees or shrubbery. Our barrels were pointed towards the east, and we *Landsers* knew that we were not the only ones waiting. Ahead of us Romanian infantry units were standing by, ready to attack. Our role, we were told, was to provide the Romanian allies with artillery support, and together we were to pre-empt a Russian attack on Germany. Though tense, we were, inexplicably, also curious.

It was still pitch black on that 22 June morning when we mounted our vehicles on the northern outskirts of Roscani. The half-tracks towing our guns were preparing for departure. All of a sudden, the piercing noise of engines starting up ripped through the air and nearly deafened us. Simultaneously, in a ghostlike column, a brigade of armoured cars, trucks, cargo vehicles and tanks leapt into motion. I never could recall how many trucks were heading up our equipment wagon, but it was an impressive number. Enveloped in a brownish-yellow cloud of dust and not encountering any resistance, we rolled forward in the direction of the Pruth.

Behind the driver and the sergeant-major, whose name was Moller, sat my friend Hans Maul with his back against the driver's seat and I, facing him, was put opposite. Squatting on wooden chests packed with wires, cables and telephone equipment, which in turn was all stored in small hard plastic boxes to protect against breakage and dirt, we began our journey. Our carbines were clamped tightly between our knees, and held upright in our hands as we stared out of the side windows, which were caked in dust. Gruesome sights of a recent battle littered the ground. We could make out several dead Russians lying in the fields with their arms spread wide open and helmets askew, or lying twisted on their stomachs, faces pressed flat into the soil.

No one except the senior sergeant said a word. 'Well, boys, the Romanians have sure done a thorough job here. If the war continues this way, I can bet you that we'll come out of it unscathed – absolutely nothing will happen to us,' he concluded, but added with a whiff of disappointment: 'So far, they haven't even requested fire support from us!'

That day our convoy only stopped once. Apprehensive, yet also filled with a sense of anticipation, we knelt down next to the wheels of our vehicles, our guns in position. 'Are we about to attack?' whispered my companion Hans into my ear. I truly had no idea. 'If our services are required in one of their forward observation posts, we'll know soon enough!' I responded tersely, but our corporal ordered us to stop talking at once. 'Silence, and don't drive yourself crazy!'

He then stood up, stared for a split second at the hand signal given by Lieutenant Stabler and shouted: 'Get back in – we're moving!'

That evening, in one of those typical Transylvanian villages one passes without even noticing whilst travelling along the interminable seeming roads in that area, we buried Lance-Corporal Hans Lindinger with full military honours. A stray bullet had accidentally hit him during our short stop-over. Apparently, he died instantly. Standing next to the small mound of earth with the wooden post on top of it, from which dangled his steel helmet, I got goose bumps listening to the gun salute which tore through the silence. In the present-arms rifle position and with our helmets on, our unit paid its respects to the first comrade killed during this part of our deployment.

After the salute was fired, our sergeant delivered a brief and rather bland sermon, of which not a single word remains in my mind. All I recall was that I stood there fixing my eyes on the wooden beam above a well, which rose into the sky and onto which was fixed a large handle that swayed back and forth in the cool evening breeze. Behind the well, I had spotted some grazing cows with their bulging eyes staring at us with what I thought was curiosity.

'I could well do without such a sermon,' I secretly thought. 'Lothar,' I said to myself, 'you most certainly don't want to be buried in this soil, it's so fertile that no one would ever come to manure it, let alone visit you.' Trying to comfort myself that I would remain unhurt, I put the loss of our comrade behind me.

Over the next few days we made rapid progress, and what with not encountering any noteworthy resistance, our mood began to lift. In fact, we advanced at such speed that our reinforcements could barely catch up with us.

At one point I overheard Baier, a senior sergeant, mumbling something about his worry as to what might happen if the heat all of a sudden gave way to rain and flooding. Even though the River Pruth could cope with large amounts of water, he feared that the road would turn into one huge mud bath. 'So far, it's been quite dry,' he mused out loud, but turning to us he looked worried: 'Who knows what the future will bring?'

The sergeant was spot on. It all began the very next day: after some rolling thunder, it started raining so hard, I had never seen anything like it before. Water came hammering down, making it well nigh impossible to move. With our guns positioned in a small forest, a comrade and I, along with two other soldiers, had been assigned to guard duty for our camp. All of us had wrapped tarpaulins over our shoulders and could hear the rain dripping down from our helmets, the water forming large pools of squishy mud below us. Within a few minutes we were wading through a ten-centimetre deep black sludge which clung to our boots, dragging us down. Inching forward at a snail's pace, often losing our footing, we really were a sorry sight, with Fritz Kohl moaning and groaning at my side and pessimistically predicting that it would only get worse. I couldn't help but agree with him. Our chief concern was for the motorised vehicles. 'How on earth will our half-tracks pulling such humungous loads be able to get a proper grip? I can bet you they'll topple over and sink deep into the soil,' Fritz agonised and then sheepishly asked, knowing full well what the answer was: 'Do you think our military gentlemen have given this even an ounce of thought back in their comfortable war room?'

The following morning a clear blue sky stretched over the vast plain in front of us and temperatures had dropped. Due to the cooler air streaming in, clouds of steam rose from the wet soil, but by mid-morning it had already turned hot and humid once again, just like the day before. There was only one difference. Swarms of mosquitoes were descending upon us like a plague, biting whatever bare skin they could find. Like all the others I tried shielding myself, wildly flailing my arms and loudly cursing the beasts, but to little avail.

Given the different nature of terrain we had to battle with as a consequence of the torrential rain, we made slow progress. Whilst our vehicles slid back and forth, frightening the hell out of us, we nevertheless managed to stick to what the Romanians called a street, an unevenly paved stretch of road lined by telephone poles rammed into the ground, some of which were dangerously leaning to one side as a result of the downpour. We could barely manage to keep up with the Romanian units, which advanced at an impressive speed. At times we would come across some Romanians on horseback heading in the opposite direction. They were relentlessly driving Russian prisoners to move along, perhaps to some labour camp, but all we could see was a sorry column of men dressed in rags and stumbling towards a destination unknown to them; these were men of all ages who could scarcely keep themselves upright, such was their exhaustion.

I had no idea what lay in store for these poor devils and could only feel compassion towards them, but made quite sure not to share any of my concerns openly. The thought that seemed to prevail at the time not only in my mind, but also in the minds of my comrades, was that we had a mission to fulfil and that a triumphant victory was waiting for us. We were convinced of our power, and our confidence was unwavering. There was indeed little that would actually have suggested that our optimism was misplaced. Much to our relief, we hadn't even once been ordered to ready ourselves to attack. No shots had been fired. Everything just seemed to remain calm and the days passed by swiftly and uneventfully. Above all, we knew that we could rely on our Romanian allies in front of us. We hadn't come across so much as a single stray Red Army unit, and thus felt quite justified in believing that Stalin's troops weren't nearly as dangerous as we had feared and that we were safe.

Soon we were but a few kilometres away from Kishinev,* the capital of Bessarabia.

We spent two very relaxing days there and our unit had a whale of a time slaughtering a pig we had 'captured' on one of our forays and which we then cooked and devoured. But sitting around on this stage on the edge of the theatre of war was certainly no mere playtime. We were kept busy with minor repairs to our vehicles and maintenance work on our equipment; meanwhile our horses, which usually had to pull the supply wagons, also got some rest, peacefully grazing in the backyard of our quarters, which this time consisted of a large empty house. The animals seemed to enjoy this break as well, relishing the attention of everyone who happened to pass by and patted their manes.

On the second evening of our stay, these two four-legged companions of ours appeared in front of our lodgings, dragging behind them a huge wine barrel resting atop a wagon, and taking up most of its cargo area as it was so massive.

---

* Now known as Chișinău, in Moldavia.

'Grab a bowl and report at the wine barrel!' The booming sound of Sergeant Baier's voice echoed back from the wall of the building. With a broad smile, our cook Erich Kaser stood on the wagon, turned the tap and was the first one to help himself, lifting his mug high up above his head. Brandishing his cup with a ceremonious circular gesture, he invited us in his local dialect not to be shy and get to it.

I too received my ration and, gabbing merrily away, I eventually tired myself out and withdrew to one of the back rooms of our night quarters. The taste of the wine was a bit too spicy and sweet for my liking, but neither I nor my comrades left a single drop in our bowls.

An hour before this very welcome break diverted our attention, we had received mail from back home. I got a letter from my erstwhile master from Waldtal, and another one from Kathi and her mother from Garmisch. Heartened by memories of my homeland and people dear to me, but perhaps more due to the alcohol we were no longer used to, I fell asleep on the straw bed that I had covered with my tarpaulin.

But my sleep was to be brief. Suddenly I felt short of breath. Breaking out into a sweat which covered my whole body, I bolted up. Surely this couldn't be due to just having had a bit of red wine, I thought to myself, and immediately answered my own question: I knew that I had suffered another of my bronchial asthma attacks. 'Gosh, I sure could do without that,' I told myself.

The following day our unit pressed on towards what we by then knew to be our destination: the city of Odessa, on the coast of the Black Sea.

I myself had been sent to the medical officer. He was a jolly sort of man, rotund but very agile and with a pleasant Bavarian mountain village accent. After a thorough examination he told me in no uncertain terms that I would have to go to the field hospital post-hate. 'We cannot beat the Russians with physically defective comrades like you. The medic will immediately issue the necessary paperwork and I want to see you off before the day is over.' He certainly wasn't going to tolerate any of my protestations. By then it was the beginning of October.

I had spent about a fortnight in the field hospital in Tiraspol when we heard on the radio that Odessa had been captured. It was 16 October 1941.

While I was beginning to feel much better, there was certainly no way I could be considered cured. The medical offer who had issued the release papers allowing me to return to my squad recommended in his letter that I urgently be transferred home and assigned to the reserve.

My journey back to my unit took me along the coastline of the Black Sea, and I recognised some German-sounding town names, Lustenau, Rosenau and others.* I wondered why I was so surprised. I had, after all, certainly heard that not so long ago many Germans had left their home country to settle in this fertile region, and to do so they had travelled down the Danube atop their Ulm boxes.†

When I reported back to Rummel, my squad leader, he carefully read through the letter I had handed to him and then, peering over his glasses, he scrutinised me long and hard. 'Well, Corporal Herrmann! Surely you'll be wanting to get back on your feet and become fit for service!'

'Yes, sir!'

'In that case,' he continued, 'I'll approve and forward the medical officer's recommendation. Until your next assignment is decided on, I'll put you on light duty.' He added that this assignment, obviously involving some travel, would give me an opportunity to get to know the military positions along the coastline and that Senior Sergeant Baier would be informed accordingly.

Picking up the receiver of the field telephone on his desk with one hand, all whilst operating the crank handle, he dismissed me with his other hand.

---

* Lustenau unidentified; Rosenau = Râşnov, in Romania. These towns had had ethnic German populations since at least the nineteenth century.
† A type of flat-bottomed barge used on the Danube.

During the following week the sergeant-major asked me to look after some of his correspondence, but since it was nothing too onerous, it provided me with a lot of free time which I could do with as I pleased. I made leisurely field trips to see for myself the spots where our guns had been concealed, and had some long chats with my comrades. Over and over again they urged me to reconsider my return to the barracks back at home. 'We've never had it so cushy as here,' they would say, 'Why on earth wouldn't you want to stay with us but instead go back to the barracks?'

I assured them that my imminent departure certainly wasn't a case of my own choosing and that, if I stayed, I would only be a medical burden to them once the going got tough. All I could do was repeat to them that the opinion wasn't my own but from the doctors in the field hospital who had decided that I simply hadn't fully recovered.

'My only wish for you guys is that it'll remain as calm here as it seems to have been until now!' I said, hoping that they would finally leave me in peace.

Once, accompanying three comrades who happened to be on leave at that same time, I took a tour through the town. Looking around, we quickly realised that quite a battle must have taken place to conquer Odessa. The telltale signs were obvious: destroyed houses next to the port, burnt-out vehicles that had been shoved to the sides of the roads, many with the black German *Balkenkreuz* emblem still visible on some of their dented parts. Ruins and debris, mounds of garbage, upended sledges, discarded trunks wherever we looked. Although we were chatting casually, the question as to how many brave men might have died in this place weighed heavy and would not let go of me for a long time to come.

Then, on the afternoon of the eighth day after my return, I was summoned to report to Senior Sergeant Moll. With a broad smile on his face he handed me two sheets of paper. 'You're one lucky guy, Private Herrmann, getting a fortnight's leave to recuperate in Breslau, your home town! Why, wouldn't you know it, it's smack on your way to Landshut!' He explained that the documents were the marching orders for me to hand in at the Landshut barracks and, wishing me good luck, he dismissed me.

My journey towards the west, travelling on a so-called recuperation train that was forced to make numerous lengthy stops, lasted for two days and nights before I finally arrived in Breslau. With my rucksack on my back, onto which was fastened my steel helmet, and my carbine strapped around my shoulder, I was hanging from the steps whilst the train pulled into the station, eager to hop off. But I was suddenly overcome by a feeling of exhaustion mixed with despondency, and though I had sent my aunt who lived in Breslau a telegram explaining the reason for my visit and asking whether I could possibly stay with her, I didn't know whether she had received it.

My joy at spotting her standing amidst the crowd on the platform was thus all the more genuine and heartfelt. She was the widowed sister of my father, and ever since childhood I had felt nothing but warm affection towards this woman. So when, once we had embraced, she repeatedly impressed upon me how much she was looking forward to my visit and that she had been deeply moved that it was her I had turned to when at a loss for somewhere to stay, she was completely honest.

'Lothar,' she said, tenderness making her voice quiver, 'You've got nobody in this world, and I just hope that maybe your father up there will look down on us two and will rejoice with us.'

Passing through the station, a guard from the army police stopped and checked me. Because of the large crescent-shaped metal gorgets hanging on chains around their necks, we *Landsers* commonly referred to them as 'chain dogs', but it didn't faze me in the least, as of course I had my papers with me.

On our way out of the station I caught the headlines of a newspaper's special edition that was being sold at two newsagents, and frantically snapped up by the crowds. Skimming the leader typed in large letters, I found out that Luftwaffe General Ernst Udet, a well-known citizen of our city, had been killed in the early hours of that same morning while flying a fighter plane of the Luftwaffe.*

Turning to my Aunt Hedwig I remarked that this piece of news wasn't exactly the happy welcome to my home town I had imagined, but she tersely responded that at least I wasn't a Luftwaffe general. 'Mind that you stay put on the ground, boy – and above all, make sure you get better soon. Your last letter to me wasn't exactly encouraging.'

I did everything I could to put my aunt at ease, reassuring her that the comrades in the convalescent company would have me fit as a fiddle in no time.

Two days later I travelled by bike to Waldtal to drop in on my old master. Dressed in full uniform, to comply with army orders, I could hardly contain my anticipation and arrived at his house where he received me with open arms.

He had aged visibly, but was thrilled to bits: 'My boy, so you haven't forgotten us altogether,' he beamed, 'but of course, I gathered that already from your letters, though there were so very few of them,' he added wistfully, then, quickly finding his usual firm voice, he demanded that I should put pen to paper more often in the future so that he could continue keeping an eye on what was happening in my life.

He wasn't the only one to be happy and in high spirits on that day. I myself had the best time. We had a long chat which made the few hours I had planned for the visit pass in a flash. When, that evening, I returned to Aunt Hedwig and had stored my bike in her shed, I handed her a large piece of beef which my former master and substitute father had offered me as a present. She was totally delighted, swiftly laid the table, and together we enjoyed a sumptuous meal.

What with catching a movie here and there, spending time with friends having drinks in coffee houses and enjoying some female company, my time convalescing flew by before I knew it. That

---

* In fact Udet, the Luftwaffe's equipment chief, had committed suicide.

changed once I left Breslau and arrived at the Landshut barracks. As I had done previously, I once again realised just how much I despised nearly every single aspect of military life. The only bright side of that assignment was my friendship with the young and very pretty daughter of a farmer who lived in the neighbourhood. This indeed offered some welcome relief.

Although my duties in the convalescent unit weren't exactly demanding, I nevertheless, from day one, gave a lot of thought to how I could manoeuvre my transfer to my beloved mountains in Garmisch. Thus, whilst allegedly busy with office tasks, I was secretly hard at work trying to put together a credible request which would convince the authorities to send me back to where my heart was. What I thought would carry most sway was if I justified my request by stating that my priority during my convalescence was to be declared fit for service as soon as possible. To this end, of course, the misty weather prevailing in the foothills was far less suitable than the fresh and crisp mountain air, or so I wrote in my request. At the time, towards the end of November 1941, foggy days were, of course, not unusual anywhere, but I sent in my application regardless and anxiously awaited the decision.

Things began to move quite quickly after that, as my plan seemed to have worked.

I could just about squeeze in a few minutes to say goodbye to Lotte, whom I had met some three weeks prior in a café on one of the Sundays when I was on leave. On that particular afternoon, there she was sipping her coffee at a nearby table, blonde, wavy hair, perhaps seventeen years old and with a pair of sparkling, bright blue eyes throwing curious, inviting looks across to where I was sitting. From the first moment I knew that this girl was my dream woman! When she got up to leave, I immediately jumped to my feet to help her into her greyish-green Lodencoat. And whilst she thanked me, I was quick to hold her attention for another moment: '*Fräulein*, may I walk you home?' For a few seconds she seemed to be thinking about it. 'No, many thanks. It's much too far.' She then explained that she lived on the family's farm in Niederviehbach, several kilometres away and that she would need to catch a train to travel back home. Not to be brushed off, I insisted. 'But surely, I can walk you to the station?' She nodded in agreement and when we arrived at the station, I spontaneously made what seemed to me the obvious decision and simply boarded the train as well. We had a wonderful chat and before reaching her home we became intimate. During the remainder of my stay in Landshut we would get together frequently and as you would expect, we fell madly and deeply in love. Had anyone from back at the garrison checked up on me, I would definitely have been demoted to construction duty.

That's all I could think of on my train ride to Garmisch. Being separated from Lotte was the only cloud overshadowing my anticipation and excitement about soon being able to take walks in the Loisach valley again.

By the time I reported for duty at the Garmisch convalescent unit, it was the second week of the Advent season. Of course the company sergeant-major immediately recognised me and seemed pleased to have me back. He had thought that I was dug in far off in the east with the other guys from Landshut and had wondered what had become of us. 'What with your asthma, you are much better off here in the mountains where we're blessed with fresh air. And as long as you're here, I want to have you with me in the office,' he continued, not wanting to waste any time delaying matters. 'Coincidentally the position of the senior clerk has just recently become vacant.' Out of politeness he then formally asked me whether I was willing to accept the offer, and I obviously was more than happy to. 'All clear then, soldier!' And with that my future in Garmisch was settled.

The duties we were assigned in the convalescent company were far less arduous than those set for new recruits in the other companies. There was a constant coming and going in our group, because, just as soon as a soldier was declared fit for duty, he was given his marching papers and packed off back to his unit, more often than not to the east. Seeing as I worked in the office, I had many such cases land on my desk, and whilst I myself was there for genuine reasons, I couldn't help but feel that others would view me as a sort of shirker. Thus I genuinely did all I could to get myself in good shape, signed up for as many outdoor activities as possible where I could breathe in the cold winter air and build up my resistance.

That didn't mean that I didn't spend many of my free hours with my erstwhile host family. I got to know Hans, Kathi's new boyfriend who was only slightly older than me. He had been a lance-corporal in the infantry, but his home town had subsequently requested that he be declared exempt and return back home to his position as a baker, a profession considered indispensable for feeding the civilian population. He suggested I sign up as a volunteer for the mountain guard, a group he described as only consisting of young men, apart from the slightly older leader, a master joiner, who wished to make themselves useful whilst not yet having been conscripted. He didn't have a hard time trying to convince me, but having got the measure of who I was, he added, 'In any event, by all accounts you're a passionate hiker and surely your doctor and superiors will be impressed if you are with us up there breathing in the mountain air that has that crisp freshness to it and will restore you in no time.' I told Hans that he had clinched the deal; I was ready and raring to go. That same evening I joined them and immediately participated in a session headed by a medical officer who instructed us in first aid.

During the war, the mountain guard was of course far less busy than during peace times, as in the winter there were fewer ski accidents and during the summer fewer injured hikers who had to be ferried down to the valley. Thus, there was plenty of opportunity for us simply to climb up to the various mountain tops, perhaps the Zugspitze or the Kreuzeck, and enjoy the panoramic views, indulge in sunbathing, playing cards or chess or watching skiers and hikers make their way up and down the slopes. These were happy times and often, whilst taking our meals in the mountain cabins or during our patrols through the Oberreintal, I literally could feel my love for Garmisch becoming more deeply rooted by the day. The Loisach valley had most definitely become home to me. I suppose another very important factor contributing to my general well-being was that I had become close to the sister of Kathi's first boyfriend, and what initially was purely a friendship very quickly developed into something more romantic.

But in spite of the strenuous outdoor activities I was so keenly incorporating into my daily routine, my medical officer, an extremely strict man, didn't consider me fit enough to return to my unit on the Eastern Front. At each of my regular check-ups he would try and calm me down: 'No, definitely not. It looks very likely that you will suffer more of these asthma attacks and I cannot have you endanger the other soldiers,' he insisted.

I, however, felt increasingly restless, as after a while I firmly considered myself fully cured and ready for service. But it turned out differently than I had hoped for. At the end of August 1943 I had to be admitted to the Alpenhof army hospital in Garmisch, this time with jaundice. After being discharged I was told back at the barracks that my position as senior clerk had been given to somebody else. Not allowing me even a moment's grief but with a twinkle in his eye, the company sergeant-major went on to inform me that as my career of an office clerk had by then run its course in any event, the superiors had decided to promote me to the position of corporal. I would, he explained, have a choice, either to be deployed as a gunner or opt for the training course as an artillery forward observer. That training was being provided in Maribor. 'They're actively looking for people, so I need you to make a decision quickly,' he urged.

In a split second I had made up my mind, stood to attention and in a firm voice replied: 'Yes, sergeant-major, I report for duty with the artillery observer training unit.' Approving my decision, which he considered most sensible, he motioned for me to sit myself behind the desk. 'We'll need this in writing from you of course.'

Two days later, I was sitting in a train which would take me, together with a sergeant and ten other corporals to Austria and then on to Maribor. While the area boasted the most beautiful mountain scenery and we should, by all accounts, have felt elated, the prevailing military discipline spoilt it for us right from the word go, mainly due to its rigour which was far more uncompromising than we had grown used to during our recruitment phase. Following strict guidelines and suffering harsh conditions with freezing temperatures, we were drilled in the techniques of operating the Model 36 mountain gun and how to register and report artillery fire, which seeing as this was our actual assignment, was of course the main focus. How to manoeuvre a telescope and trace enemy fire whilst aiming at targets on different height levels would become so much part of us that we practically heard and obeyed the orders in our dreams. We even learnt how to ride. Our horses, it has to be said, were far more gentle than our instructors.

You would have thought that the military hierarchy, with its inbuilt deference to the top brass, was set in stone, would be properly respected and fairly adhered to by one and all. But the reality was different. What we met in the field was power for power's sake, with our instructors throwing their weight around day and night. More than once we got to hear insults like: 'Why are you wasting your time here for no good reason. Even if I'm only a corporal and you think you're a big shot, don't forget that I am the instructor here and you're just a trainee! And stop wasting everybody's time with your inappropriate comments!' And there was worse still than this.

The grande finale of our training consisted of a mountain exercise, which took place close to the Judenburg, a restricted area and inaccessible to civilians due to the fact that live firing was part of the operation. Even though everything had gone to plan and all orders had been executed to the nth degree, we couldn't help but feel by the end of the day that we had been hounded at every step of the way and were nothing but losers.

Towards the end of March 1944, we all travelled back to Garmisch. Many of us, me included, fervently hoped that after all the excruciating training days we had just been put through, we would finally be granted some respite, but once again we would be sorely disappointed. At that point in the war, the criteria for medical fitness had been significantly lowered, above all due to the frightfully heavy losses in the east. Naturally, every single man was needed and not even two weeks passed after I returned from Maribor until I was assigned to a march battalion headed for the front.

CHAPTER 5

To the Eastern Front

Once again we were travelling by train. With all our equipment in our rucksacks we were on our way to Graz where we would spend three full days at the Kaiser Franz Joseph barracks. They had given us two days' leave, which luckily meant that we had plenty of time to do some sightseeing in this beautiful capital city of the Styrian province. Although our group certainly welcomed this break, I wasn't nearly as happy as my comrades were, who seemed to have no trouble finding female company whilst I still hankered for Lotte, my girl from Landshut.

On the third day our train slowly rolled out from the station, which by that time had been blacked out due to the air raids, and we left the city – also hidden in darkness – behind us. Shortly before, we had been informed that our future deployment would be with 4th Mountain Division, which had taken up defensive positions near the Dniester, but since nothing further had been disclosed we were left to make wild guesses as to what might lie in store for us. We had quite literally been left in the dark.

When day broke, a look outside the window revealed that we had passed the borders and now found ourselves in Hungarian countryside. At times the train would come to a stop so that we could relieve ourselves, but apart from some short interruptions, it kept going eastwards until we had reached the north-western parts of Romania. On it went towards the Ukraine.

Suddenly, however, the train came to a screeching halt.

'Everybody out! Leave nothing behind! Fall in, three ranks!'

We obeyed the orders without a moment's hesitation as always. The minute we all stood outside alongside the train tracks, we heard the shrill whistle of the engine and with that, huffing and puffing, the train disappeared into the distance. There was nothing around us; we had truly been dropped off in the middle of nowhere. Whilst the carriages of the train rolled past me, I had the sudden urge simply to hop on and travel back – a fleeting thought. We heard some dull rumbling noises not far away and, judging from the sun's position, we placed the noise somewhere north-east of us.

'Artillery fire!' we heard somebody saying. 'Let's hope it's our side that's doing the shooting,' mumbled Karl Kroner who was standing next to me, a pleasant sort of a fellow with whom I had had some lengthy discussions during our journey. Nodding, I didn't say a word and just pushed my mountain cap down the back of my neck. Truth be told, I was clueless as to what might happen next. The landscape around us, covered by woods and meadows, was glowing in the early morning sunlight, and it felt as if spring was on its way. The sight of such serene surroundings with the colourful flower meadows bordering the other side of the train tracks and morning dewdrops still glistening on the leaves would ordinarily have lifted my spirits no end, but that wasn't the case at that time, what with thundering gunfire going off at the front, and explosions crashing down behind us.

The grass of the field in front of us had been trampled down. Some twenty or thirty metres from where I was stood a large tent with a small flagpole rammed into the ground in front of its entrance. Whilst the tactical symbols displayed on the flag puzzled me since I didn't know what they signified, I was actually more curious about what the several assembled *Landsers* and sergeants were talking about, but I couldn't make out a thing. They seemed at ease, smoking and blowing grey cigarette puffs into the air. Suddenly a major of the *Jäger* stood in front of us, requesting we listen up.

Pointing to the man next to him, whom we recognised as a field priest from the cross hanging over his officer's jacket (with no rank emblem on it), the major started his address.

'You will now receive the blessing of our military priest,' he said, 'and whoever is a believer will surely be strengthened in his resolve to fulfil his duty. Others will come to no harm just listening.' Continuing his briefing, he then divided us into our units and advised us that, in due course, we would be taken to where we needed to be. Arm outstretched he pointed in the direction of the *Landsers* who had casually gathered at their tent's entrance and told them to stop their chattering. 'Silence!' he called.

Meanwhile, the clergyman had placed a small suitcase at his feet, unclasped the buckles and took out a shawl which he wrapped around his shoulders. Stepping forward he then pronounced his blessing: 'I will now bestow on all of you a general absolution. As you well know and if you wish, you can then come to me later for a private confession!' While very clearly enunciating a Latin benediction, he waved his crucifix in all four directions and devoutly crossed himself at the end. Many of us sank to our knees and also crossed ourselves, me included. I couldn't help overhearing Manfred Möller, another soldier with whom I had become quite close during our journey when we confided in each other matters close to our heart, murmuring: 'What with having this guy blessing us we're most definitely going to end up in a hailstorm of bullets.' This made me smile, albeit rather apprehensively.

An hour later some twenty-five men marching in formation were on their way to the front. This was the first day of us belonging to 4th Mountain Division. In front of me was Sergeant Kellermann from the 8th Battery in the 3rd Battalion of the 4th Regiment and I was soon to get an earful hearing from him everything there was to know about this unit. With my twenty-three years, I was actually amongst the older ones in my group.

Just before arriving at the front, and not far from us, we could hear the thunderous roar of artillery firing and shells crashing into the ground. Whilst I could see the guy in front of me, a veteran, tensing up ever so slightly, he soldiered on unperturbed. Only once, when a very unsettling whistling noise swished through the air, he ordered 'Full cover!' and a split-second later a shell exploded right next to us in the field. That was the first time I got to know the terrifying noise of blasting shell fire and the hissing sounds of a maelstrom of hot metal fragments which had come raining down from the sky.

'Onwards!' I could hear Kellermann shout. A few seconds later he turned to me grim-faced and said: 'Haven't we seen this nonsense before? The Russians sweep our rear areas with fire, targeting nothing, simply to harass us. Why, they can't even see us! Looks like Ivan has too much ammunition on his hands.' And, without pausing, he continued to bluster: 'They certainly haven't yet laid eyes on our camouflaged positions up there at the front. So, let's not give our game away. Let's not play tit for tat, let's hold back from targeting them directly. So far, we've been ordered not to show ourselves but remain well covered, and that's exactly what we'll continue to do.'

My new battery commander was Senior Sergeant Hoffmann. Reporting to him in his bunker, I was immediately impressed by his demeanour: here was a true soldier who inspired confidence in his men. The term 'bunker' was much exaggerated, as in truth his place consisted of nothing more than a small, airy space, hidden behind a low hill, and enclosed by raw tree trunks connected to each other by suspended tarpaulins. In it stood a simple chair, a table with the field telephone, a collapsible field bed with a wooden suitcase peeking out from underneath, and apart from that, nothing. In front of the entrance was his parked Kübelwagen,* which looked much the worse for wear, and next to it was his driver's tent.

Noticing my look of surprise, the senior sergeant made a dismissive gesture with his hands, probably indicating that I shouldn't comment, and launched straight into giving me a situation report. It turned out that they had been sitting there, in a defensive position, for quite some time, and that such downtime

---

* The German equivalent of the Allied Jeep, made by Volkswagen.

was obviously frustrating to them. 'Welcome to our sparse quarters, Sergeant Herrmann,' he added towards the end of our brief meeting. 'I can see you've been trained as a forward observer, so as of tomorrow you will be replacing Sergeant Steiner in our reconnaissance section. You're dismissed!'

Our guns were so well concealed, hidden behind the forest boundary at some 200 metres distance from the bunker, that I literally only knew where they were once I was standing smack in front of them. 'Well done,' I told the soldiers, making it clear that I approved of their skill.

Sergeant Wöhrle, the gun commander, puffing on his cigarette and leaning nonchalantly against a tree, said with an air of disdain: 'What on earth, Herrmann! Do you think we just arrived yesterday? Wouldn't you expect our commander to have put us to good use?' They had, so he informed me, heard about me and knew I was well trained. 'Perhaps you can put the fear of God into those Russians so that we'll no longer have to stand idly by,' he snorted still with a smirk on his face, and added: 'I believe the time has come to send the Russians our own little "gift".' Then he pointed to a dismal-looking trench dug nearby. The sides had been supported by bits of trees and over it hung a roof of sorts made of earth and leaves intertwined by twigs. He said: 'You'll be sleeping here in our villa with all of us lot – we've already prepared your bed.' My immediate sense was that I'd get on with those fellows and soon feel at home in the 'villa' (nobody, in truth, could make out what it was or what to call it).

'Our commander is a real artist in camouflage', commented Wöhrle with a nod in the direction of the senior sergeant, who by then was sitting in front of his bunker on a folding chair with a pad on his knees and scribbling away. Wöhrle was one of those characters who believed that he knew everyone's business and was therefore well placed to make snide remarks. 'Herrmann, don't be fooled, this guy has several women up his sleeve and he needs to answer all their letters! Obviously this keeps him out of harm's way.'

The following day I had yet another opportunity to marvel at the artistic ingenuity of my commander when I got to see his expertly concealed observation position. First I walked along the edge of the woods, ducking my head as I went to avoid the low-hanging tree branches, then I stepped into a fully covered trench at the end of which, on a slight elevation but still out of view, the infantry had installed their observation position and where a Sergeant Weinzierl received me and instructed me in my duties. He was hugely relieved, he admitted, that at long last a full complement of three was in place to make up the rota, as they had lost Heinz Klug, another gunner who had apparently been detected by some other field post and had to be removed from his position. Whether it was his fault or not, I couldn't tell. Nonetheless, it had obviously made it necessary for the team not only to relocate but also to reconfigure. Above all I was assured that there was no chance that any rays of sun would be reflected in the scissors periscope binoculars, in this new position. 'The *Jäger* have given us a really big hand throughout,' he acknowledged, clearly impressed by their skills, 'but they don't have any explanation as to why it's so calm around here, either.'

Towards eight o'clock the field telephone rang and I answered.

'Senior Sergeant Hoffmann speaking!' a strong voice boomed from the receiver, 'If you spot one, or better still, more Russian lorries driving down the short stretch of road you can see through your device, you must report this immediately. We're marooned here, and haven't yet received permission to fire, but we might well be allowed a salvo or two today. Then I want you to aim some single shots in the direction of the church steeple, but mind you don't hit it. My hunch is that the Russian lookouts are taking cover there. What we require is registered targets in case the going gets serious. All understood?!'

'Yes, sergeant!'

Twenty minutes later, whilst watching through the binoculars what impact the first salvo I had been ordered to dispatch had, I myself was surprised at how calm I was. One of the trucks had obviously just finished loading up ammunition, as I could clearly see that the explosion had caused a red-yellowish cloud to billow up into the sky. I then fired a series of single shots at the designated target, as instructed.

Pretty much at the same time the Russians responded with ferocious firing but failed to hit us, their rounds simply smashing into the ground far behind our positions instead. Admittedly, I could only vaguely make out their exact gun positions as they too were quite impressive at camouflage. I had barely filed my report on these first hits when I heard back from the senior sergeant: 'We have to keep things quiet now. Check firing!' he barked through the radio. At once, I ceased firing and returned to my underground villa.

With every day that passed we became more used to our good fortune and the feeling of being blessed that this particular spot afforded us protection. Secure in the knowledge that the *Jäger* at the front were looking after us and providing cover, we relaxed into a routine consisting mainly of waiting. But one night our captain insisted that we fell some trees and then use the trunks to construct four makeshift gun positions and camouflage them, but only just barely, in a forest clearing which was easily visible from the Russian side. We were obviously being instructed to lay a trap.

'They're herewith invited to make mincemeat out of our Potemkin battery and while they're at it we'll smother them with shells,' explained our captain. 'In my mind, it is highly unlikely that this bit of land will remain as quiet as it's been before, so I've decided to speed up the process. We're guaranteed to see some action soon.'

Clearly fed up with the waiting game, he made these predictions in a very determined tone. He then ordered that 'Every available man is required to take part in this action.'

Because on that day I was for some reason not assigned to the advanced observation unit, I was turned into a woodcutter instead, and before long four large tree trunks lay neatly on top of low mounds of earth. Stacked at an angle, they very much resembled our gun barrels. We then coloured the ends with some black paint, sloppily attached a few branches and with that our very basic camouflage was ready to do its job.

At dawn the following day, Sergeant Hoffmann inspected our work and gave it his approval: 'Well done! The Russians now have something they can shoot at. But perhaps, one never knows, they'll turn out to be savvier than we give them credit for, let's wait and see.'

The following days were uneventful, and having by then grown used to rounds hitting the ground behind our positions, we no longer paid any attention to these continuous thuds. I was thus all the more startled when, in the middle of the night, something made me sit bolt upright. What had woken me up was, bizarrely, the sudden silence engulfing me. I could only get back to sleep again once the fire picked up.

One fine day I was promoted to the position of gun captain as I was to take over from Sergeant Wöhrle who had been given permission to go on leave. We didn't find out why, but he never returned to us.* Grinning, Private Hannes Korber had the idea that he had been poached by another battalion where he would be put to better use.

Korber was in charge of looking after two of the five mules that pulled the wagons on which we would transport our guns (having disassembled them into four parts). The mules and Korber, their keeper, lived apart from us, about 200 metres further down from our gun position, where the animals were allowed to rest underneath a cover made out of branches, with Korber sleeping next to them up on the wagon. He managed to take up minimal space, always curling himself up to sleep, and I spent many an hour sitting next to him chatting, or just peacefully listening to the mules snorting, or gnawing away at their food. I found out that

---

* Records show that Wöhrle was sentenced to death by a military court, but no further details are available.

Korber owned a farm near Bad Aibling which he loved talking about, fondly telling me stories about tilling his beloved soil back at home, and about his wife and his two sons. 'They're just six and seven years old, these lads of mine,' he said, proudly adding that they were a real help to their mother. He seemed to be especially fond of the older one.

One day at the beginning of July every available soldier of our battery was ordered to report at a small clearing in the forest just behind our position. Once we had arrived there, I noticed a sergeant whom I had never seen before standing next to the captain and who, judging by his emblems, belonged to the mountain troops. When I was about to report for duty, the captain just waved me away and continued his conversation with the sergeant, but I still managed to catch the gist of what was said. Then the newly arrived sergeant admitted to our captain for all of us to hear, that nobody knew how to deal with 'such a thing', and we all grinned to each other, as it was spoken in a dialect dear to us. He obviously hailed from the Allgäu, we just couldn't quite make out whether he was from the Bavarian or the Württemberg part. He most definitely belonged to 4th Mountain Division. Our captain just nodded and told us: 'Listen up men, this is a newly developed anti-tank weapon. It's called the "Panzerfaust [Tank Fist]".' With this brief explanation he lifted up a grey tube, a metre or so in length, to which was attached something that looked like a pedal lever. The front end consisted of an egg-shaped cone of some 15–20 centimetres; the tip looked as if it had been chopped off and a two or three centimetre metal ring encircled the bottom edge.

'The *Jäger* up in front of us are already equipped with these things and are being instructed how to use them. Apparently you have to tuck the tube under your arm or carry it on your shoulder, then you need to take off the safety . . .' the voice of the captain trailed off as he demonstrated how to remove the safety, then picking up again, he continued: 'Just aim and with a little squeeze of this half-moon shaped lever, fire the projectile . . . Well, that should be easy enough,' he assured us, but warned 'You'll have to allow the tank to advance within twenty metres. Then, trust me, this will finish off every single tank, since this thing here at the front . . .', he pointed to the device at the end of the tube, 'can penetrate every enemy tank's armour. It's packed with explosives and causes such intense heat in the inside of the enemy tank that it forces its ammunition to detonate Well, guys, I don't actually know more than that, so now Sergeant Frinkäs will demonstrate how this device works. I can assure you that the Russians will literally not know what's hit them, what with those poor devils only having the T-34 at their disposal!'

The sergeant took the Panzerfaust and in his southern German dialect shouted: 'All behind me, move to the right! The Panzerfaust requires twenty metres' clearance in all directions. I don't know more than that! I'm aiming at the rock over there!' he said, pointing towards a huge bulging rock in front of us.

Sergeant Firnkäs flipped open the sight and put the tube under his right shoulder. We then stepped aside, jostling each other in the process. For a few seconds there was dead silence. Then, we heard a moderately loud 'blubb' and the rock crumbled into countless small pieces. But at the same time a horrible scream filled the air. Gunner Steiger, only nineteen years old, had wanted to observe the whole process from up close and had taken some steps forward. Before anybody could pull him away, the back-blast emanating from the Panzerfaust had hit him. With that last scream he sunk to the ground, without a face.

Angry and shocked, Sergeant Firnkäs turned around yelling at nobody in particular that he had warned us about the space that was required around this lethal weapon, but his voice was drowned out by the general turmoil that had broken out.

'Silence!' yelled our captain, and just as suddenly as it started the shouting and screaming gave way to a quiet befitting the circumstances. Calmly our captain turned to Sergeant Firnkäs, who stood in front of him, pale and stunned. 'Don't beat yourself up about it!' said our captain with a hint of kindness that surprised us all. Then, scrutinising our group, he quietly asked: 'Who was standing next to him?'

Three men stepped forward. 'Why then didn't you hold him back?'

Two of them looked down at their feet, obviously scared, probably ashamed or perhaps just lost in thought. Only Hannes Korber spoke out: 'We were all extremely curious to see how this thing worked,' he spoke in measured sentences. 'We were concentrating on the gunner and the rock. None of us noticed that Steiger was too curious for his own good.' Sergeant Hoffmann who, at least as far as we could tell was totally composed, ordered the three to fetch some spades. 'The man will be buried right here and now,' he ordered. 'Remove his mountain boots and belt!' Turning away from us we could still hear him grumbling grimly: 'We now have to economise, even when it comes to our dead. Looks like they no longer want steel helmets to be hung on the crosses either.'

For a long time, this death, which had occurred under such unusual circumstances, was a topic of conversation not only for the men of our squad, but of the entire company. Every so often one could hear a group of *Landsers* discussing it. 'This Panzerfaust is probably much less powerful than it's been hyped up to be.' 'If this thing kills our own people, I can well do without it.' 'You just have to handle it properly, then it's a marvel!' Such were the opinions whirling around for days.

On 20 July 1944 we all heard the news about the attack on our *Führer*. Information spread like wildfire through our ranks and nobody hid his reaction of shock and perturbation, me included. I kept wondering where the entire war was heading if even our top officers were breaking their oath. Discussions amongst us abounded.

'Colonel Stauffenberg is nothing short of a coward! If this highly decorated officer was truly convinced about his plan, he'd have blown himself up along with the *Führer* in that bunker and wouldn't just have slunk off! And now he's caught.'

'A bullet was wasted on him. But the same goes for a rope.'

'You'd need to strike this son of a bitch dead.'

'Gosh, what on earth are you all on about? This guy was nothing but a tool for that cowardly clique of generals.'

Indeed, it was the generals on whom so many of my colleagues focused. They were convinced that the generals were to blame, those who – thus ran their bitter complaint – had them wait for their winter clothing right from the very beginning of 41/42, and when they finally received it it was nearly springtime. 'Just try and imagine how many *Landsers* could have avoided losing their limbs in the freezing temperatures had there been a timely arrival!' was some of what I could hear, or 'It's shameful as to how many died of severe injuries because of that winter!'

Only a few amongst us kept silent and simply stared in front of us, serious and thoughtful. Generally, the troop shared the opinions held by the masses: it wasn't Hitler who was to be held accountable for the difficult war situation we were in, but his generals. The *Führer* himself would remain sacrosanct.

One thing was for certain: whilst the events of 20 July definitely didn't boost our morale, as far as we simple *Landsers* were concerned, they did indeed strengthen our resolve to at least remain faithful to our oath. For us, being duty-bound was non-negotiable. Then, when we were informed that the first V-1 flying bombs had hit England, we became even more determined than before to fight this war until we proved victorious. 'That's just the beginning,' was the rumour that went around. 'It looks like our engineers are just about to complete the manufacturing of a stupendous weapon of destruction and that will definitely end the war very soon!'

No attacks were reported, not even in the weeks that ensued. Who could have expected that the Romanians, who had always fought on our side, would switch allegiance? I, above all, thought that such a development was highly unlikely, as the days of our marching behind Romanian troops advancing along the Black Sea coastline towards Odessa were still clearly stuck in my mind. As for the devastating defeat of the German and Romanian troops during the August 1944 Jassy*–Kishinev operation, nothing at all had filtered through to us and we remained completely ignorant, trusting that all was well at the front line.

Lulled into this assurance, I, much like the others, was taken by complete surprise when the news came in on 23 August that Marshal Antonescu had been toppled. We were dismayed! That same day General Sanatescu had been charged to form a new government and, without losing a moment, he announced both that the Romanian Army would cease all warfare against the Russian Army and demanded in the same breath the immediate withdrawal of German troops from Romania.

Us lot were already feeling quite rattled, but when we got the order for instant departure, tension grew even more. Departure to where? None of us had the slightest idea. With a dour look on his face Sergeant Hoffmann stomped to his Kübelwagen, got on, and, standing upright next to his driver and looking each one of us up and down, he rode past his men, all lined up and ready to move.

I can't remember whether the phrase '*Vorwärts Kameraden, wir gehen zurück*' was coined by our squad right then and there, or whether this originated some time before that,† but all I can say is that we heard these words ringing in our ears long after darkness fell and the final signal for departure had been given.

Hannes Korber and two other privates, who belonged to our gun crew but were additionally assigned to look after our draft animals, had already harnessed them and hitched them to our vehicles. With a few expert moves we disassembled our guns and loaded them onto the wagons. When I too had packed my few belongings into my rucksack and tossed it onto what seemed to me the lighter of the carriages, I dedicated a few brief thoughts to Steiger, the gunner who had been killed in such sad circumstances.

---

* Now known as Iași, in Romania.

† 'Advance comrades, we're going back', an obvious, cynical contradiction in terms. The phrase, which became widely used, has been found in diaries and correspondence dating from at least early 1943.

'Ready for departure!' I reported in my role as first gunner.

I was surprised at how quietly and swiftly we seemed to be able to wind up everything while heading in the direction of the train tracks. Once we were rolling along the path streaked with deep tracks dug into the mud by previous transports and surrounded by the landscape now familiar to us, I turned around in my seat and was stunned: we weren't being chased. What had happened to the Russians? Had they scheduled an impromptu day of rest? We hadn't heard a single explosion for close to an hour. Such ominous silence had already woken me from my sleep once before, I thought, and to my mind it didn't bode well.

What with our horse-drawn carts, we were of course the last crew to arrive at the waiting train. While many helping hands reached out to help lift us onto the cargo train and there was lots of chattering, we were none the wiser as to where the journey was to take us. Some claimed to know that a section of our squad had departed before us together with some *Jäger*, but essentially nobody really had any reliable facts

As the train rolled towards the south, I had a funny feeling that the enemy was on our backs. But what or who lay ahead of us? We sat on the floor of our railcars next to our disassembled guns, staring out at the dimly visible landscape. Nervously, Hannes Korber chewed at his short-stemmed pipe, wondering out loud whether this signified the start of an orderly withdrawal. 'Are we actually clearing out because of the Romanians?' he asked.

'No idea, Hannes. But I do know for certain that they're not giving us a lift home any time soon.'

By 29 August our *Jäger* and artillery regiment were already in action at the Berzka–Oituz pass. A fierce battle took place and we put up an impressive fight, ferociously pulling our triggers, but what perturbed me most was not the injured and dead around me, but having to acknowledge that the Romanians, on whose side we had always been fighting, had now joined the Red Army and turned against us.

At the beginning of September it became clear that we could no longer withstand the enemy pressure that had steadily grown into a powerful and devastating advance, forcing us to retreat. There was bitter fighting by day, with us firing indiscriminately in all directions. Then, when the guns fell silent as night fell, we were forced to withdraw to a new position. Exhausted, we grabbed a piece of hard sausage or bread, gulped down a handful of water retrieved from a fountain or a river, before catching a few moments of sleep. With much the same deadly fighting taking place, the following days told on our nerves and really wore us out. Sometimes I even pitied the animals who willingly pulled our heavy wagons, but then switched to envying them for not having to think. Or perhaps they did? We, in any case, always tried to go easy on them and do the best we could to conserve their strength, so we would walk alongside them instead of letting ourselves be pulled.

On 11 September we formed a bridgehead at Csikszereda,* but sadly didn't stand the slightest chance against the lethal swarms of Russian T-34s crashing down on us, followed by tight clusters of merciless infantrymen. In the early hours of the next dawn we prepared for immediate withdrawal, with me being the first to radio our superiors that the unit had pulled out. We had already got used to the fact that we would not be provided with any clear idea of where we were supposed to retreat to. While retreating we could still hear bursting shells and the sharp whistling sounds of enemy fire zooming through the air and then smashing down not far from us.

Sergeant Moller was visibly nervous when he pointed with his outstretched arm to a road barely discernible in the dark: 'Hermann,' he yelled, 'that's the direction you must take. For Christ's sake, just get yourself moving. I've not got the foggiest idea how long the *Jägers* can hold out, and our advance detachment must by now surely have found a spot for us to assemble.'

---

* Now Mircurea Cuic, in Romania.

After Hannes Korber had managed to get the horses moving by patting them encouragingly on the back, he mumbled with obvious disdain: 'Advance detachment – God, that sure sounds pretentious. It makes me laugh.'

Our wagons struggled to roll forward, severely hindered by the deep ruts in the road, so our formation progressed at a snail's pace. We couldn't make any sense of the sudden stillness enveloping us. Why could we no longer hear any fighting? Marching ahead of the others, I regularly looked over my shoulder, concerned not to leave anybody behind. But suddenly a motorcycle emerged out of nowhere and sped past us despite the miserable road conditions. Behind the driver sat a lieutenant peering with his head bent sideways at the route ahead. Four or five minutes later they came zooming back, this time yelling something: 'Push on, keep going!' I turned to Hannes and drily remarked that this kind of intelligence wasn't particularly helpful. 'We sure didn't need this guy to tell us what to do.' But I was soon to find out that we actually didn't have the faintest idea of what was in store for us.

Seconds later I saw the dim outline of the moon shining through a gap in the otherwise thickly clouded sky and I immediately understood why the lieutenant had warned us. A sheet of dark water shimmered at a short distance from us, and while we didn't know the name of this river flowing behind a narrow reed belt, we could clearly recognise the ruins of a bridge that had been blown up. At the sight of such devastation, which clearly suggested that our retreat was doomed, Hannes Korber truly lost his nerve: 'Lothar, that clown of a sergeant has sent us in the wrong direction! Those dark spots ahead of us, they're Russian tanks – as sure as I'm standing here!'

Just in that moment the clouds swept across the moon and plunged us into a protective darkness. My head was racing as I tried to find a solution to our predicament.

Rapidly going over what our options were, I realised that our battery was nowhere to be seen. It had disappeared long before. 'We're much too slow to catch up with them and we'll no doubt just fall into the hands of Ivan,' I said, and whilst briefly nodding to Hannes, I called to the other three men back on the wagon: 'Listen up, comrades. We've been fortunate' I said, to calm their nerves. 'The broken bridge has actually saved us from the Russian tanks on the other side. What with our heavy wagons, we'll never catch up with the others.' I then ordered them to let the mules go free. 'Grab only your rifles and as much food as you can remove from the provision crates,' I instructed. 'No unnecessary hand luggage. We'll have to make our way on foot and aim to catch up with the rest!' I added that they should make haste and warned: 'No blabbering, let's march across the fields, keep west and mark my words: it could get pretty damn uncomfortable. Let's get a move on!'

With a few hand movements Hannes freed the mules from their harnesses, gave each one a friendly slap on the rump and offered some words of encouragement: 'Good luck my friends, let's hope the Russians don't cook you and eat you.' Whilst I couldn't make out his face, his voice sounded sad and I suspected that he had tears in his eyes.

I couldn't gather much from looking at my compass because it was so dark, but the moss on the tree bark showed us where west was. Had we had a starry sky shining above us, we could have orientated ourselves by first figuring out where the North Star was. But no such luck.

Keen not to lose any more time, we departed. After marching one kilometre, I suddenly remembered that with the rucksack I had left behind on the wagon, I had also lost the photos of my two girlfriends from Landshut and Garmisch. Perhaps, I thought, a Hungarian shepherd will find them along with their addresses, and with any luck, he might send them back home to Germany, a sign that I'm still alive.

We followed a path through the woods, winding our way down a long mountain slope westward. Finally leaving the forest behind us, we found ourselves in a sheep pasture that had been grazed right down to the soil. We stood still, at first shocked that we suddenly had no trees protecting us, but nonetheless relieved as we could now get our bearings.

'There, right ahead of us,' I heard from behind me, 'There! Where you can see the smoke! That must be coming from one of our depots. Looks like it's on fire', the voice unmistakably belonged to Horst Holzer, who came from Reutte in the Tyrol. 'Would you believe it, they're actually showing us the way home!' he added under his breath.

Fritz Weber doubted whether we would make it there by evening, as it seemed to be several kilometres away from where we stood. Whilst deep down I agreed with him, I felt it best to calm everyone down: 'Listen up everybody, surely we all agree that it takes these clowns an age to bring their clobber back to safety, and that's probably somewhere way behind the HKL.* Perhaps we'll reach our mates within the next hour. We've come a long way already ...' Trying to be positive not only for their sake, but for my own as well, I hoped that my words instilled some confidence.

'Lothar,' replied the Tyrolean, a slim and quite tall young man: 'When, pray tell, have you last seen the HKL? It all seems to be one hell of a mess ...' he grumbled not disguising his disgust, but then caught himself when, suddenly, we heard the noise of vehicles, rolling some fifty metres below where we were standing and moving along another track winding westwards – one we hadn't dared use. Could those be German? If we could only tag on to them, we figured we would be able to escape Russian imprisonment, something we feared more than death.

Standing there between some sparse shrubbery and staring down below without being able to make out anything much, all five of us were having more or less the same thoughts. Avoid Russian imprisonment at all costs. We pricked up our ears, but then our hopes were crashed in one fell swoop when we heard someone shouting up at us.

---

* HKL = *Hauptkampflinie* – main line of resistance.

'Those are Russians,' someone whispered behind me. I was sure that I wasn't the only one whose heart started racing. I whispered back: 'Why, these guys are in their vehicles and move even slower than we do. I reckon we can beat them. Run for it!'

All of us had been living in fear of being taken prisoner by the Russians, so my comrades didn't need much encouragement to do as instructed. I could hear them huffing and puffing right behind me, trying to keep up with my pace. After a short while I could feel myself getting extremely tired, and no longer able to run, I switched to a rapid march, breathing heavily and laboriously. The Russian vehicles seemed to be out of earshot, and I was just about to relax when I realised that our path had joined the road.

'We can't risk that,' I noted in a low voice, 'It'll get light soon. We must take another route to avoid the road. Let's make our way through the fields. I'm sure our troops can't be too far away.'

Nobody contradicted. Exhausted, anxious and always furtively glancing back over our shoulders, we stumbled on through to dusk then into the night, and were still moving along when dawn arrived. We rested infrequently and then only briefly, ducking in ditches along the terrain and wolfing down a few bits of bread. The small rivers cutting through the rocks and streaming down to the valley offered us plenty of water.

It was night again and, emboldened by darkness surrounding us, we climbed down onto the country road. Judging by the tracks we discovered and some dung, probably from mules, we thought that we couldn't be far behind our troops. Overtired, barely able to keep our eyes open, we stumbled along.

'I can't keep going.' The feeble voice belonged to one of our youngest boys, Lance-Corporal Walter, whose home town lay somewhere in the Bavarian Prealps. Nobody answered him. Some fifty metres on, all of us simply threw ourselves onto the grass but kept our eyes on a nearby hut where we suspected drovers to dwell, as we could also make out a flock of sheep cooped up in a pen.

I decided to risk it. On entering the cottage I was pleasantly surprised at the friendly welcome I received, then returned to my comrades to let them know and asked them to follow me inside. 'Mountain dwellers are rough, but a decent sort of people in my experience. I'm sure they'll let us sleep somewhere in their hay stacks or in their straw,' Hannes Korber mumbled into my ear. No sooner had he finished his sentence than one of the three herdsmen sitting at the wooden table nodded his head and with his dirty hand motioned us to a low door next to the open fireplace.

'Do you understand German?' I asked the man, a lean and tall middle-aged fellow who responded by enquiring in broken German whether we were hungry.

When all five of us shot back 'Yes!' all at once, he rose from his stool and spoke a few words to the other herdsmen, who immediately got up and with an inviting gesture offered us their seats on the wooden bench. Some moments later we devoured some stale white bread with goats' cheese and drank a diluted juice which tasted of apples and pears. It seemed that suddenly another shepherd had remembered his German, as he pointed to our rifles and asked whether we wanted to sell one of them. Cobbling the words together, he proposed that they would pay good money, that we could do with just having two guns and that they required one to shoot bears and wolves.

'Sorry,' I said, genuinely feeling apologetic, 'there is no way we can return to our troops without our weapons.' I then asked them whether they could let us know the approximate time when our men had passed by their home. Whilst both herdsmen seemed a bit disappointed not to be able to make a deal, they were helpful nonetheless. 'Think it was yesterday,' said one. 'Nahh,' the older one contradicted, 'was lunchtime today, me know exactly.'

Pulling myself up from the bench, I calculated how many hours ahead of us our troops were, and concluded that I needed to make some decisions. 'I am dead tired, but I'm taking the first night guard shift. Two hours. Then comes Korber, then Fritz. Six hours must suffice. Staying here any longer would be a pure waste of time. So, go ahead, guys, hurry up with your sleep!'

As soon as dawn broke we set off. We wanted, nay, we had to be faster than the Russians behind us – I kept drumming this into the rest. Passing one of those typical Romanian villages where the homes are lined up one after the other alongside the road, we found in one of the last houses the burnt-out remains of a German headquarters. We pressed on. By the time night fell on our second day of marching, we thought we had made good progress and had come much closer to the glow of a fire we had spotted previously. An hour later we hit on an uninhabited shepherd's lodge and we didn't think twice about ransacking it and grabbing whatever we could lay our hands on: embroidered tunics, knickerbockers and socks in the local style.

'Should Ivan catch up with us and push comes to shove, we can always disguise ourselves as shepherds,' suggested Hannes Korber, trying to justify what had been his idea. When we changed into our disguise in the nearby forest, we broke out in laughter in spite of the dire circumstances we found ourselves in. Not a single item actually fitted us.

In his very strong mountain dialect, Fritz Weber likened us to the peacocks that strutted around his farm back home, but in the end we all felt it best not to wear the clothing. While one of the tunics was much too big for me, I didn't want just to throw it away, so I stuffed it into my backpack.

After this brief masquerade we continued on our run for a further two days and nights, desperately trying to catch up with the rapidly retreating German units. In the meantime, two stragglers, *Jäger* who had lost their way, joined us so that altogether we were a group of seven. At some point, we just barely avoided a few Russian carts and motor vehicles that were sitting at the wayside, concealed by tree branches and shrubbery. We narrowly escaped falling into their hands by spotting them early on and swiftly branching off. Onwards we trudged, exhausted and scared, sticking to the fields above the road. Our fear of being captured by the Russians was greater than any other emotion we felt.

We decided to climb up the slope and finally came across a depression in the terrain. Having briefly mulled it over, we agreed that we simply had to rest and get some sleep. Once again, and in spite of being dog-tired, I offered to do the first guard duty. Leaning my rifle against a tree trunk I suddenly had this strange idea that I would keep myself awake by separating the silvery sergeant's collar badge sewn onto my uniform jacket with the help of a razor blade.

'You're not going to fall asleep, Lothar,' I admonished myself, 'no way you can do this to your comrades!' And while I kept repeating this to myself, I suddenly saw some shadowy silhouettes scurrying towards me. Immediately, I clutched my weapon.

Shock mixed with relief filled me when I heard the unmistakable Berlin dialect of one of the infantrymen asking me whether I intended to zap him. 'Naturally not, much too zonked to do that,' I hit back, 'and also I'm guarding six sleeping men behind me.'

Because the two guys appeared to me to be in much better shape than we were, I made them a proposal: 'If you want to join us, why don't you switch guard duty with me!'

'Yup, go ahead, go take a nap. If necessary, we'll wake you,' and with that one of them walked me a few steps towards my comrades who were lying on the ground, dead to the world. With a reassuring nod towards me, he returned to his mate. The moment I put my head down next to Horst Holzer, I was fast asleep – entirely unsuspecting of anything untoward and safely under the assumption that we were well protected.

CHAPTER 6

Rude Awakening

A fierce kick in my ribs startled me. Out of sheer habit I reached for my carbine but couldn't find it. Suddenly I was wide awake. And indeed, just as I had feared, looming above me wasn't one of the *Landsers* who had just joined us, but a Romanian . . . '*Hände hoch!*' he barked

We were surrounded by several Romanians, and peering sideways I could see my comrades scrambling up and, hesitating at first, but then raising their hands. A few metres away from us a Romanian officer was sitting on his horse. Compared to his underlings in their dishevelled clothing, this guy looked as if he had just stepped out of a fashion advert. I could feel one of his flunkies working my watch off my wrist. 'Legs apart,' they commanded, and I was wondering what had happened to our so-called guards. Could it be true that these Romanians had sneaked up on us so quietly and quickly that the *Landsers* hadn't had a chance to warn us? For a moment a brief thought crossed my mind: I was turning twenty-four the next day.

Within minutes each one of us was frisked from head to toe; they were obviously searching for hidden weapons. The bolts of our guns went flying in a high arc above our heads, landing in the shrubbery, while our badges were torn off our breasts. In my back I could feel one of the Romanians fumbling for my camera which I had always kept safe in a leather pouch, slung over my shoulder. Admonished by his superior to stop his pilfering, he let go of me, roughly shoving me to the side.

'Advance!' ordered the man in the fancy uniform and so I positioned myself in front of him, arms held up in the air. Then it was his turn to demand I hand over my camera followed by my compass, which was dangling from my neck. This instrument seemed to be of particular interest to him. 'Give that to me.'

Would you believe that what happened next was that Lance-Corporal Korber sidled up next to me and addressed the officer: 'Are you friend or foe?'

'Foe of Germany!'

But Korber wouldn't leave it at that. 'Surely you also have a mother at home,' he continued, trying to make his case. 'Surely you can just let us go!'

'No!'

The officer turned his horse, shouted some incomprehensible order to his men and trotted off in the direction from where we had come just a few hours earlier 'Follow me,' he ordered in a now near-perfect German accent.

With their guns pointing at us, two of his men made it clear that they wouldn't stand any shenanigans and kept poking at us with their rifle butts to push us along. One of them wore the shepherd's tunic which we had just nicked the other day and which had served me well during the previous nights. The remainder of that Romanian patrol must have been ordered to scan the area for more Germans. Surely there was a thorough search going on, I thought to myself.

The two guards behind us didn't seem quite as averse to us Germans as their superior. One of them even attempted to calm us down. In broken German he assured us that we would be better treated in the Romanian camp than in a Russian one.

While his promises might have been well-intentioned, deep down we didn't want to hold out too much hope. A gentle bend in the road where there was a clump of bushes seemed the perfect spot for my plan. I started unbuttoning my trousers and then stood at the bush making the guard believe that I had to take a leak.

'Lothar, you mustn't let this happen – mustn't allow yourself to be taken prisoner and sent to one of those notorious Russian prison camps,' I kept convincing myself whilst doing my business and, blanking out the guards behind me, I ducked, did a few quick jumps and sprinted up the slope. The higher up I got, the fainter the yelling sounded behind me and once at the peak of the hill and bounding down the other side I could no longer hear them. Gasping for air, I fervently prayed that I had made it – when suddenly a Romanian, probably belonging to a search detail, emerged out of nowhere and held a gun to my face. My attempt had thoroughly and utterly failed.

Some ten minutes later I was reunited with the other lot, slightly surprised that all I received from the officer was a scornful look of disdain whilst he tucked away his pistol in his holster. An hour later we were led through a village which we had by-passed some days beforehand. There were Russians everywhere! Russian vehicles were parked in front of practically every building, and tied to some pillars next to them were these small, robust Russian horses which by that time had impressed us with their strength; we respectfully referred to them as '*panje* horses'. The scene we encountered was horrible. One artillery piece was lined up against the next. Red Army soldiers kept hollering some incomprehensible stuff while throwing clumps of mud and horse dung at us. But worst of all were some of the female Russian soldiers who weren't attractive in any way, dressed in unflattering brown uniform blouses. These women, disparagingly referred to by our German propaganda as *Flintenweiber*,* were supposed to be proof of our enemy's moral decline.

One of them leaped up, launched her fist smack into my face, making me tumble sideways and screamed at me something in Russian which didn't sound very friendly. A Red Army soldier shoved me back.

We were relieved when our so-called leader finally pulled at the reins of his horse and came to a stop in front of the houses. Some guards stood next to a roughly hewn wooden flagpole from which hung the red flag with some kind of symbol on it. The officer then

---

* 'Shotgun women'.

disappeared behind the house. Gesturing, the soldiers ordered us to sit on the long bench along the timber wall of the house and remain silent. This didn't stop us from furtively whispering to each other, mostly asking questions or expressing our fears.

A man, clearly a Russian officer though not wearing any of the badges which should have been stuck on his neat uniform, entered the house while the Romanian officer stepped out. A little while later I was ordered in. A Russian wearing embroidered epaulettes – at that time I couldn't make out what they stood for – sat at a table with a notebook and some writing materials arranged on it. Next to that, a telephone. A uniformed soldier without rank badges stood next to him. He seemed awkward and I half-suspected that he was German. The chap, as it turned out, was the translator.

The Russian bellowed something whilst pointing at me. 'Which unit do you belong to and which rank did you hold?' the translator asked me. 'Who was your battery commander?' 'What were your losses?'

I responded to all the questions truthfully on the assumption that they knew all the answers anyway and that in any event they already had quite a bit of intelligence on each of us. Lies would only have made my situation worse.

'Did you intend to disguise yourself with that shepherd's coat?' continued the translator.

'It was much too big for me, but I used it during the night as a cover to keep me warm.'

The Russian had no further questions and waved me away.

'Send the next one in!' the translator shouted after me. Frankly, at that point, I no longer cared whether he was German or not but wanted to believe that he was neutral and had translated everything correctly.

After the others had also been questioned, two Russians with machine pistols held stretched out in front of them shoved us towards a nearby farmhouse and instructed us to assemble in its courtyard. Ordered to remain silent, we were petrified. We firmly believed that this spelt the end. We were convinced they would make short shrift of us – otherwise why would they want to look after a handful of measly prisoners?

The farm must have once belonged to an ethnic German. It was larger than the houses built along the roadside which all seemed to be of about the same size. From the inside we could hear the loud voices of men. The two Russians roughly forced us inside. All hell had broken out in that dimly lit den. A bunch of drunk Russians and Romanians lifting their half-empty vodka bottles high dragged themselves up and attacked us like some wild gang. First, they wrenched from each of us our mountain boots and trousers. Disgraced and shamed, we looked a pretty pitiful sight, standing bare-footed there in the room in our no longer clean underwear. Even during the summer the Wehrmacht rule book ordered us to wear long-johns. Then they demanded we hand them our socks.

They threw some footwear towards us to put on instead. These were essentially felt boots with the top consisting of a tightly knitted lambswool cover with short leather straps connecting this to a thin leather sole. The inside was caked with a filthy layer of putrid-smelling wet mud, and not one of us could bring himself to put his feet in them. Berserk with drink and their booty they stumbled out of the premises, leaving only some empty vodka bottles behind. The two guards remained at the door. Even if we'd still been wearing some decent clothing, nobody even remotely thought of escape any more.

Hungry, cold and dazed we lay down on the wooden benches lining the long walls of the rather large room. It had probably been the sitting room of the erstwhile owner.

Our small bunch of men grew overnight, joined by an ever increasing number of *Landsers* who had become separated from their units. Soon we resembled sheep cooped up in a pen. Luckily the guards permitted us to relieve ourselves on what once served as a manure heap behind the house. Not that we had much to digest, seeing as we had not received any food throughout our capture and we were starving. We were only allowed to fetch some water from the fountain outside.

I was actually surprised to see some *Landsers* still had bits of their mess kit, and so at least were able to use the lids of their tins. My stuff was likely way up on the hill where we had been detected. But I nevertheless considered myself fortunate as I still owned an empty can which I had found way back in that kitchen of the shepherd's lodge, along with some string and a rusty nail which had got underneath the oven. As if obeying an inner voice, I pierced a hole into the top rim of the tin, threaded through the string and then tied my new crockery around my waist. It allowed me to ladle some water into a container and then others could take a few sips.

'Bet you the Russians never thought they'd capture so many prisoners. I hear the school building across from us is also full of them. There must be a hundred of us altogether.'

I didn't see the *Landser* who had made these remarks as so many bodies were crushed against me and none of us could make each other out. In that instant the door blew open and a buxom Russian woman aiming her machine pistol at us shouted: '*Dawai! Bashli!** get food!' She then took a step back and all of us, like a horde of ravenous animals, pushed past her, me included. Brushing against her, I noticed her straw-blonde hair underneath the brown cap that she wore tilted back into her neck.

A small cart drawn by a mule stood next to the fountain, to which was attached a large cauldron sitting on top of something serving as a hotplate. I shoved myself to the front. A voice, obviously trained to issue orders, put an end to all the pushing: '*Pomalo! Padershi!*' Someone behind me translated this to 'Slowly! Wait!'

We had no choice but to obey, despite the hunger fiercely gnawing at our insides. We put ourselves in an orderly single file with one after the other approaching and stretching out our empty vessels to the Russian guy planted in front of the cart. Eventually it was my turn to have my tin filled with the undefined mix of

---

* 'Let's go! Come on!'

cabbage and carrots or something like that, I couldn't quite tell, but it was hot, if not the most nutritious. So hot in fact, that when I stepped away I had to switch the tin quickly from one hand to the other as it was scorching my fingers. With my spoon ready, the handle of which could also serve as a fork – my cutlery had luckily survived the pillage, except for the knife which one of the manhandling Romanians must have broken when we were detected – I sought a space to settle down. No sitting was allowed.

So there I was, together with all the others, stood in the courtyard, barefoot and greedily gobbling down the food. When I returned to the Russian fellow guarding the cart I stuck out my empty can for a second helping, but he just shrugged his shoulders and smashed down the lid of the cauldron.

'Well, that's that,' I thought to myself, resigned but still famished; I turned around to get inside the house along with the others when we were stopped in our tracks.

'No going in! Now *bashli!*' shouted the Russian officer with us, while two or three more Russian officers who had stood behind us darted into the house, pistols at the ready, and fetched those who had already gone inside to drag them outside again. Looking at the sun, my guess was that it must have been some time around eight o'clock when, lined up in a column of threes, we were driven through the village. All of us were barefoot and only a few of us still had our trousers on. We were a wretched sight. Somehow I managed to squeeze myself in between two comrades to remain somewhat shielded from staring eyes when it became obvious to me that this wasn't just a short walk, but that they were going to make us run the gauntlet for quite a while longer.

The guns lining the road seemed to have multiplied since our arrival. There were some positioned even at the end of the village and the *panje* horses which must have transported them were now left to graze peacefully in the autumnal meadow.

Looking at this imposing arsenal of artillery got me thinking about whether we had even the smallest chance against this much superior army power. In my mind, there seemed nothing to stand in the way of the Russians advancing – just as there was nothing that had stood in our way years ago when we invaded their land. But now *we* were the underdogs. I had been there when we withdrew, when once victorious we had retreated without method, without leadership, leaving total confusion in our wake. Why, looking back, the entire disengagement had resembled more a desperate, messy escape. How on earth would this end?

At that very moment, when it began to dawn on me what had actually brought us to this predicament, I understood what the Russians had in mind and how they intended us to pay for this. Beside the road, running along the high embankment of a river, some heavy wooden beams were piled up high in messy heaps, as if just chucked there in haste, and I immediately recognised that what was lying there in front of me were the remains of a bridge which our rearguard had exploded. Down below, water was washing over some concrete bits and you couldn't quite tell how deep the water was, though the river itself was some ten metres wide.

'*Dawai! Dawai!*' yelled a Russian officer pointing to the heap of planks and poles, then pointed to his shoulder, then to us and then in the direction of the riverbank further below. It didn't take us long to catch on, and some of us nodded to signal that we had understood. One of our group, obviously an Austrian judging by his accent, said: 'Well, boys, let's go then! We don't have a choice, they'll make minced meat of us otherwise.'

Nearly all of us were still in reasonably good shape and capable of the task at hand. We quickly broke into groups with each one hauling one of the humungous beams onto their shoulders and then transporting it down to the river, step by step. Russian pioneers stood there, ready to take over from us, and we were genuinely impressed at how quickly, right in front of our eyes and with astounding expertise, these men erected a bridge alongside the debris still floating in the water.

Not a single wooden beam was left at the roadside by the late afternoon. We received a portion of borscht, a Russian cabbage soup which I had never tasted before and which I really enjoyed, and there even were second helpings. Some of us felt emboldened to the point of daring to hope that because of our good work we would be allowed to stay the night. But it wasn't to be, as half an hour later we heard the ominous shouts: '*Dawai, dawai! Bashli, bashli!*'

We were ordered to move on.

With every weary step forward, the hammering, banging and shouting behind us grew fainter. At night, we were marched to a spot in a field where we sank to our knees, exhausted, and lay down like cows or sheep, surrounded by guards. During our trek, more and more *Landsers* who had got lost on their retreat and were roaming around until picked up, were tacked onto our lot. Some of them wore civilian clothes and were kept separate from us, closer to the road.

Someone lying near me could be heard muttering: 'Those poor sods probably didn't reckon that, judging by their plain clothes, the Russians might mistake them for partisan guerrilla fighters. Woe to them!' I kept silent but suddenly had to think back to my shepherd's coat which had been taken away from me and which had caused such suspicion at the time.

We became ever more numerous and must have already numbered several hundred men. Tired, our senses dulled, and ever more discouraged, we trudged onwards. We were so sunk into ourselves, that when some disturbance erupted at a short distance away from me around lunchtime of the second day of marching, I didn't give it much thought. We were then herded together on some field and obeyed the order to assemble, barefoot in a U-formation.

A man dressed in a very smart Russian officer's uniform, but with no visible rank badges, stood in front of us, holding in his hand a microphone. Behind him were two or three Russian officers smoking their *papirosi*, those well-known Russian cigarettes. The fine gentleman of no rank called to us in a loud and clear voice: 'Comrades! We have gathered here to enlist soldiers from amongst you. It has become utterly pointless to continue fighting for a megalomaniacal *Führer!*'

Behind me, I could hear someone saying half-loud: 'Beware comrades, this can only be some ex-officer from our ranks who has switched sides. Don't allow yourself to be fooled by him!'

In the course of his address the speaker depicted the Soviet Union as a country of workers, in which everyone made a decent living on the condition that he contributed to the common good with both his hands and his brain.

'Every day of war is one destructive day too many! If some of you are prepared to volunteer and convince your still-fighting comrades at the front that this disastrous war of ours has become totally senseless and that it would be better if they joined our side, much can be gained. It would save human lives on both sides, but above all on the German side.

'Of course we'll make loudspeakers available to you. But there is more. We will guarantee every volunteer that by the time the war has ended he will, in retrospect, have fared much better. You can be sure that he won't have to suffer as he does now. He will get decent accommodation, food will be aplenty, and he will receive, just as I have, proper clothing. And above and beyond all of that I can guarantee every new associate that he can immediately return home, come the end of the war! I now await volunteers!'

Total silence had fallen. We looked at each other with questions in our eyes and feeling completely out of our depth. Nobody amongst us wanted to step forward and become a traitor. Well, at least I didn't see anybody volunteer.

After several minutes of continued silence, the speaker took to his microphone again:

'Well, so be it. Go ahead and let yourself be driven through the land recaptured by the victorious Soviet army!'

Before our departure the next day we were ordered for the first time to form squares of ten by ten men. Each man was frisked and checked if perhaps there was still one amongst us who possessed any weapons, even if it was only a pocket knife or a sharpened spoon. Over and over again we were counted in Russian. If the numbers didn't seem correct, the whole procedure started all over again. I nearly collapsed with exhaustion, but knew that from then on I could count in Russian.

Shortly before our departure a rumour circulated. 'Apparently our destination is called Kronstadt.'*

Each one of us received a loaf of bread, which I instantly devoured but for a small leftover. It seemed to me preferable than to be robbed of my entire ration during the night, as in these few days of captivity every one had become his neighbour's enemy and was purely out for himself. None of us could have suspected in his wildest imagination that this loaf of bread was the only food we would receive until our destination, and that what lay before us was a sort of death march.

The first night was spent out in the open. While during these last days of October the nights were chilly, they were fortunately not frosty. Ten men would lie in a row, turned on their sides, each warming up by pressing himself against the back of the guy in front of him and in turn offering some warmth to the man behind. This lasted for one or two hours until I was torn out of my sleep.

'Everyone now turn over!'

No sooner had I dozed off again when the man in front of me apologised softly: 'Sorry, man, I have to take a piss . . . now.'

'Me too,' said another one somewhere further up the row.

Lifting my upper body and leaning on one arm, I could see out of the corner of my eye the glow of a cigarette a few metres away from me. It was coming from the Russian guard standing closest to our row. Instinctively, with my hand reaching for the right-hand pocket of my jacket, I double-checked that it still contained the meagre leftovers of my bread.

At dawn we slowly rose to our feet, one after the other. I too stretched, yawned and got up. Everyone felt and looked the worse for wear.

---

* The German-language name for Braşov, in Romania.

No sooner had I swallowed my last crumbs of bread than I heard the order: 'Fall in, in column of threes. We're pushing on.'

Someone amongst us, perhaps a former officer, had assumed leadership, obviously having taken over from the Russians. Who knows whether he was able to collect some brownie points for that.

It must have been after about an hour of dragging ourselves along the road that we reached one of those typical villages in Siebenbürgen. It seemed to us that the inhabitants of that particular village were ethnic Germans. Houses were crowded tightly together and mostly built close to the road. With the doors sealed and the shutters on the windows all shut, the place seemed deserted. Not a single inhabitant was on the street, obviously fearing trouble, but this didn't seem to have a reassuring effect on our guards, and they were visibly nervous. Mounted on their frisky *panje* horses both in front and to the back of us, or marching alongside our column with their automatic pistols and other guns at the ready, they drove us like a herd of sheep through the main street.

When one guy in front of me suddenly decided to break away from his line and approach a fountain he had caught sight of, he was immediately struck down by a bullet fired by a guard just two metres away from me. A short sharp burst of fire and the man lay there dead, with the guard carelessly stepping over him before screaming '*Dawai, dawai*' – he couldn't even be bothered to take the *papirosa* out of his mouth.

Once again it became crystal clear to me how war dehumanises man – both Germans and Russians.

Outside the village, vast and dense cornfields bordered the road on either side. Only a narrow ditch and a strip of grass approximately fifty centimetres wide separated us from the luscious and enticing corncobs. Our monotonous march was only interrupted by some single gunshots cracking through the air both at the front and the back of our sorry company of men. Were we committing a crime? Our sole transgression was rooted in being famished. Surely it was obvious that our barefooted comrades hadn't intended to escape, surely all they wanted was to get their hands on one or two corncobs. Why couldn't our guards understand that?

All of a sudden I saw a dead person lying on his back in front of me, arms spread wide. I didn't think twice about why or how this poor devil had met his death, all I could see was that the man was still wearing his trousers. I turned to the Russian guard beside me and signalled to him what my intention was. Contrary to what I was expecting, he simply nodded and shouted something across to the next guard. When that fellow also nodded in agreement, I swiftly slipped into the trousers of the dead man and within an instant felt human again, as if I was practically fully clothed. While the trousers were shabby, far too wide for me and moreover utterly filthy, I was grateful, mumbling a 'thank you, comrade' in the direction of the dead man.

Quickly, I threaded myself back into the slowly advancing throng of exhausted men sluggishly shuffling or stumbling forward under the watchful eye of a guard, this one mounted on a ragged horse. All I could think of was that perhaps I would trip over yet another dead body who with any luck would have shoes on his feet. I felt both embarrassed and despondent, not just because this seemed unlikely, but for even having such thoughts. What matter! During the past hours I had noticed more than once that the Russians seemed to tolerate the pilfering of the dead.

That evening we reached a larger settlement whose name I can no longer recall. Part of the group was shoved into the empty auditorium of a cinema. Were we going to be allowed to sleep in chairs? No! We were being packed so tightly in that room with all seats folded back that nobody could even lean to one side, let alone fall to the ground. A dim light bulb shed some light. Before the last door of the cinema was locked from the outside, I could hear someone ask: 'Where shit?' With a broad grin on his face the guard seemed to have understood the question, as he then pointed to a corner. The air inside quickly turned unbearably warm and above all sticky. Even though not a single one of us had eaten a thing over the past day of our march, a few still had to relieve themselves. It made complete sense to me and was indeed hugely comforting that someone designated himself as the commander in charge and as the person who would create some order; he promptly assigned a corner to become the local toilet, and I was grateful that it was the one furthest away from me as the stench would become indescribable. Hardly anyone could think of sleep and when, after what seemed an interminable amount of time, the doors were opened at dawn, I was one of the first who pushed himself forward into the outside. Deeply breathing in the morning air I got so dizzy that I could hardly take in what the Russian officer standing right next to me was yelling:

'All shitters to me at once.'

In near-perfect German and referring to the heap of shit, he ordered: 'All this needs to go out! Shovels you ask? Don't have any. With hands.'

Pointing to a garden a few metres away which surrounded a dwelling house built in the art nouveau style, he positioned himself at the door, waiting for those poor guilty sods to file past him. If I had been forced to perform this shit job I would certainly have vomited anything still left in my stomach. I'm quite sure of that.

In the course of our third day of marching there were more and more men who simply keeled over and remained on the ground. We then heard the shots of the guards finishing them off. 'Lothar, this cannot happen to you! You must do all you can to keep yourself on your feet!' I told myself over and over again.

When the guard next to me started having a conversation with the one behind him at the top of his voice whilst half turning around, I disappeared with one swift jump into the cornfield alongside the path. Undiscovered, I slipped back into the column with several corncobs clutched in my hands, but was instantly robbed of most of them apart from one or two which I immediately gobbled down. Encouraged by my success, I suspect, several men behind me attempted to do the same, and we could hear a few shots being fired. I myself could barely believe that none of this seemed to affect me emotionally, and I continued chewing the cob unperturbed. My stomach, though somewhat calmed, still ached from hunger, and I felt anything but full.

That day I saw two further incidents in which a comrade was shot and wounded as he hobbled out of the cornfield with cobs clasped in his hands. Though his mates would try and drag him along for a short distance, their own strength was also waning and so they would just let go of him; we stragglers at the rear were too weak and helpless to lift him up again and we stumbled on; our hearts were hardening. Shots echoing from behind the miserable mass of silhouettes signalled to us that he had found his death.

It rained towards the end of that day. We were herded into a field. Along with some others, I at first resisted lying down on the ground, seeing as it was already colder and wetter by that time of the year, but we watched how others just sank to the ground in total exhaustion whilst wondering how many of us would be able to get up the next morning. In the meantime, I had long lost contact with my own troop of men. Were my comrades still alive, or had they perished on this most dreadful of death marches? But such thoughts came and went in a flash; what I had to focus on was my own situation.

I too felt completely broken and stopped caring much about anything, but I was shaken out of my stupor by one guy whose ingenuity, typical for the *Landser* he was, once again came into play. This pal, he wasn't terribly young any more, said in a clearly recognisable Berlin accent: 'Why fret, comrades, the situation here is as clear as the raindrops coming down. Why don't we sleep standing up! All we need to do is lean against each other, just the way we stacked our shovels in our RAD days. Split up in four, and each pair leaning against each other and standing opposite the other pair, place your hands and heads on the shoulders of your partner in front of you!'

Without trying to figure out whether or not that made sense I tried this arrangement and it worked, even though our pyramid often threatened to cave in when one or the other man's legs buckled underneath him. The next day the Russians drove those men who had managed to get themselves up and standing into a nearby field. Shots were being fired. Obviously the weak had been taken out. Again we had to fall into formation, squares of ten by ten, and after a brutally long roll-call our starving and tired lot was ordered to move onward.

Did the Russians actually have no food provisions for us or did they just want to take revenge on the damned Nazis who had hurt their people so much? The distances which we put behind us during those days became ever shorter, for a reason unknown to us.

On the fifth day of marching, late in the afternoon, we arrived at the outskirts of Kronstadt. Before us lay an immense space surrounded by coils of barbed wire. Behind it stood some largish tents which in our eyes seemed like luxury. Wearily taking in the sight, our column, by then greatly reduced, ever so slightly picked up its pace.

Eventually we stood outside the camp entrance and it took an age until a number of Russians set about frisking us from head to toe, searching every inch of our bodies. I was allowed to keep my tin can, my spoon, my fork, and even the string I had tied around my waist. With the search over, we passed through the wire-mesh gate. We had some mixed feelings. What lay ahead of us? Some civilians standing around turned out to be ethnic Germans. A sense of relief?

'We have to cut your hair,' one of the older men explained to us. He was some sixty years old and standing right next to me. He immediately lifted his right hand in which he held a pair of manual clippers and, not missing a beat, he continued: 'We'll also have to shave you under your armpits and in the intimate areas. The camp commander fears lice and epidemic outbreaks.'

Before setting to work he jovially told me that I wasn't the first customer to whom he had to give a bald head. 'The others who arrived here looked no better than you. In fact, some of them could barely still stand.' His voice had turned sad when he mumbled: 'What on earth has become of our once proud German Wehrmacht? I can still barely believe it.'

Later on I was assigned to a tent not too far away from the camp fence, and to a fairly fresh-seeming straw bed next to a surprisingly cheery chap from Berlin.

'Mate,' he orientated me, 'every morning and for lunch we'll be getting some watery soup and a small piece of bread. Sometimes in the evening too.' He paused briefly before asking: 'Don't you have anything apart from this tin can? Mark my word, that old guy next to you won't last too long. He was an artillery gunner somewhere around here. His head is on his bread bag and he keeps a complete set of cutlery in that. If we're fast enough when the moment's right, we'll get our hands on that in the next day or so.'

Although I was extremely tired, I was curious nonetheless, but kept my mouth shut and let him carry on. 'Maybe there'll be some soup for us today and a bit of cornbread. You sure won't get full on it, I can tell you that much.' Whispering, he then added: 'The comrade who occupied your spot before you arrived was taken in this morning for questioning. I'm pretty sure that we'll never see the guy again, as otherwise the top dog of the tent wouldn't have assigned you his spot. These honchos are selected by the Russians. We lie here, shoulder to shoulder, and my space is right here against the tent wall. There are times we crawl outside from underneath the tarpaulin, are you game?'

'What's there for me to do outside?' I whispered back, my curiosity now piqued.

'Remember what I'm telling you, mate. Every morning the ethnic Germans throw some bits over the fence to our side, always to the same spot – bread, sometimes even butter. Without these extras I wouldn't be as fit as I am now. Four of the guys from our neighbouring tent are part of this as well. But you'll also need to know that the Ivans themselves aren't exactly leading a lavish lifestyle, so they also want their cut. The ethnic Germans have bribed the guards, so rest assured, there's something in it for them as well. Up to now, they've been turning a blind eye. Well? Will you be joining us?'

'Absolutely,' was all I could bring myself to say before sleep overcame me.

That afternoon there was no 'little soup' as my neighbour had predicted. My poor stomach ached with hunger, but I fell asleep nonetheless. Towards morning my neighbour shook me awake, whispering into my ear: 'Be as quiet as possible. Maybe our ethnic German friends will turn up with their food bag. We have to be extremely careful, because if others get wind of it, there'll be nothing left for us. As for the old man next to you, he can't hear or see anything.'

We slipped out without making a sound. Once in the open I could hear the Berlin boy muttering something softly to two silhouettes I could barely make out. I only caught some snatches of their sentences: '. . . they'd have to arrive soon . . . outside just two Russians . . . they probably are in the know . . . have no grub either . . .'

Things then happened very quickly. Some twenty or thirty metres away from the camp stood a house attached to a farm. I could see an old man emerging from the building accompanied by a boy about fourteen years old. They stopped in front of the barbed wire. I then heard the old one growl in a husky voice: '*Achtung!*'

Stretching his arm out wide he hurled a dark item over the fence and I was full of admiration of my night companion at how speedily and adeptly he caught the bundle, which he then handed over to me. It was a paper bag filled to the brim and securely fastened, and I pressed it tenderly to my breast. Then the man tossed over the second instalment, which was caught equally adroitly but without a syllable being uttered, and then entrusted to two other prisoners whom I didn't know.

'We don't have anything more,' whispered the young lad, with the gruff voice of the man chiming in: 'We'll return tomorrow. Make sure that the bags disappear.'

'Well, of course,' I heard one of the other two assure him. 'They'll disappear in our shit hole. Thanks very much!'

'See ya tomorrow,' whispered the Berlin chappy, and off he trotted in front of me, my mouth watering all the while.

'We'll share inside. Crawl in, ahead of me. But be quiet so that nobody catches on, otherwise all hell will break loose.' He took the bag out of my hand and seeing my worried look, he quickly added: 'I'll slide it through to you in just a minute.'

Two or three minutes later I was sitting on the floor, ravenously gobbling down two covered pieces of cornbread thickly smeared with butter. My companion even still had his flask on him. Filled with water, he passed it over his lap to offer me a drink. 'For you to wash it down,' he whispered softly, I could barely understand him, but nothing mattered. My fourth slice of bread was topped with butter and some hard cheese. I could hardly remember a time when I felt so satisfied as then, and I immediately fell asleep once more.

It must have been about eight o'clock when I received a piece of bread and watery soup served from the Russian kitchen cart. On that day the roll-call wasn't half as difficult as usual and thus standing didn't seem as painful as it had done previously, especially seeing as I wasn't that hungry. To this very day I think back to those times with gratitude, and to the ethnic Germans who stood by our side.

A comrade lining up next to me remarked, with disdain in his voice: 'I don't think Russians know how to count properly. That's why they have to constantly go over their numbers again. They'll never get the right result.' Without any obvious connection he continued: 'By the way, the ethnic Germans usually give away some food up there where the guards stand. But us lot don't get to see any of it, or not much, because the distribution is unfair!'

I didn't respond to him. Instead, and not for the first time, my eyes wandered longingly up towards the mountains, which I could clearly see from where we were stood, and one of them looked terribly similar to the Kramer with its peak the Königsstand. My yearning for those mountains of mine nearly choked me. My neighbour seemed to notice this, as he lightly nudged me in the ribs, remarking gently: 'Well, well, don't be like that. We stand a good chance, we do, to survive this whole shit. But, yes, these mountains also make me think of home.'

The moment we were back in our tents, my name was called. A very young-looking Russian, his pistol aimed at me, took me to a small building situated at the end of a road about a kilometre long, the very place where we had been head-counted that same morning.

Once inside, we found ourselves in a corridor where the young guy knocked on a door, opened it, and with his pistol motioned me to enter. The officer interrogating me was comfortably seated on an old high-backed chair behind his desk. He too was shaved bald, but judging by the growing hair stubble he must have had black hair. Two dark eyes scrutinised me through a pair of thick horn-rimmed glasses.

He was distinguished-looking, obviously an officer, but I wasn't able to tell from his epaulettes what his rank was. Meanwhile he cross-examined me for two hours straight, asking me every single detail, pumping me for more and more information, questions upon questions.

'What's your profession? Where were you at such and such a time? Who was there? The captain of your battery, what's his name?' and so it went on and on. He also queried the unusual length of my stay at the garrison. After I responded truthfully to everything, he suddenly waved his hands impatiently across the table to the door and gestured for me to leave. '*Dawai! Bashli!*'

This time round a rather pretty Russian woman, though forbidding in demeanour, led me back to the tent. Whilst trotting back I asked myself whether the interrogation officer was Jewish, and therefore might have been especially harsh with me. It made me think back to our arrival, when armed Romanian Army men had treated us with an intense animosity. I too had received a whack with a stick on my back because the man didn't think I got myself to the hairdresser quickly enough. Screaming, he spat at me full of venom:

'You German pigs! You sure didn't get a hold of *me*! But you've murdered my brother and my parents in the concentration camp. You damned Nazi swines just called it "chasing them up the chimney"!'

Others in my group got a similar earful.

There was a constant coming and going in our camp, and the explanation we were provided was that it all had to do with Romania's unexpected change of sides. Batches of men from our Romanian deployment, mostly from the tank repair units and similar facilities dotted all across the country, were transported to our camp and the prisoner population grew by the day.

Every now and again names were shouted out in our tent, followed by several men slowly rising to their feet . . . people who would rarely be seen again, whilst others took their place. By that time the camp was holding some two or three thousand men, but despite the interminable daily roll-calls, we couldn't ever establish an exact number.

I wasn't quite sure from where my neighbour had procured for himself a scrap piece of paper along with a pencil butt, and he never told me. He simply whispered: 'Jot down your home address. We don't have more space. What we want to do is wrap this piece of paper around a stone, throw it across the fence to our German friends and hope they manage to circulate a flyer back at home – give our families a sign we're alive, though it's unlikely this will work.'

CHAPTER 7

Forced Labour by the Sea of Azov

We had been camped at the outskirts of Kronstadt for two weeks and the weather was turning cold when one morning the order came: 'Attention, outside for roll-call! Followed by transport!'

Where to? The Russians hadn't even let their aides in on the secret.

On that day we didn't just have to endure the interminable head-count, but also one of those thorough body searches which took place at the camp entrance. But of course there were no dangerous objects or valuables for them to find. Falling into a column of fives, we departed. I couldn't quite tell how long our column was, but in front and behind me the ranks seemed to stretch on forever. Judging from his dialect, my marching companion to my right was Franconian.

'My oh my!' he exclaimed, 'The inhabitants of the town sure must have put the fear of God in these guys! Just look at this, every ten metres there's a guard who's meant to stop any of us from scramming and seeking shelter with them.'

Silent, we mindlessly stared ahead of us, hundreds of sluggish men stumbling through the town along a two to three kilometre road and not setting eyes on a single inhabitant. Once we had arrived at the station, we were chased onto freight trains, crammed on covered cargo wagons in groups of forty. The door slammed shut behind us.

Someone, I didn't know who it was, issued the order: 'Everyone who has to go must do his business in that right backhand corner next to the door, so that the remainder of our wagon remains clean. You can piss through the small gap, they've left us for ventilation.

As not a single one amongst us had eaten anything much during the previous days, our emergency loo was not used very frequently. After a few hours, and since I was still barefoot like many others, I was shivering in the cold despite the sticky air inside.

The train stopped. Some cried, full of hope: 'Will we finally get some grub?' Sadly that was not the case.

The doors were rammed open. 'All out!'

Dazed by the light, we staggered outside. Someone in front announced: 'We're in Jassy at the Romanian border. Next stop will be the Ukraine.'

There was no reaction, none of us had it in us, and I was profoundly shocked at how inured and apathetic I had become. I was in possession of some cooking ware following the previous day, and all I was missing now was a knife. All my thoughts were focused on the mess kit, my container. It should be filled to the brim. Nothing else seemed to matter at that minute.

Once again we were herded like sheep through the town, guarded by Russians on horses. We ended up at an actual camp, and after a surprisingly hasty body search we were marched towards a long row of wooden barracks. Suddenly we became aware of groups huddling in one direction only. Held back by the shrill screams of the Russians and some hefty whipping with their riding crops, we could just barely be prevented from attacking three Russian kitchen carts. The camp commandant, a former German officer who had been designated to his position by the Russians, ordered discipline.

Sadly, my pot wasn't filled up to the top as I had hoped, and my stomach wasn't even close to being satisfied with the meagre amount of thin potato soup I had been given. That day we received a further two portions of the watery soup which, although not nutritious, at least warmed us up. Regardless, we greedily gobbled it up along with the small piece of bread we had been allocated.

That night, closely pressed one against the other, we lay on our cots, trying to warm each other up. In our row we were all lying on our right side when, in the pitch dark, we suddenly heard the sounds of a harmonica. The stifled coughing, the heavy breathing and sighing – it all stopped. Melancholically we listened to the Viennese melody '*Ich kenn ein kleines Wegerl im Helenental*'.*

Emotions believed to have been long lost or buried surged up in us, woken by this tiny instrument. I cried desperate tears inside myself and could only imagine that the same was happening to the men all around me. But strangely, inexplicably, and despite feeling so hopelessly despondent, I somehow managed to start drawing on a new energy.

'Give up? Never in a thousand years!'

Instead of visualising the small Helenental path of the song, I conjured up an entirely different path – the one I knew from the Loisach valley which trailed up the slope to the Waxenstein.†

'Lothar, listen, the mountain tops all around Garmisch, your home and its inhabitants – they're all waiting for you. Hang in there – you must and will see them again despite it all now looking so bleak. At some point this miserable war and this awful captivity will come to an end.'

Whilst the sounds of the melody whimpered through the barrack, I just wondered to myself how this man had managed to keep his harmonica through all the searches and frisking. Surely he hadn't been able to do this all on his own? I suspected that this object must have been secretly passed from one man to another.

We were restless that first night, the next day was 1 November, and it occurred to me that on that day back at home my people were celebrating All Saints' Day. That's when everyone visits the gravesites of their relatives and friends. Had I already been declared 'missing'? I couldn't really believe that it would not be the case.

---

* 'I know a tiny path in Helenental', by Alexander Steinbrecher.
† The Waxenstein is a group of mountains near Garmisch-Partenkirchen. The highest is Großer Waxenstein at 2,277 metres (7,470 ft).

We were counted, and counted again. Gradually the cold crept up from my feet, deep inside me and spread throughout. Suddenly I pricked up my ears: 'All those with bare feet, step forward!'

I pushed forward. We seemed to be the majority, we were forced to undergo a separate head-count but at the end of it, and much to our pleasant surprise, received a pair of sandal-type shoes. The soles of our new footwear consisted of a layer of wood, approximately three centimetres thick, whilst the toe box consisted of some leather straps leaving enough room for the toes to move around and for these clogs to fit all foot sizes. A small leather band on both sides connected the front to the back, holding the heel in place.

With each day passing by the atmosphere amongst us prisoners became increasingly tense. Hunger stared out of each pair of eyes, everyone was a bundle of nerves. Sometimes three times, but mostly only twice a day we received that thin soup with so few grains of barley you could count them on one hand. The piece of bread to go with it arrived less regularly as time went on.

Many gave up, some acted up. 'The Russians seem to want to delay our hero's death as long as possible! Why, it looks like they want to stand by and observe how we slowly but surely rot away!'

But there were others who countered this by trying to be more objective, maintaining that our guards didn't fare much better when it came to food supplies. 'Just goes to show you, the Russians took too many of us captive and too soon. And that's now their method to decimate us!'

I kept myself separate from such discussions, feeling they did nothing for me. I was looking to preserve my energy and didn't budge from my position during the day. It was getting increasingly cold in the barrack. We all knew it: winter was just around the corner and nobody had enough clothes to wrap himself in. Would my determination, my ironclad intention of one day returning home help me get through the winter?

A few days later we were herded to the station. Many were too weak to walk by themselves and had to be assisted by their comrades on either side supporting them under their arms. An endless worm of half starved silhouettes, dishevelled and slumped over, writhed along the road. Impatient guards kept driving us on: '*Dawai! Dawai!*'

Screaming Russians then crammed us into cargo trucks, fifty men per wagon. Behind my back the door was slammed shut, locked from the outside but leaving a narrow two-centimetre gap to allow some icy wind to blow in. A long shrill engine whistle pierced the air and after some short pulls and bucks the train departed.

The man next to me, who obviously knew a bit of Russian, turned to the rest of us: 'When I asked the guard during our march where we were going, he told me it was a large factory by the Azov Sea. We'll have to work for the Red Army!'

'And why would he be in the know?' asked somebody.

'Don't have the faintest. You should've asked him yourself.'

'Don't speak any Russian.'

'That's your problem!'

The bad mood seemed briefly to replace the omnipresent apathy and already you could hear someone else shouting: 'For God's sake, nobody can stand up straight for all this time!'

'Well, there's nothing we can do about it, we'll just have to take turns sitting on the floor, once again define our shit corner and try keeping ourselves warm by crouching closely together.'

'Easier said than done! Can't you see, for crying out loud, that we're already rammed together shoulder to shoulder and the wind blowing into me is ice cold. I've nearly turned into an icicle.'

'What do I care, why don't you swap with someone else!'

Nobody budged. But we somehow managed so that a few of us were able to sit down, pull our legs up close against our chests, while the others remained standing. Being crushed together in these tight quarters was frightening. Moisture from our breath covered the ceiling and the walls of the wagon with a thin sheet of ice crystals due to the freezing temperature.

I made quite sure to avoid leaning against the freezing side, but found some warmth by resting against my neighbour instead.

The train came to a halt and I fervently hoped that we would get some food. A low murmur of anticipation spread through the wagon. But I and my suffering comrades would be sorely disappointed. Instead we heard some undefinable shouting and Russian hollering some wagons ahead.

'All they're doing is filling up the engines with water,' suggested my neighbour, the same guy who had had the conversation with the guard. That same moment the door was flung open and a German voice yelled: 'We're informed that one of you scumbags in this wagon still has a watch. Hand it over!'

No one moved. One voice yelled back: 'You've been had, sorry, nobody can help you out here!'

The Russian seemed disappointed. He cursed and rammed the door shut, except for the gap already mentioned, then bolted it from the outside. We peed through that gap, and what with the freezing temperatures, the air immediately turned our urine into ice. Because we hadn't even as much as drunk a sip of water during that first day of travel let alone had anything to eat, I actually didn't notice whether the corner designated as our latrine had been used at all.

The train came to yet another stop. This time the doors were pulled wide apart, with three guards standing right outside our wagon, brandishing their submachine guns in our faces. I could immediately sense my envy, seeing them standing there with their feet warmly wrapped up in fur boots that peeked out from underneath heavily lined coats and reached up to their knees. And to top it off, they wore hefty leather caps, even lined with fur, with the earmuffs turned down and protecting their cheeks and necks. How I wished I could get my hands on those.

'That's what I call proper winter outfits,' I thought to myself.

Our wagon had come to a stop near a wooden shed, which we could hardly make out with the onset of darkness. Nobody paid any attention to the clicking noise coming from the train engine with water being syphoned off from a fountain, through a tin pipe and into the steam boiler. Our attention was rather taken up by a carriage, drawn by some ragged horses on which stood several zinc pots containing something still unbeknown to us at the time. One of those carriages stopped in front of our freight wagon. Out of nowhere a translator, probably German himself, appeared behind the guards and yelled:

'Everyone to remain inside! Only those who want to die instantly may jump out! Form a circle inside, have your bowls ready! What we have are small, nutritious salt fish rich in protein, and a piece of bread for everyone. No pushing! Everyone will receive his portion!'

It was actually surprising how most of us still had a grip on ourselves. Only a few surged forward regardless. I gulped down my ration of heavily salted fish, and the bread was also gone within seconds, even before I could once again reclaim my spot right in front of the still open doors. Nobody seemed to heed our calls for a bit of water. Doors were rammed shut again, the whistle of the engine echoed into the night, and we could feel the train with its unusual cargo rolling onwards.

A voice, obviously used to issuing orders, echoed in the dark: 'We must roll ourselves up as we've done before! It's tried and tested. Get some sleep!'

Nobody bothered to contradict him. Eventually you could hear quiet scraping all through the carriage, cursing alternating with sighing. We rolled up next to each other on the floor, sometimes even lying on top of the man next to us. The guy in front of me was taller and bulkier than myself, and I could therefore rest my head on his shoulder, which was tilted slightly forward. This is how I gradually and uneasily dozed off, but nature soon had its way, and I fell into a deep slumber, interrupted by nightmares interspersed by shouts to turn over.

Was it morning already or still night time? I, for one, was wide awake when I noticed the train slowing down. At the same time my hands could feel my neighbour's body: it was cold. Having spoken to him but briefly, I knew that he had been older than me and that he had been a foreman in a repair workshop in the Romanian hinterlands, in charge of overhauling and adjusting lorries. Without a moment's hesitation, I took his much larger coat off his body knowing that I could make good use of it as an additional protection against the cold, all I needed to do was roll up the sleeves. Just when I had finished pulling his thick woollen socks over my legs, I realised that with these last garments there was nothing more for me to take from him. Meanwhile I heard somebody else mumbling: 'Sorry comrade, you don't need anything else.'

The wagon door was flung open and an unknown voice loudly inquired: 'All good?'

'No!,' I shouted back, 'I've got a dead man lying here.'

'Bring him out!'

Once we had discarded the large uncovered corpse – he must have been quite well nourished – out in the open, there was another call: 'Here we've got another one.'

'He too will no longer have to freeze,' I thought to myself when his naked body was moved across the wagon over our heads. Suddenly I noticed that not a single one of us was still carrying his identification tag around his neck. The Russians or Romanians obviously had uses for everything. We had become nameless.

This was another moment when I demanded from myself a total and utter determination to survive. This time round we were handed some bread that had been brought to the train in baskets, and our co-prisoner who spoke Russian begged one of the food distributors for some water only to be told, 'They apparently have none for us, they need it for the engine, looks like. Perhaps we'll get some later!'

The man who translated all this for us had been a school principal in civilian life back at home in Upper Silesia, that's at least what I was able to find out about him in the meantime.

It was only on the third day that the Russians finally distributed some water out of tin basins. It was ice-cold and, careful not to catch a cold, I drank it as slowly as I possibly could, restraining myself from gulping it down in one go, all whilst chewing on my piece of bread weighing maybe 300 grams.

'Lothar, you've got to survive!'

In the midst of the constant darkness surrounding us, I had lost my sense of time. Some among us claimed that we had already been travelling for six days, others countered that by insisting it had only been five. But macabre as it might seem today, not one of us regretted the fact that day by day our wagons became more spacious, seeing as at every stop two or three corpses were transported away. These men had starved to death or had perished of thirst or exhaustion. The Russians, visibly undisturbed by this, trotted down the sides of the train and counted the dead. Our school principal at one point made a remark, softly, barely audible: 'One wouldn't have expected anything different. After all, we've not come at their invitation.'

We were ordered to get off in Taganrog.

Wobbling, lacking any sure footing, we hobbled under strict observation along the train tracks towards what seemed like factory halls, which had been badly hit by the battles. Even though I could barely keep myself upright, I counted ten buildings all lined up in a row along the tracks. Their roofs had largely been demolished, but above three of the furnaces I noticed dark smoke emanating from the long chimneys and darkening the grey winter sky above.

We had long before that realised that the Russians were expert inventors. At our arrival we would be given hard proof, as we could already hear the clattering noise of machines at work coming out of the other halls. Signs above each hall entrance in Cyrillic script obviously indicated what was going on inside but other than the school principal from Upper Silesia, nobody could read them.

Our lot had gathered at the last hall while our guards, leaning in small groups against the remains of some wall, carried on chatting loudly while puffing their *papirosi* and blowing smoke into the air.

A somewhat plump middle-aged woman dressed in a white and almost clean coat was sitting on a chair in front of the wide open entrance door; next to her sat three young women in Red Army uniform behind a long table. Each one had a list in front of them where they registered the names and details provided to them by the plump one.

My linguistic neighbour confirmed my assumption: 'The plump one is the doctor. She'll need to inspect all newcomers and based on her judgement she will allocate us to one of three work groups. I think there must be some factories around here, perhaps numbered one, two and three. But I couldn't really catch much more than that.'

After about a minute it was my turn to stand in front of the doctor. 'Open mouth!' Then while still casually inspecting the inside of my mouth, she ordered: 'Name? Turn round!'

She felt through both pairs of trousers I wore, one on top of the other, and examined my buttocks. She turned her head and called to the Russian sitting next to her my name and the work category she had decided to put me in. It looked like I had been allocated to category two, which the school principal was assigned to as well.

Together we shuffled over to hall one where workers, mostly women, were operating the many machines. There were only a few men amongst those labourers, mostly older Russians. Thick quilted jackets along with woollen caps and felt boots protected the Russians from the freezing temperatures. In between them, clearly recognisable, crouched the prisoners of war in their ragged uniforms and their skimpy footwear.

Shouting above the noise of the machines, the school principal tried to lift my spirits: 'Lothar, it seems that in our misfortune we've somehow lucked out with this assignment. Looks like category one has to go to halls one and three and operate the furnaces, which means that they'll contract a lung infection or something like that once they're out in the cold. But what do the Russians care about us – we're not human to them!'

I could only briefly thank him with a quick nod for this information as in that same moment we had reached a group of prisoners assembled at the end of the hall. It was an empty section of about 200 square metres, above which one could see the grey sky through a hole in the roof. There stood the *natchalnik*, the manager of the hall, atop an upside down wooden crate. This well-fed man had a longish narrow face, which seemed all the longer because of his elongated and slightly bent nose. Indifferently scanning us with his black gleaming eyes he finally exclaimed in near perfect German which was only faintly tainted by an unfamiliar accent: 'Have I finally got one hundred men?'

Someone whispered behind me: 'Well, if that man isn't Jewish, I'll eat glass.'

'My guess was that I wouldn't be getting more than a hundred today.' He seemed quite satisfied with that state of affairs and, pointing to the concrete floor, he shouted: 'You can make yourself at home here. The roof is already being worked on and there is wood waste outside – help yourself. You have two days – then work on behalf of our victory will commence. We're producing grenades for the front! Anyone who moves more than one hundred metres away from the hall gets a bullet in his head! Anything else and how to operate the machines will be explained by the foreman!'

While uttering the last words of his address he turned around and pointed to an older Russian, who had until then stood waiting behind him. Without losing a beat the foreman yelled: 'First clean! Who hairdresser?'

Three men reported. The Russian then inspected us circle of men and shouted again: 'Heads bald already! Good.' Then he pointed to his arm pits and between his legs, handed a clipper to each barber and roared his next orders in his booming bass voice: 'When finished, back to I. Must be! If no, more sick quicker!'

What then followed, and it was not without some pain, clarified for us once and for all, that here, we were no longer human beings, we were nothings. It wasn't that we had lice, it was the lice who had us. I was one of the first ones finished and leaned against the wall opposite.

'Now coming with me,' the old guy said in broken German. 'Can bring wood for underneath sleep. But before, clothing must be hot in steam cabin. All seams full . . . lice! Must make quickly dead. You! Coming with me!'

He pointed to the three bare brick walls around us and then marched in front of us through a gap in the wall about a metre wide, that might have once been a window which reached down to the bottom. By coincidence, two amongst us were professional joiners and were happy when the foreman provided us with a box of nails, a saw and several plaster hammers.

'Want all back!'

That was about the sum total the apparently quite good-natured foreman left us with.

I never found out where the small cylindrical iron stove suddenly appeared from, but when the men dragged it in, there was a huge relief. I was even more surprised at how swiftly rows of plank beds, or something near enough, were cobbled together out of the wood scraps and before we knew it they stood ready along the two side walls.

'Lothar, at least we don't have to sleep on this ice-cold concrete floor. Gosh, do I ever hope we are allowed to keep that oven. Fritz, what a devil of a fellow, has even ensured that we have some left-over wood to burn in the oven, plus a stove pipe. Looks like the pitch is deep enough for the smoke to rise and nothing can actually go up in flames around here!'

Already the foreman was issuing further orders: '*Dawai! Bashli!* Now lice make dead!'

He led us to a cube-like concrete building, with a tin pipe rising out of the roof. In front of a steel door a heap of coat hangers lay around with white labels fastened around the top. Pointing at them, he yelled: 'Each man put clothes on it and remember number. Not long you naked. Not quickly freeze to death. Inside, first very hot steam, break lice in folds of clothes, then hot wind dry clothes. Then nice. Do quickly. *Dawai.*'

At that point an old, sullen-looking Russian took our literally threadbare uniforms. Some of us had to help him put our hangers on several racks arranged parallel and next to each other. There within the delousing chamber it was pleasantly warm, but when I left the cold penetrated right through to my bones. We huddled closely together and didn't much pay attention to the Russian women who were standing next to their machines and, pointing at us, were laughing their heads off.

The chamber was heated from outside and an interminable time seemed to go by before we could finally hear the hissing noises of steam escaping the steel door. The old Russian opened the door and after first vigorously wagging an empty bag around to allow some fresh air to blow in, he motioned for us to pick up our garments.

I most certainly could never have stepped onto the boiling concrete flooring had I not availed myself of the worn-out shoes a dead comrade had left me the day before.

It was so warm inside that we cheekily took a whole lot longer to hand our clothes to those waiting outside, quite a different story to before, when we had been ordered to get them up on the hangers. And when I slipped into my pleasantly warm clothing, it really felt good. Some of my comrades, however, had a pretty bad surprise when they got hold of their braces and the leather bits started crumbling in their hands.

That evening, for the first time, we were to receive our cabbage soup along with 300 grams of bread. Our stove, in the meantime, had claimed a 'lover':* while all of us tried to keep ourselves warm by pressing ourselves one against the other as we were now used to doing, this one man never got up the following day. Two comrades dragged out his corpse, a frail naked body and this time round I couldn't put my hands on even as much as a thread of his tattered inheritance.

The following day I was instructed by a Russian who had a surprisingly good command of German how to operate the turning lathe. He actually seemed pleased with my deftness. From that day on and in my position as a labourer I received 600 grams of black bread and often, but by no means every day, three portions

---

* The man must have wrapped himself around the oven and burnt to death.

of some kind of soup. The machines were not left standing idle. We had shifts from 6 a.m. to 2 p.m. and from 2 p.m. to 10 p.m. and from 10 p.m. to 6 a.m.

The Russian men and women usually worked in twelve-hour shifts and were compensated with food supplies based on their performance, the so-called production target they were meant to reach. I am sure we weren't wrong in believing that their food supplies were larger than ours, yet in spite of that obvious fact, I once saw a Russian woman leaving the hall crying loudly and screaming in desperation. Because she hadn't reached the quota she apparently received nothing or too little to take home for her children. That's at least how the school principal, who shared the turning lathe with me, translated the incident.

One day, out of the blue and before the much-dreaded cold Russian winter descended upon us, we were pleasantly surprised to be informed that we would be receiving new clothing. Instructed to queue at the Red Army lorry which had stopped alongside our pit, we then each picked up a traditional grey-green quilted jacket on the back of which the letters WP were painted – standing for *Woina Pleni*, 'prisoner of war' – along with warmly lined trousers.

'Well, I never would've expected so much welfare coming our way from the state. Seems like the Russian prefers a labouring Nazi to a dead one,' was the wry remark my neighbour made under his breath.

We had no choice but to get used to our new circumstances, even to the repetitious inquisitions. After I had a few tense hours of being questioned, it turned out that I actually got away rather lightly, because neither my unit nor therefore myself had been guilty of any war crimes and thus no blame for anything untoward could be pinned on us. But others didn't fare that well and quite a few disappeared, never to be seen again. Rumour had it that the crime must have been the slaughtering of a cow or a pig, that in other words the perpetrator had appropriated state property. Reason enough to cart him off to Siberia.

Many of us lost a frightening amount of weight in a very short time and it happened ever more frequently that one or two from our group would have to be carried away before our shift had even started. I too had to tighten the string around my waist repeatedly. But I never failed to remind and admonish myself: 'Lothar, you must persevere, you must hold on and survive and don't pay any attention to your constantly grumbling stomach. You must overcome the hunger, because the mountains in the Loisach valley are expecting you.'

Then there was the first victim of a new scourge. Shortly before Christmas a guy shouted to nobody in particular: 'Move out of my way, I can't hold it in any longer!' He staggered towards the standing latrine some twenty or thirty metres away from him, and even before he could reach it we could see his bottom turning bright red. Our school principal, as usual knowing the score, warned me that the poor chap was suffering from dysentery. 'That's all we needed,' he added in exasperation. The following day the fellow's emaciated corpse was discarded.

The ensuing weeks, with two or three or even more dead every few days, only dispirited us further. At one point I overheard a *natchalnik* comment sarcastically: 'Now you Nazis know how is when man shits himself dead. Like this, you so many of us killed.'

This is how we vegetated from one day to the next, from one tiny ration to another, like animals, and having lost all sense of time. It was only when we were allocated to a different shift that we became aware that yet a further seven days had elapsed. Once, we had just finished our night shift and had collapsed dead-tired onto our planks, someone asked half-heartedly: 'Christmas ... has it come and gone already?' The response he received sounded angry: 'Dream on, man, do we really give a damn? I count myself lucky if I can keep myself upright on these hunger rations!'

Only our school principal seemed to have the wherewithal to care about other things, things beyond our malnutrition. Still of strong voice he declared: 'Christmas 1944 has just passed. The Orthodox Christians celebrate the holiday on 6 January. But because the Communists refuse to tolerate any kind of religion, the Christians and their priests are now obliged to perform their services in secret. What's important at this moment is for you to conserve your strength and get some sleep.'

It was an icy day in January when it was my turn to be asked whether I wanted to bury a guy. There was an extra portion of soup in it.

The school principal, shooting me a glance, was prepared to help me, and so together we lugged the cadaver outside. A guard pointed us in the direction of a yard filled with rubble, located just behind the pit. There was nothing, of course, in the form of a burial. The ground was frozen solid. The two of us were chilled to the bone, but did our best to remove some hard clots of soil and stone with our clammy fingers before chucking our corpse to join the heap of others already piled there. We then covered the bodies with some debris and chunks of clay. Only God could know what spring would bring. The wind tore at our clothes and with the job done we hurried to get ourselves back to the sheltered side of the unheated hall.

Towards the end of February, I too showed symptoms of having contracted dysentery and was moved to the sick bay, fortunately in a heated space which was therefore more bearable. I was actually pleasantly taken by the friendly manner of the female doctor whose maternal approach had a soothing effect on me. At the very start of my therapy she ordered that I first get myself cleaned up thoroughly, and a former German medic scrubbed me from head to toe; sadly he didn't allow me to remain sitting in the warm water of the tub any longer than was necessary. 'Man, we don't really usually have that much warm water here,' he said.

Before being allowed to wrap up in a blanket and lie down on a plank, I even got a portion of soup, which I devoured instantly. This one was more nutritious than what we received as our daily ration after our shifts, and it was even supplemented by a piece of white bread. All in all, I nearly felt well within myself. There were some further twenty patients spread out on the wooden floor alongside the brick walls. Many died and were carted away, others recovered, and others still were immediately dispatched back to work. After about a fortnight the doctor assigned me to labour category three, which translated as me being sufficiently fit to work, but only for lighter labour in section ten.

As I was making my way to my new assignment, the rays of early spring lingered on our dismal surroundings, warming me up. But the sun seemed to shine right through me into my heart, and all I could do was fervently hope that this miserable war would soon come to a close. Maybe, just maybe, those miracle weapons that had been promised to us would turn the tide and again bring good fortune to Germany. All I really cared about was seeing my beloved mountains once more.

Hope surged and was further boosted by the fact that some days prior I had been given permission to go to the camp's shoe workshop where our cobbler had been working. I was able to get my totally worn-out clogs replaced by a pair that themselves had been mended several times already, but were quite handsome things compared to the old pair. And what joy when I also received some old but still usable footwraps. Thus equipped, I marched towards my newly allocated post and felt as if I was being carried on wings.

Following my orders I reported to the *natchalnik* of section ten, a man quite similar to my previous superior. With a few words he assigned me to a charge-hand, a German, much to my surprise.

'Here in my work squad we always unfailingly meet our production target. This is not a place to recuperate.' Those were his welcoming words, and he continued: 'Daily deliveries of empty gun crates come in from the front, more or less damaged stuff. Our duty is to put them back in working order as best we can. So, off with you! Get to work! Otherwise they'll cut our bread ration.'

Though put off by this obsequious display of diligence, I was of course aware of why this guy was putting it on. From the other prisoners I had learned that our boss had been a sergeant in the Luftwaffe and was out to endear himself to the Russians. Looking around me I noticed that all the comrades in my squad were prisoners of war, which clearly meant that with local Russians not deployed in this section, the conditions and provisions would be worse. But I didn't let this bother me further and set to work, albeit not putting in a great deal of effort. Because by that evening I had only managed to turn out six crates for the ready-to-use line-up, our boss was well and truly annoyed. 'I'll not get stick from the Russians because of you!' he blustered. 'What I need is twenty or more units per day per man. You better shape up – if not, I'll make damn sure to get rid of you and cart you off to another work place!'

Furiously I fumed back: 'Stop showing off, man. Why . . . can't you see that just by having you the Russians are saving themselves one more paid labourer. Don't be fooled – don't think for a moment that the Russians will let you go home sooner than us because of that!'

At that moment I felt the soothing touch of a hand tapping my shoulder from behind, and turning around I could have screamed with joy. My school principal from Upper Silesia stood in front of me. 'Just landed here,' he chuckled softly, 'and I intend to stick around with you. Suffered a bit of a funny spell at my machine and our female doctor decided to put me down a level. Lothar,' he then whispered with a nod towards the ex-sergeant, 'don't even try and talk sense to this one.'

When on the following day several wagons full of damaged ammunition crates were unloaded and I carefully observed the ensuing sequence of events, I quickly found out why some of us were easily able to fix ten or more of those boxes per day. The minute the wagons came to a stop, these cunning guys pushed forward and grabbed only the lightly damaged crates, leaving the badly damaged ones for the rest of us. Our school principal had also caught on and we certainly followed suit, eventually also managing to meet our target. When the oaf of a charge-hand, who must have assumed that he had put the fear of God in us, praised us for having worked harder, my Upper Silesian friend simply looked him straight in the face and remarked: 'Ah, you fool, haven't you noticed what's been happening here? The Russians have been waiting for idiots like you.'

The first days of March were once again bitter cold. We were freezing, toiling away at our workstations, though on one occasion (which still remains in my memory) we found a way to sneak unnoticed into the heated chamber of the Russian manager. Not only did the elderly man not turn us away, he even showed us to a wooden bench next to his small stove while mumbling into his chin some Russian words we couldn't understand. But then, when my comrade addressed him in Russian, a hint of a smile flickered across his wrinkled, unshaven face.

My school principal translated to me the question he had asked and the response he had received. 'Boss, Russia is so vast and rich in minerals. Why then is it so poor?'

'It's not Russia which is so large,' the manager replied, 'it's that the Jewry is so large. And that's why so many of us here are poor.' This came as a surprise to me. I was taken aback that anti-semitism, which had been incessantly drilled into us by our political leaders back at home, obviously also had many followers here in Russia, and that there was a tendency in this country too to pin all the evils in society on the Jews.

On our return to work our German boss was extremely annoyed. 'And where have you two been loafing around?' he asked.

'I'll give you three guesses, you bully' replied my school principal unfazed. 'Lothar must look after his dysentery and I was helping him in his efforts. And now – don't hold us back from continuing our work.'

One dreary day followed the next. Although the physical demands made on us weren't as fierce as before, we nevertheless suffered from hunger. During our night shift of 7–8 May we suddenly heard the howling of sirens all around us. Stepping outside the door we could see the female Russian labourers in the halls of the ammunition factory hugging their much older Russian male colleagues and screaming with joy. The school principal embarked on his translation:

'The war is over. We've won! The red flag has been raised above Berlin. *Woina, kaput.*'*

My whole world collapsed. Was it really true that all the sacrifices we had made, all the deprivations we had suffered, should turn out to have been for nothing? At the daily roll-call some four days prior, the school principal and I had estimated that at most one-third of the originally imprisoned inmates were still alive. Hunger, dysentery and exhaustion had ensured that our initial group had shrunk to just a fraction of what it was before. And had it all been for nothing? In the meantime, the hunger didn't let up, sapping our last bits of energy and continuing to claim its victims from amongst our ranks.

Whilst the thunderous Russian songs of victory rang in my ears, I quietly took a moment to gather my last bits of energy to convince myself as firmly as before that now was not the time to give up on myself. Who knew? Maybe the victory of the Allies would bring us home sooner. What I yearned for most was to return to my loved ones and to my mountains – I wanted to see all of it once more and at all costs.

---

* *Woina kaput*: 'the war is over'.

CHAPTER 8

An Unknown Destination

Over the following days we were ordered to repair stuff and clean up. Every so often, one or two guards would come round, pick out groups, sometimes they were smaller, sometimes larger, and take them somewhere, though we couldn't ever find out where the 'somewhere' was but suspected it was the railway station.

One sunny day – it was warm and pleasant outside – an Asian-looking guard led me and nine other men through the wide open entrance gate of the ammunition factory, which by that time had been shut down.

'Pity, that,' my neighbour mumbled in a low voice, 'if there were more of us, one could half hope that they were taking us home. Why, the war is over now, isn't it?'

'Dream on!' another guy at the back retorted. 'What's happening here is that we're being squeezed dry like lemons. As long as we're still capable of work, not a single one of us will return to our homeland.'

'Sure,' another fellow chimed in. 'We're all Nazis to them, and now it's us poor devils who have to clean up the pigsty those idiots of ours have created back behind the front line. Who cares about the fact that we never volunteered . . . the Russians tar us all with the same brush. That way they'll make damn sure they don't have to feed useless mouths.'

A guard, waving us impatiently to a passenger train, herded us up the steps to a carriage which was obviously reserved for our lot. Taking a seat behind us, he placed his machine pistol with its typical round magazine across his thighs, and stared straight at us with an undefinable expression. We rolled on inland, passing through two or three towns without stopping. I'm not sure how many kilometres we had put behind us when the train pulled up at a wooden station building in a remote village and, once more, we were shouted at to get out: '*Dawai, Bashli!*'

Pointing to one of the typical Russian country roads, alongside which roughly hewn telephone poles had been rammed in, the guard made it clear that our route would continue on foot. No tree, no bush, nothing broke up the dull countryside as far as the eye could see. But the surrounding farmland was fertile, boasting vast fields for cattle to graze, and crops were aplenty.

Depressed, exhausted and weary, we dragged ourselves along the road, wondering what would be in store for us at our destination. At long last some straw-thatched roofs loomed on the horizon. 'A *kolkhoz*,'* mumbled the comrade to my side. 'That's where they'll put us to work then. Hope there'll be something there to sink our teeth into. I can already make out a pump well.'

Our guard handed us over to the *natchalnik* of the *kolkhoz* and moments later I saw a Russian woman in a horse-drawn cart ferrying our man back to the station.

A deep-red sun was setting in the western evening sky when I, by then much strengthened thanks to a portion of borscht we had received, tried to find the sleeping quarters which had been assigned to us in a shed close to the main building where some straw had been piled up.

Trying to make myself as comfortable as possible, I learned a bit about my neighbour's fortunes, and he volunteered to help me get my bearings. 'We're some 200 men here, tasked to weed beet fields with our bare hands and some hoes. It's generally fine. As for me, the Russians got hold of me on 6 February when I was holed up in the Breslau fortifications,† then I was in a truck factory near Moscow and now, here I am, barely a week.'

---

* Collective farm.
† Breslau was besieged by the Red Army from early February 1945 to the end of the war.

'Would you believe it,' I responded, 'I was born in Breslau, I'm a true *Lerge*. What's it like there, now?' I was really curious.

He looked at me with sadness in his eyes.

'Dreadful! Gauleiter Hanke, that pig, waited as late as 20 January before he finally allowed the women and children to be evacuated. The trains couldn't hold more than a few loads of refugees, and the rest . . . he just sent them on foot towards the west. Thousands were wandering around, homeless, freezing and hungry. We ourselves were rapidly running low on ammunition, but, curiously and we couldn't understand why, we always got plenty of meat and sausage. No idea how that came about. When the Russians captured the airfield in Gandau in the west of the city our Ju-52s couldn't reach the runways any more. So, the deputy mayor then in charge, a Herr Spielhagen, keen to avoid further casualties, advised that we capitulate to the Red Army. But what happened instead was that the SS ordered him to be shot by men of the Volkssturm.* And how did Gauleiter Hanke apparently comment on his death? "He who fears an honourable death dies in disgrace!"'

My neighbour obviously noticed the look of horror on my face, as he fell silent for a moment before continuing with a look of visible disgust:

'This Hanke criminal only had one runway built behind the Kaiserbrücke, blowing up everything and anything which stood in its way and leaving old men and women and fourteen-, fifteen-year-old lads to clear away the rubble. I myself was still around to see the runway, it was just before the Russians herded me away into captivity, and it measured some 300 metres wide and 1 kilometre long.

'I heard rumours that in fact only one aircraft ever took off from there – with Hanke, that pig, on board. You see my friend, it's these sorts of shitrags we paid obedience to for years.'

---

* The Volkssturm was a militia force roughly equivalent to the British Home Guard established by the Nazis in the final months of the war.

The daily regime at the *kolkhoz* was one we knew from before, when we were imprisoned at the factory. After the early morning roll-call, we got our portion of soup, this was followed by labour in the fields, then a bowl of borscht. When, on the fourth day they were looking to select two drivers, we didn't know for what reason of course, I didn't hesitate for a moment and put up my hand. I simply wanted out, to move on.

I and the other fellow chosen were directed to report to a hall-like construction, also covered by straw and some three kilometres away. We walked there unguarded, chatted about our hopes of soon being released and for that reason alone never even thought about fleeing. On our walk I confided to my comrade, who was somewhat older than me and who indeed was a trained driver, that I had lied.

'No matter, Lothar,' he replied cheerfully, 'if they ask us to drive tractors, I'll show you how simple it all is. Bet you, nobody'll notice.'

Once we arrived at our destination, we received our instructions from the manager of the hall who could only speak some broken German.

'Here four tractors, come from everywhere. All need wheels change. *Dawai, Dawai.*'

Watching my fellow prisoner, I quickly picked up how to exchange old wheels for new ones. We stacked the old wheels next to the so-called repair workshop and replaced them with the new ones, which we picked up from the rear area of the building where they had been stored according to two standard sizes.

After our one-hour lunch break we would usually leave hungry. That's why, unsupervised, I took myself to the nearby village whose inhabitants consisted on the whole of women now living on their own, mostly sitting in front of their huts in the sunshine amidst their children. No one really seemed to be living in comfortable circumstances and I had to take a deep breath before mustering up enough courage to ask them for *khleb*, bread. The old couple sitting in front of the first hut didn't, or didn't want to understand me.

But then the old woman sitting in front of the second hut nodded at me kindly, filled both my jacket pockets with sunflower seeds, and then went inside to bring me a large piece of bread. She likely didn't understand my German words of thanks, but showered me with a torrent of exclamations accompanied by imprinting a cross on my forehead with her thumb.

Our Russian foreman was a man of about sixty who had a slight limp, and when I returned from my escapade, he wagged a warning finger at me but it definitely was more in jest. 'You out beg? No good. Not do again. Now work!'

After seven days we were told that our services were no longer required at the repair workshop. Two days of toiling in the fields followed then, one morning during roll-call, I saw a small horse cart with a *panje* horse harnessed to it. An old Russian man was leaning against the vehicle, legs crossed and smoking his *papirosa* with obvious pleasure.

It turned out that this man was asking for two labourers for his own *kolkhoz* which was situated some distance away. Without giving it too much thought I volunteered and moments later I and another comrade, this time a Saxon, sat atop the cart, headed once again to an unknown fate. My new colleague mentioned how he was yearning to return back home to his farm near Leipzig and to his wife and three children.

'At least, Lothar,' he mused, 'this senseless slaughtering has finally come to an end and frankly, the Russians cannot keep us here forever. I bet that they'll let us go just as soon as their victorious menfolk have returned home.'

The small Russian horse trotted merrily along. An hour had gone by when the horse suddenly neighed, shook its mane and increased its pace. The straw-thatched roofs of a cluster of huts appeared before us and after another few minutes' drive our coachman artfully swung round in a semi-circle before coming to a stop in front of a building we thought was a barn.

He pointed his whip towards the entrance door and immediately gathered his reins ready for departure. We jumped off the carriage and watched the driver as he continued on to one of the several stables standing fifty metres apart from each other along the road. Before we entered the building, we could see his cart rolling past the fifth stable, after which the terrain gently dipped down towards the reed-covered banks of a thin river with a small rickety wooden bridge. Behind nestled a village. 'Goodness, what a fertile area we've landed in! This is the stuff of dreams!' exclaimed my comrade.

I couldn't agree with him more. 'Otto,' I asked him, 'Do you think these women over there riding on their carts are bringing in the first cut of hay or already the second?'

'You're asking me too many questions. But let's just say, if a wheat kernel dropped from your pocket anywhere around here, looks to me you'd be able to harvest an entire field in no time. By Jove, I wouldn't mind such fertile ground back at home.'

We then both entered the barn-like building where we had been dropped off and were surprised at what we saw.

A youthful looking woman, obviously the head cook, beyond whom two elderly women and a young girl peered at us with unconcealed curiosity from behind the large table, greeted us in a very friendly manner. Only the cook spoke German. 'I am Natasha. Your *natchalnik* has brought you to us.'

With these words she handed us a small piece of bread and some salt (a traditional gesture of welcome), which surprised us even more. Then everyone was given a glass of vodka and a small gherkin. I couldn't help myself but spontaneously burst out: 'Otto, we've landed on our feet here. Surely the work they've in mind for us cannot be that strenuous. I can easily see us happily remaining here until we're released.'

'You might well be right there, Lothar.'

That's when the *natchalnik* entered the roomy kitchen, in which obviously food was being prepared for all the farm's labourers. First, in broken German, he turned to Otto: 'You farmer. You look after pigs. Important for everybody. Allowed to free run little bit in grass. After, not necessary much feeding, also better taste.'

Briefly sizing me up, he then astutely remarked: 'You other profession. But now, must learn look after mother pigs. Important too.' I nodded obligingly even though I was disappointed, as I hadn't expected to end up here as a pig farmer.

'Lothar,' my comrade tried to console me, 'it really doesn't matter. I'm sure we won't have to exert ourselves too much around here. If we're fed reasonably well, we'll be able to return home recuperated.'

The Russian obviously understood us, because, shrugging his shoulders, he turned back to Otto again.

'Young boy work here until now. He today in army. You be careful, animals not run far away. Stay together. Night in stable. You responsible.'

Then, addressing me, he felt he owed me an explanation. 'Wife do it, but now sick. Not come back. Now I showing you mother pigs. One mother have babies already. Others will come. Stable you always make clean, fresh straw. Animals not outside, not! *Ponemai*, understood?'

That same afternoon I mucked out the stable and with the help of a wheelbarrow carted the pig shit away to a nearby manure heap. After I had finished those chores, I distributed straw to the sows which were kept separate in an area surrounded by a very sturdy wooden fence, and behind which Otto's animals were meant to find shelter at night and in bad weather.

Towards the evening Otto and I were sat at the end of a long narrow bench at a large table, and, hands washed, gratefully devoured the barley soup that had been ladled out for everyone together with a chunk of bread. The *natchalnik* was seated next to four older men at the other end. Except for them, only women had joined the table; they were of all ages and carried on a loud conversation which obviously concerned the two of us. The looks we received differed widely: some peered at us in curiosity, others shot stern, searching and even hostile glances in our direction; then there were those who seemed to be sorry for us, and some who didn't seem to care one way or another.

Otto and I left the table as soon as it felt proper, and we couldn't remember the last time we had felt so full. With a brief nod to our boss, the *natchalnik*, we hastened to leave the kitchen. Nobody seemed to be very interested in where we wanted to sleep or if we could even find a spot to do so, but seeing as neither of us two had been born with a silver spoon in our mouths, we didn't let this worry us too much.

The night was turning warm, so we decided to sleep out in the open, just above the river bank. A hitherto unknown feeling nearly approximating freedom and relief rose in us, but was mixed with worry and wistful thoughts about our homeland far away.

'Lothar, what d'you think will await us back in Germany? Have our loved ones survived the madness? This uncertainty has plagued me for some time and I fear that at home people are also suffering from food shortages and lack all the necessities in life.'

'Otto, me too, I keep having to think about these things, even though I have neither wife nor children who would expect me to return.'

The second I had uttered these words, we heard engine noise from very close by. Slowly a lorry rattled down the road, which was badly damaged by countless potholes, and, swaying lightly from side to side, it crossed the nearby bridge. Women were sitting in the cargo area. They had worked here during the day and were now returning to their lodgings somewhere in the neighbourhood. Listening to their singing of mournful yet at the same time melodious tunes we had never heard sung before, we involuntarily felt goose bumps all over our bodies and shivered with emotion.

Softly I whispered to my fellow prisoner: 'Otto, looks like this is the other face of Russia: melancholia and indifference, empathy and cruelty – all seem to lie next to each other, side by side. And us? What did we do? Bring nothing but calamity upon these people, that's what we did.'

'You might well have a point. As for me, when I hear these tunes, I just get homesick.'

In the following weeks we would quite often get to hear the same dreamy and lyrical tunes resonating far across the countryside. Sometimes there were older men sitting amongst the womenfolk and their vigorous tenors or sonorous bass voices would harmonise beautifully with the female altos and meld into a melodious chorus.

At times the tinkling sound of a balalaika accompanied the evening songs. The two of us would simply sit by quietly and in spite of our longing for home, we could feel our hatred against the 'Russian sub-humans', the so-called 'Ivans', that had been instilled in us for so many years fade away while making way for some recognition that, in fact, more connected us to the simple Russian folks than separated us from them.

Two large fields growing cucumbers and tomatoes stretched from just opposite the *kolkhoz* to beyond the horizon. At our first breakfast Natasha, with a mixture of words and gestures, explained that everyone could eat from the crops as much as they wanted. From what she said I gathered that this wouldn't be considered theft of Soviet property, and I certainly didn't need much convincing to make good use of this unexpected offer. Otto seemed to have much the same view. 'Lothar, all I'm hoping for is that this continues. We sure had the luck of the draw,' he remarked cheerfully.

That evening both of us bathed in the river and, for once, took our sweet time while also realising this was a good opportunity to give our filthy clothes a wash. It was long overdue. We then lay naked in the grass, drying off in the warm wind before slipping into our threadbare but clean garments.

The following day, in the kitchen after supper, the *natchalnik* took us aside and pointed to a woman sitting next to him who offered to cut our hair. 'Your *natchalnik* – my husband,' she said in broken German. 'I professional hairdresser. You two will much better look after, also with clean hair like now.'

She then resolutely reached for a manually operated hair-cutter and set to work shortening our manes, which in the past months had grown to a significant length. Once she briefly asked: 'Hurt?' While I laughingly assured her that it was fine, she started chatting and told me that her brother who was in the Red Army and in Germany had returned to his wife in the village for a week's leave.

'Is tank in Beslau – does city exist?' she inquired.

'*Breslau*, yes!'

She then jotted down the address of my aunt and assured me that her brother would look her up on his return there. 'Piotr very responsible. Will visit, certain.' She also wrote down the address of Otto's family.

But when nothing happened in the following weeks and no letters or news from the Russian soldier arrived, we gave up hope and once again were filled with the familiar uncertainty.

On one particular day we had some light rain, so Otto and I spent the night in one of the straw-roofed huts, but we didn't much care for the experience as we were woken by the constant rustling of mice and miaowing cats and the dust-filled air bothered us. We quickly decided to build a small hut for ourselves, using straw – of which there was plenty – and placing it close to the bank of the river, which was a tributary of the Mius.

After three evenings of concerted effort we had completed our night shelter. It was hardly bigger than a two-man tent but served our purposes. Because the wind largely blew from the west, we had placed the open entrance on the east side, which also meant that it was sheltered by the cowshed opposite. We then dug a shallow pit and filled it with stones to create a fireplace. We felt quite contented with what we had achieved and even our *natchalnik* grunted something approvingly while chucking his *papirosa* butt into the fireplace. He then turned on his heel without saying another word.

'Lothar, the two of us really did win the jackpot. Think about it – we're receiving a spoonful of sugar every five days and on top of that five grams of tobacco.'

I couldn't agree with him more. 'You're right – I still remember that when we received tobacco back at the ammunition factory,

I had to find some heavy smokers who'd want to agree to exchange it for sugar – and here? Here, we have our *natchalnik* right at our doorstep and our deals obviously keep him happy. I can only hope that they'll retain us here through the winter.'

'Well, Lothar, here we differ. Don't you remember, at our last work post there were rumours that we'd be allowed to return home before Christmas?'

'May your words reach God's ears. But right now, I feel like going bathing. Want to join me?'

'Not really, I've already washed myself. I'll have a lie down.'

'Sleep well, see you later.'

For a long while I just sat there enjoying the balmy evening, watching as the water idly weaved its way over the riverbed which was only five metres wide. Lying in the shallow bit, elbows perched with just my head popping out above the water and totally naked, I felt peaceful and at one with nature, observing the dragonflies whirling around me and the glowworms luring other insects. A soft noise from across the river made me look up. A young girl of around seventeen or eighteen had approached and then, stopping short for a few seconds, just stared at me in disbelief with her bright blue shimmering eyes, perhaps also somewhat frightened. She was barefoot and wore her blonde hair in a tight plait nearly reaching down to her slim hips. We eyed each other and I could sense that she suspected who I was. Lightly shrugging her shoulders, she continued on her path without looking back. Were Russian girls forbidden to speak to prisoners of war, I wondered? Surely not. But, no matter, I thought it wise to behave with as much restraint as possible. I might be lucky enough to meet this blonde beauty again one day.

But the sight of her reminded me so much of Lotte back in Landshut that it physically hurt me, and the pain literally pressed on my heart. Nevertheless, the brief encounter with this magical creature confirmed to me once more that I was still capable of feeling emotions other than simply homesickness. I felt normal and alive.

When I returned the following morning to the stables, I stopped at the entrance in surprise. One of the sows I had been put in charge of greeted me with a very friendly grunt and my eyes instantly fell on eight small piglets sucking on their mother's nipples, squealing and smacking their lips delicately. I sat myself down in the straw next to the mother pig and stroked her neck. By then, the pig had got used to me and didn't mind.

One morning at the beginning of September, I felt tired and weak and broke out in a cold sweat, but seemed to run a fever at the same time. Otto took me to an old man in the *kolkhoz* whom we knew sometimes acted as a healer. After one look at me he seemed to be able to pinpoint what was wrong. 'Fever not good,' he diagnosed, 'but I not have much medicine.' He gave me five or six tablets, instructing me to take one each day. 'Sleep much!' he advised and sent me away.

After I had swallowed my first dose, Otto led me to the far corner of the barn which was quite private. 'Sleep tight, boy. Don't worry about your animals, I'll take care of them. I'll check in on you this evening at the latest,' he said soothingly before having to return to work.

In my feverish dreams I climbed mountains, skied downhill into the valley and heard cannons explode. I am not quite sure how long I hovered in this state with only my Saxon farmer to care for me, provide me with water and feed me with anything he could lay his hands on. The *natchalnik* couldn't care less how or even whether I improved; all he cared about was the welfare of the pigs in the *kolkhoz*.

Gradually I regained my strength and could once again look after my sows, which in the meantime had given birth to two further litters. It had become necessary to keep each sow and her litter in a separate shack.

A Russian woman would come by three times a day carrying large pots of fresh milk which she had picked up from the cowsheds and was meant for my animals, but as soon as she had poured it all into the piglets' troughs and stepped out of my pig shack I would whip out my spoon from my jacket pocket and help myself to as much of the still warm milk as I could. It wasn't the most hygienic, but I was determined to do anything which would restore me to full health. One day, surely, the longed-for return to our home country would have to be announced, I thought, and once that happened, I wanted to be fit enough to undertake the journey.

It was mid-September and the warm nights had come to an end. Otto and I set out to look for some wood, and found enough to get a fire going to keep us warm. Nobody seemed to be bothered by the flickering glare of our small fire. Then, one night, our hut was suddenly ablaze and we both just managed to get away in the nick of time. It was probably a sudden gust of wind which had kindled the embers and must have blown some sparks into the straw roof. Unfortunately this incident forced us back into the barn, which we didn't enjoy at all.

It was one of the last days in October when our *natchalnik* informed us that 'now finish' – our rather pleasant assignment had obviously been terminated and we had become goods to be returned – and drove us in his *panje* cart in the direction of our first *kolkhoz*. He didn't care one way or another, or if he did, he certainly didn't show it. Once back, our comrades told us that during our absence that summer there had been no deaths: we were still some 250 strong. That same evening of our arrival we were sent out to collect dry wood so that the kitchen could cook us some tomato soup. It turned out thin and watery.

We then spent the following week with practically no work to do, but eagerly gobbled up and digested the inevitable rumours referring to the prospect that we would soon be dismissed. 'What do you want – there's just no employment for us around here. Surely the Russians won't be wanting to feed men who aren't of any use.'

In my heart the hope of returning home soon was rekindled, but rationally I couldn't justify such dreams. 'Don't you think that this vast country which we harmed so much contains more than just *kolkhozes,* and will find ways and places where we can be useful?' I asked myself. I had to admit that it was much more probable that the Russians would deploy us for precisely what I suspected: to rebuild what we had destroyed.

CHAPTER 9

The Escape

Thin wafts of cloud during the last days of October 1945 heralded the arrival of winter, when one chilly morning during roll-call a Soviet Army man did a thorough body search on each of us and did indeed find quite a few bits and pieces, which made him, of course, feel it was all worth it. No earth-shattering valuables, but some of my co-prisoners had, for example, sharpened their spoons in such a manner that enabled them to slice bread.

Every now and again, whilst the guard marched up and down the rows, we would hear him say: '*Nix gut.*'

It was surprising how exacting they seemed to be with their counting on that particular day, and even jotted down our names on their lists. Were these signs pointing to our imminent release, or did the Russian officer have to justify that his next delivery of us men to god-knows-where was all in order? Even if many of us dreamed about an early release, I for one considered myself to be amongst the realists, who figured that this whole procedure only served one goal: to transport us to a different location where we would be put to work. I was to be proven right.

After the head count, we were ordered to report for departure. For the next four days we would be dragged through the vast Russian plains but no shots were fired, seeing as our guards had no reason to want us dead. Every morning we were handed one portion of tomato or potato soup, or a liquid which resembled borscht, and a piece of bread. The march had every appearance of having been well thought through, as on each evening we would arrive at a straw bunker where we spent the night. The fields around us had been harvested. The most hair-raising rumours travelled through the ranks, but one of them actually hit the mark as far as I was concerned:

'Boys, looks like we're approaching the coal mines of the Donets basin. That's where the Russians will likely be needing us.'

'Ha, so now we know why we're being fed just enough so that no one is left behind. Too little to live on, but not enough to kill us.'

We reached our destination on the fourth day, just as night was falling. The site already housed one thousand *woina plenis*, POWs. It was situated on the outskirts of Makiivka and, as we had suspected, was close to a coal mine. The settlement consisted of several houses of a similar build, previously populated by the families of Russian miners. They consisted of a ground and first floor, were empty, and what with all of them being a uniform dull greyish colour, their drab appearance was depressing.

Two houses were allocated to us 250 newcomers. They had no heating, and with the nights having by then become significantly cooler, the prospect of us being able to live in even minimal comfort was bleak.

Without looking around I and about fifteen other men, simply lay down on the planks we had discovered in one of the small rooms on the ground floor and were grateful at least still to have our well-lined quilted jackets and trousers which afforded us some warmth.

But before even entering the house we noticed that the latrine was located outside – in a kind of courtyard that connected the buildings. It consisted of a concrete slab which had been cemented into the ground and into which had been cut twelve equidistant holes underneath which a sump collected the faeces.

'Bon appetit,' my neighbour commented sarcastically. 'This might do for the moment. But when the cold winter wind swooshes the piss over that concrete, you're sure to break some bones when you fall onto the freezing sheet of ice.' The subsequent winter months proved him only too right.

On entering the house, I had made sure to mark out my sleeping quarters and only then stepped outside for a moment so that I could get my bearings. Where were we actually? Not far from where I stood I could make out a low single-storey house standing next to the entrance of the colliery. Next to it, as far as my eyes could tell in the darkness, was what I suspected to be a slag heap.

One of the veteran POWs who, judging by his looks, must have been interned here for what I suspected had been quite a while, had just used our loo and was about to walk past me when I grabbed his arm. 'Comrade, can you tell me what this construction over there is intended for – is it a storage space?' I enquired.

'No! Let me fill you in . . . You can't imagine what we look like when we see the light of day after our shift down below is over. It's where we take a shower. The Russians you see,' he told me, confirming what I had suspected all along, 'want to keep us here for quite some time. But by Jove, this pit is the most primitive one I could ever have imagined. It's not at all like what we know from back home. I'm from Wattenscheid in fact. Around here, you can only dream about things like lift cages and suchlike. They've no clue. Here, you have to descend on ladders, heft the chunks of coal into your back basket and climb up again. May I wish you good luck, so they don't stick you in the notorious pit number six, as they did with me when I was a newcomer. On top of everything else, it's wet and slippery there. We have dead and injured on a daily basis – all registered by the Russians. Keep well, comrade!'
He disappeared, leaving me, the new POW fresh from the last transport, deep in thought.

But after roll-call the next morning, my worst fears didn't materialise. Together with my 250 comrades, I was allocated to a detail at a stone quarry which several guards took us to immediately after the headcount. Arriving at the site, I once again could only marvel at the rich natural resources this country possessed. Not far from the collieries lay pink, solid rock layered high in substantial horizontal beds so that you could hack away at each of them for several days and get a good yield.

A Russian foreman collected twenty men from our group for his gang. In broken German mixed in with some Russian bits, and accompanying the whole palaver with some gestures, he explained how with the help of crowbars and chisels we should be able to break the rock, and extract from this seemingly inexhaustible supply preferably only large slabs. I, meanwhile, out of the corner of my eye, took a closer look at the guards in charge of us. While our foreman didn't say how many cubic metres of rock they expected us to stack ready for transport, he certainly made it quite clear that our daily ration directly depended on our productivity.

'*Dawai! Dawai!* No rest here, even if weather one day not good! Better here than in coal pit!'

Nobody doubted that his last comment was the truth.

During the first days I was tasked, together with a comrade who came from Swabia and turned out to be quite a crafty guy, to haul the broken slabs onto a simple wooden stretcher and cart them away to the storage space, and then to unload and pile them up on top of each other. The bars sticking out at the front and back of these stretchers pressed heavily into our hands and we soon worked out that if we didn't load too many slabs in one go we could just about manage the weight.

Trudging back and forth, we kept a close eye on both our foreman and the guards. I wanted nothing to escape me. I also took close note of the river, several metres wide, winding its way through the landscape and then disappearing to the horizon.

'Lothar,' the Swabian turned to me and observed in his unmistakable dialect, 'what we have to do is once in a while place some smaller rock pieces in between the slabs, just when the overseer isn't looking at us. That'll give us some empty cubic metres, enough at least to spare our ribcages.'

The two of us weren't the only porters, and while it went without saying that we, of course, let our comrades in on our technique, we sadly didn't get away with it. Our Russian foreman would often come up to us and poke his stick through gaps that appeared too large to him, and if he successfully caught us out, he would adjust our quota, explaining that he too was being checked.

'*Nix* cheat! Because Russian very angry!'

The Russian winter, with its temperatures falling well below minus thirty degrees, did nothing to ease our lot, nor to help us towards meeting the quota our daily rations depended on. We were continuously plagued by indescribable hunger, but at least didn't suffer any deaths, whereas down in the colliery where our comrades laboured underground, this was a near-daily occurrence. While it would obviously have been warmer down there, we were sure glad to be able to see the sky and be assigned to above-ground labour.

This advantage, however, also had its downside. Several times, after snowfalls, our soaking garments had to dry against our bodies as of course we didn't own any change of clothing. That in turn would mean reporting to work the following day with damp shirts and trousers still clinging to us.

Twice that winter we were chased out of our cabin and ordered to assemble at the station to unload tree trunks from the flatcars. We dreaded these particularly cruel and backbreaking assignments, and it further weakened many of our men who were suffering already from constant hunger and thirst. However despondent I felt, it surprised me how resilient I had become whilst here in Russia.

But when, during the second of these deployments, we had to shovel away some two-metre-high snow banks that the wind had swept into our region during that night and which made it impossible to get to the trunks, with our hands protected only by threadbare gloves made of rough linen, I too believed that I had reached my limit. I no longer felt able to carry on, yet somehow I automatically did. The top layer of the tree trunks was relatively easy to lift off and throw to the ground, whereupon comrades lugged them over to the waiting lorries which would then drive them to the colliery. An ice-cold wind blowing in from the east whistled around our ears. But when we were ordered to unload the pit props from the wagon, heave them across the rakes and then onto the lorry freight beds, we soon felt unbearably hot. There we were, an outdoor human assembly line of shivering and emaciated silhouettes covered in rags and slaving away throughout the night. At dawn, once again having to let our clothes dry against our bodies and despite the night spent without sleep or a moment's rest in between tasks, we were forced to report to our day shift straight away. There was no letting up.

On a February morning – by now it was 1946 – and under a bright blue sky, though conditions were freezing, we listened to an announcement at roll-call requesting anyone who was a painter to come forward. Without giving it a lot of thought I volunteered, and within the hour a guard took me and a comrade from Frankfurt on Main to a bakery in Makiivka. It wasn't a bakery as I knew it from back home, rather something more like a bread factory. It was, of course, state-owned, and I was quite impressed by both the high hygienic standards and the smooth operational efficiency being maintained. In the first hall I saw men and women standing over large tubs mixing and kneading the dough with their bare hands, which they then carried into the second hall, a large baking area where we were told to start our job.

Instructed to paint all the walls but without interrupting the flow of work, we followed the *natchalnik*'s detailed orders as to how we should go about our job. The aroma of freshly baked bread was most pleasant and the *natchalnik*, who surprisingly spoke an excellent German, handed each of us a large piece.

Ravenously gobbling it up, we could, in the meantime, watch how several women with sleeves pulled up high, wearing white aprons that reached down to their ankles and clean kerchiefs wrapped around their hair, gathered the dough from the tubs before distributing it equally into tin loaf pans, which I estimated must have been some fifteen centimetres square and fifteen centimetres high. Once filled, the tins disappeared into the ovens, which were fired by coal, whilst other ovens were being emptied by two women who then laid the freshly baked loaves onto long wooden boards that had been scrubbed clean, before, in a final step, moving them to racks on which they were stacked to cool off.

Another assembly line working like clockwork, I thought, though far more bearable than the one back at the quarry.

The walls in both halls were not in terrible shape, just slightly dulled by the smoke, but obviously the state official checking on these matters had found them wanting. Showing us where we could find the carbide mix and lime plaster – both held in storage in a cool but rust-free metal shed in the courtyard – he then handed us brushes that basically resembled reed-like mops attached to long rounded wooden handles, and ordered us to set to work.

Though closely scrutinised by the curious eyes of the women working in both halls, we nevertheless felt comfortable in these warm surroundings, and did all we could to spend as much time as possible on the job without it becoming too risky. That same afternoon we had already progressed to the baking area, and I was the first one to use the men's toilet, which by that time was freshly painted and sparkly clean.

Always scheming and making the most of every opportunity that came my way, I tucked the ends of my trousers into my shoes and then tied these up as tight as I could. Having previously noticed that once all the baking tins had been scraped clean of the bread leftovers that had got stuck to their sides these were then swept up into little heaps in between the ovens, I sneaked over and stashed away as much of the precious crumbs as I could. My companion from Frankfurt was a much more timid sort of a fellow, but at least didn't mind shielding me with his body as best he could. Enviously eyeing me with both my trouser legs stuffed to the brim, my buddy finally plucked up enough courage to follow suit, this time with me serving as his screen. After our shift, which lasted about nine hours, had ended, we slowly waddled back to our gang under the surveillance of our guard. He didn't catch on. The guy from Frankfurt was housed in the second building, and it was only when we returned to the quarry the next day that I bumped into him again.

'Lothar,' he whinged, 'they practically tore every last crumb out of my trouser legs. I was left with virtually nothing!'

'Oh, you poor sod!' I replied without much compassion in my voice. 'It was actually quite different for me,' I said somewhat smugly. 'I made it crystal clear to the guys that all I did was my work and that it wasn't my fault they hadn't learned a proper trade.'

On that day – it wasn't a particularly cold one – I as usual paid close attention to the line-up of the guards. Would I be able to detect even the tiniest gap in their formation? To my great dismay, I discovered that on that day the guard even had one of the watchdogs next to him, something which was usually only the case at night when they surrounded our housing complex.

Meanwhile, all of us had just about given up hope of being liberated in the foreseeable future. While the story of one of the miners having successfully escaped had filtered through, providing us with a measure of encouragement, it was quickly shattered by the repercussions. His co-prisoners were punished by having their rations cut and sadly, a few days after his escape, the collier was found and forced to be the literal whipping boy in between rows of the comrades he had betrayed. My guess was that he never left the sick bay. And yet, while it seemed absolutely impossible to escape from this place undetected, and in spite of the awful incident with the collier, I simply wasn't prepared to give up on my plan. I had been hatching it for too long for me not to believe confidently that it could work and that I would prevail in the end.

In the middle of March, some six weeks after our painting assignment, me and my comrade from Frankfurt were yet again dispatched to the bread factory, the same one as before. Both of us knew what the score was, what they expected from us, when and where, so no explanations were necessary. And once again, both of us were very skilled in smuggling leftover bread back to our billet.

But on that day a Russian lieutenant had arrived in our camp, assigned to be the new commander of the guard detail. Self-important and overbearing, he put us off immediately. When, however, on 15 April he requested that 'the two decorators' be brought to him so that he could instruct them to paint his own quarters, which weren't too far way from our camp, both me and my colleague were only too willing to oblige. The guy from Frankfurt was looking forward to a change of scenery, a bit of a break from our dull daily regime, whereas I spun hopes of quite a different nature, oddly sensing that my moment had finally arrived.

A guard took us a short distance down the street, lined by houses each as drab as the next, all grey and built in the same bland style. The people we walked past were similarly sombre-looking; all dressed the same, they actually hardly looked any different from us, the *woina plenis*. I had long ago rubbed away the WP which had been painted onto my quilted jacket and which could now only be made out if one looked really close-up. I firmly believed I blended in.

The lieutenant's room was situated in the rear part of the third or fourth house on that street, and his particular building was of an exceptionally imposing size. The guard remained with us for the time it took us to move all the furniture into the centre of the room, and then disappeared without another word.

We had just started scraping off the peeling paint on the walls, which had obviously been sorely neglected for many years, when I turned to my comrade and casually said: 'Look here, Hannes, I'm going to have to take a piss. I spotted the loo in the corridor when we walked through.'

'Fine, Lothar. But don't stay away too long. These walls look like a hell of a lot of work. We've got to get moving on them if we're to have them finished by tonight. You know the type of lieutenant we've been landed with – that sort of conceited brat will act up if we're not done with the job by the time he returns this evening. The walls at the bread factory were so much easier than this mess here!'

Already through the door, I called back over my shoulder: 'Don't worry, Hannes, just keep at it in the meantime,' and waved my hand to reassure him.

Once outside, I dashed down the hallway to the front door, opened it just a crack, only enough to look outside and scan the situation. Looking both ways and not detecting any guards and only a few civilians, I stepped out into the road and quietly shut the door behind me. At the same time I patted my pockets to make sure that my most valuable possession – a large chunk of bread – hadn't got lost. My heart was in my mouth, but I forced myself to remain composed. Striding unhurriedly and purposefully towards the quarry, but carefully making a wide circle around it to bypass the camp, my only fear was the fierce guard dogs.

Following my meticulous plan, I walked towards the river. Under no circumstances were the dogs to follow my scent, so I had to get myself into the water as quickly as I could.

Wading in, I pulled the bread out of my pocket and held it high above my head whilst still in the shallows and not yet forced to swim. This worked until I got to the middle where the water was much colder than I had expected.

I was not allowing myself to become discouraged, and repeating to myself over and over again that, whatever it took, I had to make it, I struggled onwards downstream. Thankfully the water never reached above my chest, but some twenty or thirty metres down the river the freezing temperature forced me to climb up the opposite bank. While encouraged that I had managed the river well enough, I also knew that I was still far from being out of danger. I started running, literally for my life, terrified in case I was followed and couldn't tell whether my whole body trembled out of excitement or the cold. Furtively looking over my shoulders without stopping, I eventually could feel myself becoming breathless and decided to alternate between walking at a fast pace and running. My direction was Stalino* yet my intention was to work round the city.

I didn't know how many metres or indeed kilometres I had put behind me when I saw from afar a small forest and decided to go through it. By where the sun stood, it must have been towards noon. Very quickly I spotted a heap of leaves behind a tree, which probably had been swept up by the wind and seemed made to measure for me to crawl deep inside. While of course

---

* Now Donetsk.

the foliage from the previous year was no longer fresh and actually consisted largely of dry clumps, I was, however, finally warm again, though I couldn't tell if it was because I had found some shelter or because I was nervous and frightened. My heart was still racing and, taking deep breaths, I tried to calm myself down. Though feeling far from safe, I nevertheless thought it best to remain in my hiding place and wait for night to fall before pressing onwards. Chewing slowly and carefully, I finished the bread ration I had allocated myself for that day before drifting into an exhausted semi-conscious doze, not exactly a deep sleep, but refreshing nevertheless.

It was already dark when I got up and, brushing off some of the leaves still sticking to my shabby clothing, I was ready to continue on my route towards Stalino. A strange sense of euphoria filled me, probably because the first leg of my escape had been successful.

Some two to three kilometres further on I arrived at a railway embankment, just as I had expected whilst planning my escape route. The single track seemed to run westward and, not hesitating even for a moment, I followed the line. About an hour later, some five kilometres further along, a station building appeared ahead of me and, behind it, the outlines of several houses. Sniffing the air, much like wild animals might do, I stood still in one spot to get my bearings and scan the surroundings. Some soft voices were audible, emerging from the entrance of the station. Inside was, as far as I could make out, an unlit space, probably the waiting room. Could it be possible that, since everything around me was shrouded in darkness, there was no electricity in this area? Who cares, I thought, all that mattered was that the situation was ideal for my purposes since I suspected that, as soon as the train pulled in, all passengers would push towards it and I could tag myself on to the crowd unnoticed.

I couldn't really say how I plucked up the courage to go through with my idea, but I simply wanted and had to try at least once to see if I could pass as a Russian amongst Russians, without immediately drawing attention to myself as a *woina pleni*. I had to do so before boarding the train. With an air of feigned nonchalance I entered the waiting room. Standing for a few seconds right next to the door so my eyes could adjust to the darkness, I was eventually able to make out an empty seat available on the bench which ran along the walls of the rectangular room. Men and women of all shapes and sizes were sitting there, all wrapped in the same quilted jackets and enveloped by an atmosphere thick with the smell of onions, garlic and perspiration.

I was beginning to feel relatively safe amongst all the crates, parcels and sacks – which the Russians tended to use for luggage – and had just sat down when suddenly a flash of torchlight from the rear shone in my direction, accompanied by the quiet but strict words: '*Propas jest*' – 'Your papers.'

'I gotta get the hell out of here,' I thought and, panicking inwardly, rose from my seat as slowly as I could. After nearly tripping over a bag lying on the floor, I reached the door just a split second before the torchlight could land right on me. Gently pulling the door shut behind me, I quickened my step and walked along the tracks before finding a hiding place in the shrubbery. It was still dark. Relieved, I took a few deep breaths, inhaling the mild spring air, which helped bring down my heart rate.

As soon as dawn broke, I got up and could see a signpost not far away from where I stood with an arrow pointing to the word 'Stalino', reassuring me that my sense of direction had been correct. My intention was to hop onto a train and hop off again just before it reached the city.

The first freight train rattled past me at such a high speed that it was impossible for me to jump on. As I could under no circumstances risk breaking any bones, I decided to walk along the tracks to a place where the train would be forced to slow down for a bend. But luck was not on my side, and both the second and third trains were unsuitable as they were all made up of closed freight cars. 'Looks like only cargo is being transported in this coal district, not a single passenger train has passed by so far,' I thought to myself in total frustration.

Another two heavily loaded freight trains followed after short intervals but, though they were slower, they were headed in the wrong direction.

. A little while later I came to a turning of some 90 degrees, and this seemed the perfect spot for my plan. Ten minutes must have gone by when finally another train approached. The chug-chugging noise of the engine indicated to me that it was slowing down, just as I had hoped it would. I therefore had no problem jumping onto one of the empty cargo trucks and then immediately crouching into a corner, and what with the side boards being some one metre high, I was kept safely hidden from curious eyes.

But there was an aspect I hadn't considered, namely that seeing as this was, of course, a coal basin, the freight was nearly exclusively coal. The airflow of the accelerating train blew the coal dust around the cargo area and I could barely breathe for the constant black whirlwind blasting small coal particles into my eyes, which then became sore from all my rubbing.

However, this didn't prevent me from occasionally peering over the wooden sideboards. Thankfully this allowed me to realise, probably just in the nick of time, that the clusters of houses now lining the route had become denser. Was the train approaching the city? A sudden hissing noise along with the screeching of wheels seemed to confirm my fears. The train was just about to come to a complete standstill when, unplanned, I jumped off.

Watching the last wagon travel by me, I saw straight across the tracks one of the shower huts I was familiar with from back at the colliery, and which I knew was meant to serve miners. Cautiously I inspected my surroundings and realised that I was on my own – no one to be seen as far as I could tell. But where there were shower huts, the pits couldn't be far away, I figured, though nothing except for the huts supported my suspicion. I wondered whether POWs had been enlisted to transport coal here as well.

Then my eyes travelled down and looking at myself, I got a big fright. Whilst my clothing had been dirty before, it was now thickly cloaked in coal dust. Searching in my pocket for the piece of broken mirror I had picked up a while ago, I held it up and staring back at me was a totally black face, except for two gleaming-white eyeballs; my hair was black, my three-day old beard, my nostrils – everything. But in spite of my precarious situation I couldn't help but grin – what a sight I was! An unpleasant itch all over my skin told me, however, that the fine film of coal dust had also penetrated through my garments, and my amusement came to a quick end.

Peering around me like a timid deer sensing imminent danger, I assured myself that nobody was about. I then crept up towards the shower hut, pressed down the handle of the entrance door and, much to my surprise, found it was unlocked.

A wonderful smell of curd soap drifted towards me, the concrete floor was wet and drops of water still clung to walls stained in a dark-red oil paint. Yes, a shift must have recently taken their shower here.

'Hope the next shift isn't about to enter,' I prayed, while swiftly discarding my shoes. Much to my disgust, I realised that the coal dust had seeped in through the neck of my shirt, and not able to escape anywhere at the bottom, had formed a ghastly sticky layer which covered my footwraps. They resembled black rags, and my feet didn't look much better either.

Before getting undressed, I held my shoes underneath the shower and discovered that the water was pleasantly warm. Next, I cleaned the wraps before peeling off my other garments, which I then also rinsed under the stream of water. Only then did I discover a piece of curd soap that had been left in a corner. What joy! Grabbing it, I rubbed both my threadbare garments and myself clean. After that I felt reborn, even though my clothes were still damp.

'Lucky once again,' I thought, whilst stretching out in the warm sunshine of that early spring day.

Feeling rather cheerful, I continued on a path winding its way more or less alongside the tracks, and before too long I approached buildings obviously housing the miners; they were dull, grey and uniform in structure. My intention was to ask them for some bread. Having long before that day envisioned that I would find myself in such a situation, I had learnt and imprinted in my memory the proper Russian sentence: 'I am a *woina pleni*; today, I have my day off, I am very hungry and would like to ask you for a piece of bread.'

When I knocked on the first door, a gruff elderly man closed it right in my face with a curt '*niet*'. But at the second house, I was greeted by a friendly woman, in age she could have been my mother, and not only did she ask me in and offer me a piece of bread, but most generously presented me with a mug of milk as well. When she went to her kitchen cupboard she pointed to a photograph of a very young Russian soldier. Unfortunately, I couldn't understand everything she said, but gathered that her son was stationed in 'Leipsh', which probably meant Leipzig.

A bit later on, though reasonably satiated, I continued knocking on other doors with the same patter – and on the whole I was successful. It seemed that it was predominantly women who lived in the houses, or perhaps the men were away, working in one of the surrounding collieries.

Fortified, I continued west whilst trying to avoid the city at all costs. Asking anybody whether I could stay overnight was of course out of the question, as this would have certainly raised suspicion.

Several cargo trains rattled past, but train hopping had run its course for me. Aware of the fact that travel documents were being checked everywhere, I couldn't consider using one of the few passenger trains either, and thus I had no other option than to continue on foot until some other mode of transport presented itself.

That day I marched until my feet felt numb and my eyes could no longer see a thing. Just when I was about to seek a deep hollow, or anything that could lend itself to a reasonably well-suited spot to sleep, a large growling dog appeared before me. Was a *kolkhoz* situated nearby, or a village? Hardly, I thought. Crouching down to the level of the inhospitable prowler, I murmured some soft comforting words.

'Why all the noise?' I asked as if speaking to a young child. 'Surely you're only putting on a good show of being dangerous . . . what, and you can also bark?'

I couldn't tell whether the animal really was quite as black and menacing as I feared, or whether it was simply down to the bad lighting, but he started wagging his tail, then whimpered meekly and slowly trotted towards me. As he settled in front of my feet, his eyes pitifully staring up at me, I started to pat him, at first cautiously, then with more confidence and tenderness. All of a sudden his mouth pushed hard against the pocket of my quilted jacket containing a bit of my begged-for bread. Clasping his large head between both my hands I looked straight into his eyes: 'Sorry, fellow, this food is off-limits for you . . . I need it for myself.'

I rose to my feet, took a step forward and nearly tumbled right into a ditch filled with leaves and twigs and measuring some two metres long and one metre wide. Might someone before me already have spent the night here? Without hesitating, I took ownership of my new lodgings and made myself as comfortable as possible. I calculated that surely the temperature would plunge right to freezing point that night too, and so I didn't mind one bit that the dog joined me in my temporary dwellings. Squeezing himself right up against me he provided me with much appreciated warmth. Making sure that I lay in a position which safeguarded my pocket with the bread inside, I could feel my canine-shaped hot water bottle at my back.

Rudely awakened by the cold I realised that dawn was breaking. I stretched my limbs while my companion bounded around and, moaning happily, jumped up my legs as if he had always been mine and was now looking forward to our regular morning stroll. It truly pained me to fend off this poor shaggy creature, but I just had to do it: 'So sorry, old chap! I've hardly anything to put between my own teeth – sharing is not an option.' Pointing my finger in some direction, I urged him to run along. 'For God's sake, don't make it so hard for me, scram!' I finally shouted, then turned and walked away.

After some fifty steps I glanced back and, wouldn't you know it, the animal sat right next to the little campsite we had shared the night before and looked at me with a sad, disappointed expression. Or was it accusation in his eyes? I feared for a little while that he would follow me, and was relieved that in the end he didn't.

The following night I huddled up next to a stray cow, which didn't seem to mind this, and I only regretted not knowing how to milk it. I was famished when I woke up early in the morning under a grey sky, but remained determined to press on.

After more than an hour of marching at a good pace I reached a solitary cottage, which I observed for a while, trying to figure out what exactly the deal with it was. Eventually, I surmised that the only person living there was a middle-aged woman. Obviously not suspecting that she was being watched, the woman washed herself, leaning over a wooden tub filled with water that trickled thinly out from a pump. She seemed carefree and at peace.

I decided that my usual twaddle of being a *woina pleni* who had a day off wouldn't stand up in these circumstances, and that nothing but the truth would do.

Therefore, I was really pleased by the friendly way the woman reacted to my confession. Admittedly, the skinny cow, tied to a long string attached to a pole dug into the ground, and grazing peacefully, had not escaped my notice either. Coming up close and able to peek inside the hut, I saw a picture of a Russian soldier hanging on the wall, but what with my limited vocabulary in Russian, I didn't dare enquire about his welfare. She asked me in.

The woman was certainly not blessed with any riches, but this didn't prevent her from placing a small wooden bowl with cabbage soup in front of me as if there was nothing to it. Then she noticed how I stroked my chin with the back of my hand in embarrassment, ashamed of my unshaven look, and she resolutely got up, ladled some water from her boiler on the stove into a small tin container and handed me a shaving blade, a piece of curd soap and a well-used shaving brush. It felt to me that she was chuckling inside as she watched me struggle with my shave to get rid of my beard. Inevitably it occurred to me that perhaps these few objects which the woman so generously shared with me belonged to her absent husband. Was he with the Red Army? Was she waiting for him? Not wanting to dwell on assumptions or questions, I decided that it was best for me to move on, and that's what I did.

Back on the road, I felt rather proud of myself for having up until then successfully circumvented larger towns, but unfortunately, this also resulted in me no longer really having my bearings. No alternative other than getting myself to the next train station seemed practical. There, with a bit of luck, I would find a map of the area that would indicate my exact location, or so I figured. Without further obstacles and one hour later, I had reached a station.

Confident that nobody would recognise me as a German POW due to my bland uniform and Russian look, I purposefully strode up to an information sign standing right in the middle of a long platform. I had to pass five young chaps, perhaps three or four years younger than me. One of them grabbed me by the sleeve, showering me with words, probably mostly questions. Did he suspect I was a returnee who could give him some answers as to what might have happened to the Soviet army?

I certainly wasn't the person to do so, and before I knew it, I heard some loud screams: '*Woina pleni! Woina pleni!*' I had been found out.

Instantly I tore myself loose, and was about to run away when two *militsiya* (police) men blocked my path. There was no way out. Off I went, or rather off I was dragged by two burly guys who took me to the local *militsiya* base about a hundred metres away from the station. I was duly locked in a large prison cell where some other guys, who had obviously broken Soviet rules in one way or another, sat huddled together on the floor. They weren't in any way what we would have called hardened criminals.

The following morning I could not fail but notice with envy that each of my fellow prisoners had been provided by their relatives with food, whilst I sat with nothing but some watery barley soup doled out by the prison. Merrily they were carrying on in loud Russian interspersed with much laughter and merriment, and intermittently pointing at me and to a toilet bucket half-covered by a tin lid. Two of them decided to take the lead and, in broken German, gave me the dreaded order.

'You empty every day – then we give you food from us. Do it!'

Slightly resistant, but having no real choice, I obeyed. After carefully shoving the heavy container towards the door, which a cop had opened on the raucous shouts of my co-prisoners, I then followed the man to a trench covered by a slimy wooden plank, and into which I could at long last pour the putrid-smelling contents of the pail. The man made absolutely sure not to leave my side while I grabbed the rubber hose from which came a sparse flow of water to rinse out the bucket. I of course thoroughly washed my hands after that, and fortunately the guard seemed to understand.

Back in the roomy prison cell where everyone rested on his own straw bundle, the two men who spoke a few bits of German turned to me: 'Fritz, you now *pogushert** eat! And with that he excitedly gestured to me to return to my sleeping area where, indeed, there lay three thick slices of bread and some cheese.

'Here better than Siberia,' he said, 'You soon be there!'

It was difficult for me to interpret the tone underlying his words. Was he ridiculing me or trying to be sympathetic? Whatever the case, it left me scared to death about the future. They would deport me to a place from which there was no return. No! I forced myself not to panic, forced myself to be determined and remain resolved to survive.

They kept me in that cell for about a week, in miserable and awful conditions. Then, one morning, the *militsiya* man led me to the station and together we boarded a train that had pulled in minutes earlier. Sitting there with the guard opposite me I hardly dared look up, too embarrassed about my circumstances. But I

---

* *Pogushert* (Ukrainian) = hurry.

was probably not the first nor the last *woina pleni* en route to an unknown destination. Only a few of the passengers eyed us with curiosity, most of them seemed unbothered by our presence. Even though my companion didn't carry with him a visible weapon, I never even for a second entertained the idea of escaping. Around here, in this more urban area, they would surely hunt me down like a dog, and what would follow could only make a bad situation worse. That much was clear to me.

When the noises of the train wheels started sounding hollow underneath us, I knew we were crossing the wide River Dniepr. I couldn't help imagining how easy it would have been, had my escape plan worked, to cross the river as a stowaway on a train – a river that, even before my escape, had always filled me with great awe and respect.

The train gradually slowed down and the guard got up from his bench, signalling with his hand that I do the same. We got off.

About a quarter of an hour later I found myself standing in the corridor of an imposing building in front of a table, behind which sat a Russian soldier, obviously a clerk. His demeanour relaxed, his broadly rimmed cap pushed far back onto his neck, he rather lazily exchanged a few words with my guard, the only ones of which I could understand were *woina pleni*. Then, waving somewhat indifferently towards a sturdy-looking wooden staircase behind him, he indicated for the guard and me to make our way to the upper floor. My companion knocked on one of the doors.

My heart was in my mouth as I entered the room. Standing upright in front of a large desk, behind which I could see the portrait of Stalin hanging on the wall, I felt as though the Russian dictator with his steely eyes controlled both the room and my fate.

Speaking fluent German, a Russian officer, or he might have been a sergeant, bellowed at me: 'You've been picked up and identified as a POW who's escaped. What number is the camp you broke out of?'

At that moment, when I had to gather all my energy to remain calm and concentrate on what to say, my thoughts went to my comrade in the pits who had escaped, was re-captured and whose co-prisoners nearly flogged him to death because of the shortened rations they had been punished with due to his actions. I had to avoid that at all costs. With the most innocent expression I was capable of, I responded: 'I would gladly inform you of that, *Pan*,* but I've forgotten.'

The officer stared at me, eyebrows raised, and I literally felt like shitting in my pants, though I had hardly eaten anything.

'He doesn't believe you, Lothar,' I was thinking, whilst trying to convey the impression that I was doing my very best to remember. Counting out loud I responded: '200 ... no, it could have been 300 ... perhaps. ... I'm truly sorry, *Pan*, as hard as I try, I simply cannot recall that number.'

It was only then that the officer seemed to become aware of the *militsiya* man still waiting at the door and, gesturing at him with an impatient, stern hand motion, he made it clear that the cop was to remove himself. Gazing at me long and hard with searching eyes that conveyed a mixture of disdain and disgust, he reached for the telephone standing on his desk, barked some words into the receiver, then slammed it back onto the fork.

A few minutes later I heard the door behind me opening and, my heart sinking yet again, got the familiar earful: '*Woina pleni! Dawai! Bashli, Bashli!*'

Tightening my hands flat along my trouser seams, I sort of bowed in deference to the officer before slowly turning on my heels to leave, but caught out of the corner of my eyes how the visibly furious officer got up from his chair. Before I knew it, he gave me such a forceful kick on the behind that it catapulted me outside before the door crashed shut.

Once I landed in the corridor, which seemed to go on forever, I gesticulated to my new guard along with some Russian words I had picked up in the meantime that I desperately needed the loo.

'*Ubornaya, Pan!*'†

---

* *Pan* (Ukrainian) = Sir.

† *Ubornaya* = lavatory.

The Russian obviously understood and grudgingly jerked his head in the direction I should go. Walking behind me, he then yelled: '*Stoy!*' 'Stop!'

I looked back and saw him pointing to a door on my right. By all accounts he must have had bad experiences with German prisoners, or perhaps he just strictly adhered to the rules, because when I was about to draw the door to the squeaky clean toilet closed behind me, he rammed his foot in between. Out of the blue he then pulled out his Tokarev pistol, and wagged it in the direction of the toilet bowl.

Once again I became painfully aware that prisoners of war just couldn't expect any consideration for their human dignity. While I was doing my business, three Russian women in pristine uniforms passed by outside and laughed, clearly much entertained by what they saw. Moments later I was allowed to wash my hands, and was quite surprised to find a clean towel hanging ready next to the basin. Well, all I could say is that these particular authorities certainly seemed to place great importance on hygienic standards.

Next, I endured an hour or more of walking next to my guard through the streets of Dnipropetrovsk,* where one could still see signs of past battles. After arriving at a barracks beside an endless-seeming field big enough to hold perhaps a thousand men, my escort filled in some paperwork in a sparsely furnished guardroom, and with the handover completed, he departed without addressing me with so much as a word or a glance.

For the first few minutes I felt lost. Though the surroundings were familiar to me from my service with the Wehrmacht, my circumstances had changed violently; additionally and more than ever before I felt humiliated and depressed. My escape had failed miserably, and even though I counted myself lucky to have landed in the southern part of the Ukraine with its mild climate, I was gripped by panic and fear of possibly being deported to Siberia.

---

* Now Dnipro, Ukraine.

The high-pitched voice of an ex-Romanian sergeant tore me out of my gloomy thoughts. Surely his once elegant uniform must have seen better days, I mused to myself, noting that while it was clean, it was threadbare and missing all military insignia. He addressed me in German:

'I have remained a friend of the Germans and that's the reason they've interned me. I've been made commander of the camp. Of course, I have a Russian sergeant above me and it's he who has the final say.' He was calm and reassuring. 'But that surely won't be of any interest to you,' he continued as if he had spoken too much about himself. 'Have you learnt a trade?'

'Yes, sir. I am a professional decorator. More precisely, I'm actually a trained decorative painter.'

'The last bit you said is less relevant for our purposes. But they're looking for painters in the car plant where you'll be working as of tomorrow. Quite lucky, really! Tomorrow, first thing, report to the *natchalnik* in charge there, and he'll hand you over to the foreman who's got the final say.'

Glancing briefly at a note he was holding in his hand, he quickly added: 'Herrmann, you'll be lodged in barrack number five. Tomorrow, you're to get yourself to the plant with the first shift!'

The morning food distribution that took place in front of the barracks had already reached the end of the queue by the time I arrived, but I still managed to get some leftover soup, which calmed my aching stomach. The barracks, with their long walls facing the camp road, were built close together, but between barracks four and five, right at the back, I spotted an outhouse positioned just as one had been back in my Wehrmacht days.

'You seem to have made yourself quite at home here,' I commented to my neighbour. 'It's how you look at it,' was his response, resignation churning in his voice. The man, ashen-faced, his hair greying, was not of the talkative kind.

Beds as such were non-existent in our barracks; we slept on the bare floor to the left and right of the middle corridor, our quilted jackets serving as pillows. Quickly scanning the room before settling down, I estimated us to be some fifty men in all.

'This morning they identified your precursor as an SS man based on the blood group tattooed into his armpit,' was the unsolicited information my neighbour on the other side provided me with. 'He and his unit must have committed some crime – in any event, there's no way this guy'll return. You probably know as well as anyone how fast they'll condemn you to ten years in Siberia.'

'If he doesn't, he'll know soon enough,' I heard someone else butt in. 'Don't think for even a second that you'll be working in a car plant tomorrow. You can just forget about that straight away! In real life it's an honest-to-god ammunition plant and tank smithy.'

'What do we care,' objected another one, 'the war finished ages ago. What's it to us what the Russians require these tanks for or why. All I'm upset about is that those poor devils who are forced to slave away at the furnaces must suffer unbearably what with the scorching heat – my heart goes out to them. Only yesterday they had to drag two of our men and one Romanian out of there – dead, all three of them.'

'We're both trained car mechanics,' said my immediate neighbours, 'and work in the engine department. Do you also have a profession?'

'I'm to report tomorrow as a painter.'

'Well, seems luck is on your side. There are worse things, for sure.'

'Maybe we'll also get a break today. Why, it's already late afternoon, and we usually get some food before the night shift moves out. Bread? Well, that seems to be a precious commodity around here – and in Ukraine of all places, can you believe it?'

After the nerve-wracking experience I had just lived through, I slowly relaxed, eventually drifting off into a dozy sleep when, suddenly, a kick to my ribs tore me abruptly out of my semi-consciousness: 'Go, Lothar, there's soup to be had!'

The following day the guards led us to the plant some thirty minutes' march away. Keeping my eyes and ears open, I noticed that there were some clusters of Hungarians and Romanians amongst our shift who had obviously not changed sides or, if they had, it hadn't been done in time. 'What d'you think of that?' I asked my march companion, who was also sharing my barrack.

'No idea,' he responded, shrugging his shoulders, 'but I can't feel sorry for them if they were so stupid.'

Barely an hour later, standing next to my Russian foreman, the scene before me in the long hall with high ceilings was rather encouraging; it felt like any busy workshop, filled with the sounds of hammering, welding and riveting. The noise was so deafening that the foreman could only make himself understood by yelling – albeit in near-perfect German.

'Two are already up there. But they could really do with some support, because we can't have our trolleys and cranes stand idle for more than three hours. In two hours, the absolute latest, we've got to dispatch our heavy-duty transport! Hurry up!'

With that, and shoving a heavy bucket filled with anti-corrosion paint into my hands along with a brand new paint brush, he pointed upwards. His finger indicated a steel ladder propped vertically upwards and precariously supporting a narrow scaffolding plank. I could see two silhouettes standing towards the very end, dressed in the same overalls that I had been given just before. Judging by their sweeping hand movements, I gathered they were busy using a wire brush to scrape the rust off a crane trolley attached to a metal track. 'If you need more red lead, then fetch it from here. I've had enough delivered,' yelled the foreman into my ear, and I just nodded to show I understood.

Once up there, I first had to steady myself with one hand on the metal track, which I thought was rather flimsy, and as for my other hand, I couldn't let go of the bucket, firmly gripping its handle.

'Listen, boy, don't overdo it here! Believe me, these future T-34s ain't worth it. No need to exert yourself for the Ivans.' Reassured by the matter-of-fact advice of my new work colleague, I sat myself on the edge of the platform to catch my breath and tried to unstiffen my fingers that still clutched the bucket.

'This bucket won't be sufficient for all three trolley cranes,' declared one of the workers. Still rubbing my hands, I assured them that there was plenty more at the bottom of the ladder. 'The buckets are too heavy for one man. Let's help each other get them up here,' said the other.

Still rubbing my hands and looking at the three cranes, I said, thinking out loud: 'Surely the manual scraping is the most difficult part of the job. Why don't you both bring me a bucket up here and, in the meantime, I'll get started with painting.'

'Ahh,' scoffed the guy who had first calmed me down and whom I knew by then to be called Karl, 'Ivan will forever be grateful to you – but you'll not live to know it.'

'Why don't you swop Ivan with the word "homeland" – that'll hit the nail on the head much better,' I sneered.

Then Erwin, the third amongst us, started chiming in, and there was something foreboding in his warning: 'Stop this immediately. If we don't finish these three things here in the time given to us, they'll shorten our daily rations!'

Both of them climbed down rung by rung, whilst I began skilfully applying the red lead to the trolley crane furthest away from the ladder. We were finished just within the time allocated to us, and the *natchalnik* praised us with something which made us chuckle inside. It sounded like *'Nemze djelo'* – 'Germans can do anything.'

'Instead of compliments, a big chunk of bread and a square helping of soup would go a long way!' Kurt exclaimed for all to hear, and not in the least embarrassed, but the *natchalnik* blithely ignored him.

The last few hours of my shift were spent along with some others painting the anti-corrosion stuff onto the insides of tank turrets.

Towards 14:30, having barely arrived back at my camp and still at the gate, I was told that the following day I would have a different job, painting the windows and doors in a new-build not far away.

Early next morning, the guard who was leading me and three other decorators to the new-build, was, for a change, a good-natured Russian not continuously driving us to move faster. He must have known full well that not a single one amongst us thought about escaping, as he wore his submachine gun nonchalantly slung across his back, trudging along and puffing on his *papirosa*. We were sure that during the day he had a rest somewhere in the shrubbery, just once in a while coming by to watch us at work. Meanwhile, thoroughly enjoying those few unusual days and being able to work without pressure, we genuinely felt our nerves settling down a bit.

I'm not quite sure how the Russian cook got wind of what I was working as, but when on the first day of my new enlistment I returned from work back to the camp, he waved surreptitiously for me to come to the door of the large camp kitchen of barrack number one.

'You can bring small white paint for me?' he asked in broken German. 'Need here, for kitchen. You paint – I give you soup in break. Paint also my house for child and wife – I give you food for this.'

Feverishly, I tried to figure out a way to smuggle paint into the camp. After all, we were talking about state property, and theft was generally most brutally punished. I reckoned that I could perhaps hide a small jar of paint underneath my quilted jacket, seeing as even in warm temperatures I carried it with me every day folded over my arm so that nobody could steal it. But usually this garment was thoroughly checked at the entrance gate to the camp – too dangerous, I concluded. I then recalled those times in my first camp when I smuggled bread. That would work, I decided.

'Every day, but small amounts in closed jars,' I tried to explain to the Russian.

With a satisfied grin the Russian thumped me on my shoulder. 'Goot. Come in. Small deposit always goot. Come eat!'

A minute later, there I was, sitting at a table in the camp kitchen facing my benefactor, happily spooning up some hearty potato soup with even tiny bits of meat in it. Out of the corner of my eye I observed the cook's assistants, and though obviously prisoners, they seemed to fare much better than us lot. Without anybody hearing me, I asked the Russian: 'Could I also work here – always?'

With visible regret he shrugged his shoulders: 'Already commander give jobs to other. Nearly all Romanian. Only one German.'

'Well,' I thought to myself, 'why should it be different here than anywhere else in this world.'

The following day I managed to fill up two jars with paint and deliver them to the kitchen. That went well for six days running, after which I got caught during the search at the gate and was summoned to the office of the camp commander in barrack number one. I felt nauseous while the man addressed me in a severe tone. 'What were you up to with that paint? Planned to exchange it for food, were you?'

I quickly decided that coming out with the truth was my best bet. 'But, of course not! This paint and the rest of it, which I already organised, were meant for painting the kitchen windows.'

Obviously reassured, the Romanian's face lightened up. 'You're in luck, Herrmann,' he said, his tone considerably friendlier. 'Why don't you start at once and give our kitchen a new look. I'll let it go this time round. And now, get out of here. Once the kitchen is done, you can renovate my office. But I'll go down the legal route to acquire the paint!'

My small enterprise, so promising at the start, thus came to an abrupt end, and from that day onwards I didn't dare to divert even the smallest drop of state property from its intended purpose.

I devoted a huge amount of time, equal to about a whole week of time off between shifts, to fixing up the camp kitchen, but had meanwhile also become creative, having suggested to the cook that I decorate the bare white walls by painting flowers on them. 'Goot, but where colours?'

'Don't worry,' I replied, 'Leave it to me. We've got carbide and some red and yellow clay and we'll add some carbon powder. All I'll need is a small paint brush.'

'Shaving brush, goot?' he asked, and when I nodded yes, he exclaimed: 'I have – I bring it you tomorrow!'

The following day I found some empty tin containers and mixed up several colours. It didn't take long before I magically had a beautiful sunflower appear on the bare wall. I was so engrossed in my job that I hadn't noticed the camp commander join some others who stood behind and watched me. With his unmistakable dictatorial tone which was hard to miss, he ordered: 'That's what I want opposite my desk in my office!'

Not taking my eyes off the work I was doing I obligingly responded: 'I'll be happy to do this for you. But I can only paint if I'm not hungry.' He seemingly didn't hear my last comment, for as I was turning around, I could already see him leaving through the door.

In exchange for a little bread I procured a second shaving brush from a comrade, one eminently suitable in my eyes for painting fine lines. Disappointingly, all I received in return was some approving words. The Russian sergeant who was our commander's superior also seemed to be impressed by my work but once again '*Nemze djelo*' was all I got. I wondered where this sort of comment came from or what it was based on.

'The Russians obviously brought back with them cargo trains filled with captured goods, but simply didn't know how to operate any of the machines or any of the other technical stuff, thus rendering it unusable for them,' explained one of my comrades who worked in the new-builds. 'We could, for example, see broken sewing machines, lamps, or bicycles lying next to the tracks – everything you can imagine,' he carried on. 'If someone amongst us volunteered to fix any of those things in return for some extra rations, you'd always hear: "*Nemze djelo!*" So that was the long and short of it. Germans can do anything.'

Another change in routine came a few days later when I and a few other comrades were marched along a dead straight road leading to an airfield designated for gliders. Needless to say the road had been built by prisoners of war. Even before arriving at the field, which was surrounded by barbed wire about two metres high, my march companion pointed upwards, noting: 'Looks to me like this is where Stalin's future air force pilots are being taught to fly.'

Following his example, I also looked up towards the dark blue and cloudless summer sky and spotted several olive green sailplanes with the red Soviet stars painted on their wings and slim fuselages. Watching them as they drew wide turns, diving and climbing alternately, my thoughts once again drifted back home, to the airfield I worked at back in the early days of the war.

The task we had been ordered to complete was to clear the sandy road next to the hangar of debris and stones that had accumulated due to the wind.

Some of the young pilots in training were busy covering the frame of a glider's fuselage and wings with canvas. The loud orders being shouted at them by their instructors reminded us of the brusque way in which our own superiors had addressed us in our German barrack courtyards. But what caught my personal interest was the small heap of off-cuts, all of it good solid sailcloth, which lay next to the plane parts being assembled.

On the spur of the moment I asked the instructor whether I was permitted to take some of the cloth pieces. While scrutinising me with unconcealed animosity, he obviously understood, and much to my delight nodded in agreement.

'Why on earth are you begging from that guy? What would you be needing these rags for – surely this hero of the skies is asking himself the same question.'

'Well, you see, I'll be using these to cut out templates for my decoration works.'

'Cutting? What'll you cut with?'

'Leave that to me, don't worry.'

'Just don't get yourself caught with these tailoring tools of yours. Surely, you didn't miss what happened to the poor sod from barrack number five. They caught him with a bread knife this past week, in other words with Soviet state property. I don't need to tell you that it got him ten years in Siberia! We'll never see that one again – nobody can survive it.'

'Fiddlesticks. I don't even own a knife. Just a spoon I've sharpened into shape.'

'They'll confiscate that as well.'

'Definitely not, as I also use it for my jobs for the Russians.'

We fell silent as the instructor dismissed his recruits, walked over to where I had crouched down over the canvas, and because he was about a head taller than me, he peered over my shoulder and watched me select a rectangular piece which I quickly tucked under my shirt.

'*Charasho!*' 'Good!' he muttered contemptuously and turned his back.

Without further delay, we set to work sweeping and hauling away stones, feigning eagerness and hoping that the wind would settle down and not bring more rubbish our way.

August, meanwhile, had come to an end. One morning roll-call was especially long, and the head count more precise than usual, making my neighbour draw his gloomy conclusions. 'Lothar, this doesn't bode well. If they check their inventory so thoroughly it surely means that we'll be dispatched to some other place.'

'I'm also feeling sick about this,' I said, but another co-prisoner felt more up-beat.

'Maybe they'll let us go home?'

His optimism was met with derisive laughter. 'You dimwit, do you also believe in Father Christmas!'

'As long as repairs still need to be done in this country, that's as long as we'll be here.'

'Look at us though, we're just 200, perhaps 300 men from our camp – the others are already at work doing their morning shift – surely they would've assembled the whole lot of us in one go if they wanted to announce imminent plans.

'Who the hell knows what they're scheming against us.'

CHAPTER 10

An Endless Expanse

———•———

Our march to the station passed under strict surveillance. On our way we couldn't help but notice a number of German POWs, and though it is difficult to recall how many of them there were, what struck me then was the hard labour they were forced to perform by lugging about and removing the last debris of past battles.

One of our lot shouted out for all to hear: 'Didn't I predict that our comrades were allowed to remain here when they've obviously selected a very special location for the likes of us!' This guy clearly anticipated that what lay in store for us was even worse than this.

Nobody responded, but I was quite certain not to have been the only one feeling queasy when we were herded across the tracks to where a freight train waited. It was so long we couldn't see either the engine or the last wagon, which remained hidden around a bend. The carriages right behind the engine, which was already puffing away and eager to ferry us to an unknown destination, were reserved for our group.

We weren't the only Germans, as other POWs had also been sent along, but before any of us could catch our breath we were bundled onto the train.

'The world hasn't ever seen the likes of this,' I heard a young voice from behind me say. 'Looks like Ivan is transporting us in double-deckers!' Soon we were to find out what he meant.

'*Dawai, Dawai!*' yelled one of the guards while counting off twenty-four men by gestures of his left hand; he then motioned with the submachine gun in his right hand for the group to board one of the wagons before starting counting all over again. A tall East Prussian guy was the first to hop inside, then briefly recoiled and, turning to the young guy who had made the previous comment, reported in his harsh dialect that he had been spot on. Obviously, the young fellow had been on one of these trains before.

'How right you are, mate. Six wooden planks on the right, six wooden planks on the left and above them, the same story. Wouldn't you know it – they've even provided us with a round hole to use as a loo. Guys, just you wait and see: one hell of a stinking ride lies ahead of us!'

When three or four burly Russians with their guns strapped across their backs pushed shut the sliding doors behind us, we were left in semi-darkness. Sizing up the situation within a second, I had my strategy down pat by then, and quickly laid my quilted jacket on one of the lower planks near the opening. 'A bit of fresh air won't hurt me,' I mumbled to myself, 'Why, it's already feeling hot and stuffy in here.'

The fellow from East Prussia overheard me and quickly grabbed the spot opposite me. 'Nobody can predict where they're planning to take us,' he cautioned. 'It may well take longer and you'll freeze to death over there in the draft. By the way, my name is Hannes.'

'I'm Lothar. Hannes, do me a favour and don't think the worst,' I begged him.

'Wasn't my intention, I swear. But mark my words, nothing good will come of this. Nothing.'

After some twenty minutes the train was on the move, slowly at first, then picking up in speed. A lone voice then broke the quiet: 'Looks like the Russians have got their heads around operating the engines. Boy, would I give a lot to find out what they've got in mind for us!'

'They'll definitely not let you know; you can count on that!'

'Never mind, we will and we want to survive this bit as well,' I said, sounding so determined I even surprised myself. The reaction I got was some indistinguishable mumbling.

According to where the sun was, it was late in the afternoon when the train came to a halt, and we listened as our locomotive was filled with water. Suddenly the door was shoved wide open and two Russians poured salt fish onto the floor of our carriage. Quietly I thanked the good Lord that this time round we all also received sufficient water to drink, along with a hunk of bread. 'What a noble lot we've been landed with this time,' commented the East Prussian fellow.

'Depends how you look at it. I'd prefer them to be properly dished up and fatter!' responded another guy who, judging from his accent, came from Hamburg.

'My sense is that they've been instructed to keep us shipshape, ready to take on larger jobs. If this continues, we sure won't have any dead among us.' This was the unmistakable voice of our young friend.

'Mind what you say, boy, the larger the job, the longer we'll be at it.'

A long silence followed. We all felt downcast and depressed.

With a few violent jerks, the train started moving again, and though none of us felt like joking, someone's comment still made us smile: 'No doubt about it, they've most definitely replaced the engine driver with an apprentice. Can't really blame the driver – the poor comrade must surely be entitled to catch a nap at some point.' We stared into the night, into the vastness of a country we had thought we could bring to its knees.

We travelled for several days and still nobody knew where we were going, or even where we were.

I saw my East Prussian comrade stand at the gap by the door as he often did, peering outside. Suddenly he became quite agitated and, with his voice breaking with emotion, he shouted: 'Fellows, look, I can see the Volga over there! We must be somewhere near Stalingrad!'

'I sure hope we won't be ordered to clear up the mess you've left behind; the ruins and the bomb craters you and your lot have created!'

'Stop joking – I feel sick.'

Our train rolled on. Later we thought we were travelling along the banks of the Caspian Sea, but couldn't make out why we also kept receiving, pretty regularly, fresh water, bread and small fish. Nobody was around who could tell us where within the enormous region under Stalin's control we were.

At the start of the third week the train stopped a few hundred metres from a lake. The doors were pulled open and at long last – it was the first time since we had boarded – we were allowed to get off. We stretched our bones into every which direction while guards instructed us to move down to the lake – a still, gleaming expanse of water which somehow struck us as surreal in the barren steppe. 'What, are you being serious? Are we actually allowed to go for a swim?' asked our youngster, spreading his arms out wide in a breast-stroke.

Much to our bewilderment, the guards nodded, and we all staggered and stumbled rather than walked down to the glittering water, the sunlight reflecting in its smooth surface. Like the others, I quickly got out of my clothing, wrapped my things in my stinking quilted jacket, which I then lifted above my head and waded into the delicious wet of the lake. Laughing along with the rest of them and shouting in delight, we splashed our way to where we could barely stand, behaving like small children.

'May our lice drown and suffer a swift death!'

'Agreed, lets dunk our bundles deep into the water, surely it will get rid of these pests!'

'Go ahead, little guys, drink, drink up you beastly creatures! There's plenty of water for all of you!'

Some two hours after our refreshing swim we were back on the train. Through the open gap the outline of a building not far away from us appeared, and it didn't take us long to determine that it was a de-lousing station. 'Look at that – Could it be that our hosts are now really looking after us? I would've never given them so much credit. Looks like they've realised what valuable resources they have in us.'

'Let's treasure this moment!'

'But, fellows, is this really all meant for our own good? Let's wait and see,' cautioned a voice of reason from a corner of the wagon.

'Let's stop driving each other crazy, for God's sake. Don't worry!'

'Easy for you to say. And by the way, tell us good man, how on earth have you managed to remain looking so fit and well?'

'Take a look, fellows, take a good look over there! Don't these chimneys belong to a factory!? I can bet you anything, that's what they are! These smokestacks definitely belong to a plant!'

'Yes, there's no doubt about that.'

'Children, listen up, even had we been able to hold Stalingrad and take Moscow, you can bet your life that, regardless, they'd have continued manufacturing all their weapons around here and without stopping. This land is much too vast for anybody to have been able to defeat and occupy it in its entirety.'

'I can only pray that that's not where we'll be spilling our last drop of blood – I've no energy to spare!'

'If it's not here, it'll be somewhere else!'

Premonitions and fears abounded and swirled through the air. I tried to peek out the open slit as much as possible, and my guess was that we were approaching the city of Alma Ata.* We had, there was no doubt in anybody's mind, reached the Altai mountains, the border between Russia and Mongolia. Longingly taking in the contours of the mountains that truly reminded me of back home, I tried making guesses as to which one was Peak Lenin and which one Peak Stalin.† But the sight alone sufficed to strengthen my resolve to return to my homeland one day, whatever it took. Painfully aware that because of the insurmountable distances any plan to escape would be doomed to fail, I quickly banned any such thought from my mind.

The journey, seemingly interminable, continued. While stopping and starting, watching day turn into night and into day again, over and over, and staring out at scenery which barely changed, we felt like cattle locked in cages and transported for slaughter. Rumours kept circulating from one carriage to the other.

---

* Now Almaty, in Kazakhstan.
† Now known as Ibn Sina and Ismoil Somoni Peaks respectively.

'We've just passed the Kazakh steppe.'

'I believe that our destination is Karaganda and its collieries.'

'We're heading west.'

At some point one of the men asked whether the Russians actually intended to drive us through the entire Soviet Union. But in truth, nobody had a clue where we were in that great big land controlled by the iron hand of Stalin.

One day we stopped at a large city. Crowding around the narrow open strip of the carriage door, we marvelled at seeing the turquoise-green cupola of a mosque, above which rose high into the sky the minaret, but I, for one, remained anxious. While yet again the engine was being filled with water, the clamour of merchants peddling their wares and trying to sell them to our guards penetrated through to us. One of our lot in the wagon, trying to decipher what it said on the sign hanging over the platform, thought we had arrived in Samarkand.

'You idiot!' retorted someone furiously. 'Don't pretend that you can read that damned script!'

'If that is so, why, we must have landed far down to the south-east of the Urals, in the dark recesses of Asia!'

'And is that my fault?'

'Let's just hope they'll not order us to get off!'

Suddenly we fell silent. The locomotive emitted a high-pitched whistle and we were off once more. Strangely, I felt relieved.

When, after four weeks, the doors of the cargo train were opened and we were allowed to leave this cage on wheels behind us, we found ourselves on a deserted platform with no building in sight except for the lonely station hut. This saw us once again asking questions that would remain unanswered, and spreading rumours that would remain un-quashed. When we were ordered to fall into column of fours, fears of a march loomed.

'Will we have to continue on foot?'

'Look at us, miracle of miracles, we haven't lost a single man. There are no dead bodies!'

'We're close to Jezkasgan.'

'Not far to China then . . .'

'Oh for goodness sake, stop your clever waffling. D'you really want to make us believe in your shit?'

'Never mind, all I know is that the Russian guy I spoke to told me that we've reached our destination.'

'How many men are we? Six hundred? Five hundred?'

Our column soon resembled a worm of exhausted bodies mindlessly stumbling along. Progressing at a mere snail's pace, it took us a long time before we finally reached our destination. In front of us and in the middle of the barren steppe lay our campsite, surrounded by a barbed-wire fence about two metres high, and with the entry gates wide open. I was standing in one of the last rows of four and saw two Russians shutting the gates behind us while I listened to the harsh order of a man dressed in a tattered German Navy uniform who stood up straight in front of us.

'Comrades! The Russians have appointed me as commander of the camp. Of course, I have a Russian officer above me. So far, only our office quarters, the camp kitchen and the sick bay in barrack number one are up and running. We have a Russian doctor supported by a German doctor and a medic. But be warned, you must at all costs avoid falling seriously ill as we barely have any medication. The Russians want to keep us alive and healthy, but, above all, they want to protect themselves from any illness that could have been brought in. That's the reason we're being quarantined for four weeks, and no contact with the outside is permitted! So, watch it!

'We'll first tackle the delousing station, which you've always referred to as a *banja*, and what you need now is to get it functioning. Then you'll work on your lodgings and everything else we'll require, such as a tailoring workshop, a cobbler's and a clothing outlet. But we only have four weeks to get it all done, the Russians won't allocate more time than that for us to set up shop. We've even got electricity. Any of you who've learned a trade – anything, plasterers, electricians or other craftsmen, report to me as soon as possible. That's it for today!'

Immediately, murmurings erupted, comments, questions and assumptions whirling around whilst our commander, a rather strange fellow, left us to it. 'This loser from the Kriegsmarine is spouting total nonsense. By golly, haven't the Russians picked a right dud!'

'Leave it be, Heiner, the guy's just trying to clarify stuff for us – it's what he's been ordered to do. I think he is A-okay, myself.'

'Werner,' somebody else added, 'I think you were right first time around. I'm pretty certain that what was here before was a so-called *gulag*, a camp for Russian prisoners!'

'There are others apart from us!' said someone. 'Japanese, guys from the Spanish Blue Division, interned Swedes, also Koreans and people from the Baltics.' All this turned out to be true.

'So, we're not supposed to meet up with any of them?'

'Somewhere round here there's also a camp for women!'

'I've heard rumours that some top-secret Russian outposts are supposed to be constructed in this part of the world!'

'No wonder . . . that's why they've dragged us all the way here.'

As I stared up at the grey sky, with a light flurry of snowflakes dancing to the ground, all kinds of crazy thoughts spun around inside my head, which was starting to feel like a veritable beehive. Did winter set in that early around here? Hadn't we travelled through the steppes just a few days prior with summer-like temperatures soaring to forty degrees? It was late September and the following day was my birthday.

As in the past, I swore to myself not to give up, ever, to defy the hardships and survive against all odds, even though escape in this wasteland was not an option.

Our lodgings were the most bizarre we'd ever come across. A group of some twenty men went to each hut; ours felt chilly and dank. Each had a rounded tin roof, on top of which a layer of earth had been spread with grass growing on it and even some small bushes and a few young birch trees. Facing the camp road was a large window located next to the entrance. The floor consisted of compressed mud, and in the middle of the approximately ten metre long room, dangling from the centre of the ceiling, a single bulb emitted a faint light.

'Next to the entrance gate I saw planks and beams lying around. Surely, they're meant for us,' our tall East Prussian guy exclaimed in a cheery mood. 'I'm a joiner, so that'll be handy. But first, I heard we're to be given supper, or whatever they call the meals around here. After that, I'll report to the captain and ask for permission to cobble together something resembling sleeping quarters!'

Together with our master carpenter I then went up to the captain and reported my skills as decorator. We got permission to pick up a few planks and beams and take them to our hall, 'but not a sliver more than is strictly necessary'. Against a receipt, we even received nails, several hammers and two handsaws. 'You're only permitted to build in between your shifts. We work two shifts, from 0600 hours to 1400 hours, and from 1400 hours to 2200 hours. If you want to start today, it's up to you!'

'This guy definitely can't hide the officer in him,' commented my East Prussian mate the minute we were outside. 'But he doesn't seem to want to be difficult with us, he seems okay to me.'

Meanwhile I told our fellow men in our bunker: 'Onwards, guys! We can start immediately and won't have to sleep on a bare floor!' Seeing as we benefited from Hannes's expertise, we only selected the choicest wooden bits, ripping them out from the loose heap, and we sure didn't hold back. During the first night we managed to put together an impressive part of our new furnishings, all the while organised by our in-house joiner.

'Boys, we'll have time to be tired tomorrow too. So let's do a thorough job. My guess is that the mud here on the floor will turn pretty chilly once night falls. The higher up our plank beds, the better for us.'

'I heard they're looking for barbers,' said Franz, who I knew came from a village in Odenwald. 'I'm already dreading this ... having our entire bodies sheared tomorrow morning will be another nightmare. It bloody hurts, and these guys only use blunt shaving knives.'

'Not only painful, but definitely disrespectful,' I agreed.

'As for me, I couldn't give a shit whether or not the damned *banja* is completed by tonight,' a comrade behind me snapped. Emotions were running high.

We did in fact manage to complete the first stage of our carpentry job so could then spend the night on top of a bunk-bed construction raised about half a metre above ground.

Everyone was surprised that after only three days the *banja* was fully operational. That was the first time we got to see the Russian camp commandant, who inspected the place and whose now familiar words '*Nemze djelo*' did little for us, other than sounding like an overused proverb, and many could be heard grumbling that what they would much prefer was more food.

But the commandant, a dissatisfied and haggard fellow who seemed exhausted from his job, ignored the comments. Rumour had it that he hadn't willingly transferred to this corner of the world, having been forced to uproot his entire family; but he had ruffled feathers back in Moscow, resulting in his superiors exiling him as punishment. We weren't to draw any conclusions from that, advised our captain. The man, he warned us, apparently scrupulously managed every single food item allocated to him and never smuggled even so much as a morsel through shady channels, as was the custom in other places in the Soviet Union. Apparently, he just couldn't afford to risk being caught. 'The man is singularly upright! We get everything he's sent, well, saying that, everything from the allocation which ends up arriving here!'

By then, we had become hawk-eyed, counting and measuring, judging and scheming. The first thing we noticed was that every fourteen days we would get a small portion of sugar and the same amount of tobacco, something I remembered from back in my days at the *kolkhoz*. Was our Russian camp commander behind all of this? Some of us were such nicotine addicts that it was easy for me to exchange my tobacco ration for sugar. I welcomed this additional amount of sugar as it definitely contributed to keeping me healthy.

Some of my comrades were gifted craftsmen and I got to admire how they magically created tobacco pipes out of bits of metal scraps, and, using every second of their meagre spare time, they hammered, banged and forged artistic tobacco tins, which they would often even decorate.

Due to an injury to my left hand caused whilst trying to fix our roof, and which wouldn't stop bleeding, I was forced to take myself to the sickbay after a few days. 'Looks bad, but all I can do for you, mate, is dress it. Don't expect any more than that.'

Paul, the medic, originated from Upper Silesia, and from day one we got on extremely well. Whilst he was taking his time looking after my wound, I was observing our German doctor who, working at the other end of the ward, had the unwelcome task of needing to explain to a miserable looking elderly man that he would have to amputate a finger on his right hand without anaesthetic. 'Sadly, there has been no further supply of anaesthetics. But we simply can't ignore a finger looking like this as it will definitely cause blood poisoning.'

Behind the doctor I caught a glimpse of the lovely young Russian doctor, the German doctor's superior, and her wavy hair and beautiful eyes caught my attention. 'Does she look at everyone with such empathy in her eyes?' I asked Paul.

'Yup, Lothar, we sure struck lucky with this lass, she's brilliant to work with. She's the first to be upset that so much of the medication falls off the back of the lorry, so to speak, though allocated to us. Our own doctor gets on well with her.' Taking me by surprise he abruptly turned to me, asking: 'Would you still be able to paint with one hand only? One thing is certain, you're not going to be able to do any heavy work, our lovely medicine lady has just now put you down to the lowest labour category. But hey, listen, we could well do with having this bare wall here decorated and . . .'

'Do you have paint and brush?' I quickly interrupted, eager to remain in these calm surroundings.

'Not exactly, what we've got is lambskin, and we could make brushes out of that. But how would we make the paint?'

'With coal dust, and to that we'd add yellow, white or reddish brown clay and I can mix different shades. And all of that I could do for you for an additional portion of soup.'

'We've got all of that stuff, even some small containers for the paint. And as for your nutritious compensation,' he added, lowering his voice, 'I'm sure our ward doctor won't object. I've seen her several times stand in front of the bare wall, lost in thought.'

Paul had finished bandaging my hand and walked over to the doctor, who sat behind her desk at the far end of the ward. I could see her nodding, and even thought I could detect a fleeting smile light up her pretty face before mouthing the reply: '*Charasho,*' 'That's fine.'

'All sorted, Lothar, you're good to go for tomorrow morning!' confirmed Paul, shouting back to me the welcome news.

That same evening the guy from East Prussia and a fellow from Odenwald turned the lambskin remnants entrusted to me by Paul into paint brushes as per my instructions. Our master joiner, by now terribly skinny, quite skilfully attached the handles, which were made out of rounded fragments of wood.

The following day, hungry but in good spirits nonetheless, I set to work, whilst my thoughts wandered back to my master back at home. It was to him I owed a debt of gratitude, as he had not only spotted my talent but supported me in my professional career, and I quietly thanked him for that. I never forgot him.

I worked swiftly and with utmost concentration as had always been my habit, and it wasn't long before some large, lanky sunflowers began to emerge on the wall; brightly gleaming in the daylight, and slightly leaning to the side, they spread a bit of cheer and colour through the otherwise dismal ward. Elated by my progress, I filled the still empty-feeling 'canvas' by adding the greyish-black contours of our Waxenstein mountains, above it a dark blue sky and in the foreground, green forests and meadows.

After my last brush stroke I stepped back to have a final look and suddenly realised what had been annoying me all the time I was painting the scenery: the soft whimpering of the man whose finger the German doctor had to amputate. The poor guy, bathed in perspiration, was flat out on his bed just a few metres away from me. Paul was sitting by his side, trying to comfort him.

'What a surprise!' exclaimed someone behind me suddenly. 'Wouldn't you know it, these are unmistakably the Waxenstein mountains from Garmisch! No doubt about it!' Turning around, I realised that the voice belonged to the German doctor who was standing in front of the mural, transfixed.

'Do you hail from Garmisch or perhaps its surroundings?' I asked him.

'No, I come from Rosenheim and have ...' halting briefly, he then continued, 'perhaps I should say, *had* a girlfriend in Garmisch. But let me congratulate you. It's turned into a real welcoming atmosphere around here. I'm sure everyone will take pleasure looking at it.'

It was only then that he noticed the Russian doctor, who had also approached without us having been aware of her presence, and who joined us with one of her warm smiles on her face to admire the now embellished wall. Tucking both hands into the pockets of her white coat, she produced two pieces of bread and handed them to me with a flourish. 'Good picture. Are you an artist?'

'No, I am just trained as a decorative painter, one who cannot help but remember his mountains from back home.'

'Beautiful, nonetheless. Would you be prepared to do something like this for our lieutenant in your time off?'

'But, of course, with pleasure,' was all I could bring myself to stutter, before she had already turned away but not without giving me a friendly nod.

'Goodness, she seems in a rush today,' the doctor from Rosenheim couldn't stop himself from commenting,

'My hunch is that she's due for a review by our superiors, based on the high number of ill patients we had to report as of late. Well, thank goodness, that this isn't part of my remit. But this little one is a real trooper. As for you, I must take my hat off to you once again. I can only hope that our guardian angel over there will get you some more commissions, and before you know it, we'll turn into a kind of picture gallery. I feel it'll do us all great deal of good, but especially our sick patients.'

The following day I was busy covering the mud flooring of our lodgings with a layer of strongly diluted clay with the help of two patients who hadn't quite fully recovered, whilst one of my comrades watched on. 'These Russians would be better advised to come up with some more food,' he huffed angrily, 'rather than bother us with their exaggerated craze for hygiene. That sure would do much more for our energy and health!'

'Do we really have to lay it all out for you and explain how much of the provisions which are allocated to us go missing on the transport, or rather, get diverted?' my other comrade tried to reason with him.

'I entirely agree with you, Christian,' I butted in, 'and not only that, can you imagine how little we'd end up with if our lieutenant and his team also skimmed off a bit for themselves?'

'Frankly, the smidgen they'd take for themselves wouldn't fatten up our soup in any event,' moaned yet another one. 'I wouldn't mind finding out for whom we're actually constructing the houses and roads in this god-forsaken steppe!'

The guy who had started the whole argument wouldn't be calmed down, whilst the fellow from Odenwald tried to put an end to it. 'I'm quite sure that the Russians won't fail to let you know in writing what they're up to. All you need to do is to ask them nicely.'

Then, abruptly, we heard Paul, the medic, shout: 'Lothar, get yourself over here, looks like you're needed! We've got the boss of our captain, the Russian lieutenant, standing in front of your paintwork. He wants a word with you.'

Stomping together through the few centimetres of fresh snow that now covered the short path to our sick bay, my good friend had a big smile on his face when he muttered: 'Lothar, I can bet you that this spells a few extra rations for your good self. I can assure you that you're in for a treat.'

'I'm not so certain,' I curtly responded as I caught sight of a red Opel P4 parked in front of the sick bay's entrance, reminding me with a pang of sad nostalgia of its blue counterpart in which I, a mere apprentice at the time, had been allowed to drive my inebriated master home in spite of not having a licence. It seemed an age ago and profound sadness overcame me.

What a different situation I was in now with a uniformed Russian soldier in front of me, leaning against the car, nonchalantly blowing little puffs of smoke from his *papirosa* into the crisp winter air.

A few moments later I found myself in front of a rotund little man who was wearing his much too large officer's cap pushed far back and looking at me with an undeniably friendly expression in his eyes.

'Since you're currently not suited for heavy labour,' he started off in near faultless German, 'I'm requesting that you now turn your hand to decorating my private home. These are the exact mountains I desire to have on my living room wall. They remind me of my youth in the Caucasus. I'm being told that this picture here represents the Garmisch landscape?'

'*Da*,' I replied hastily and could see Paul grinning from ear to ear whilst the Russian lieutenant just smiled.

'I'm told that you have brushes you can use. And apparently you mix the colours yourself?'

'Yes, that's so, but I make them up on site and would require different types of clay and some carbon dust.'

'Good! Tomorrow, at eight in the morning I'll come and get you. My wife also has some things she wishes to be done in our house.'

It was only at that point, and probably just as a matter of form, that he turned to the German camp commander who had followed the entire conversation while remaining silent.

'Now, you're informed, all understood? I still have to go across to the Japanese. That tough slit-eyed lot are on strike, refusing to work, they claim they're doing it because they're always hungry. If they keep being so stubborn, they can starve to death is what I say. Then there'll be more left for the others.'*

The Russian straightened his cap and left without so much as a goodbye. Our commander shot a glance at him as he walked out, and it wasn't hard to second-guess what was going through his mind.

The following day I was picked up and sat next to several paper bags filled with clay and coal dust, all gathered beforehand by Paul, on the back seat of the small motorcar. Much to my surprise, the comrade lieutenant was actually driving himself. 'Do you live far away from the camp?' I asked.

'*Niet*, we'll soon be there.'

But I couldn't keep my curiosity at bay. 'Is it really true that the Japanese are on strike?'

Whilst throwing me a look of annoyance mixed with disdain through the rearview mirror, he simply shrugged his shoulders. 'If these boys insist on leaving the camp as corpses then it's up to them. As for us, they can forget it! We'll never comply with their mad requests, and Moscow is far away.' Staring grimly at the snow-covered highway, he made it clear that for him the conversation was over and done with, leaving me with my thoughts. I couldn't help but secretly admire the courage, and just generally the attitude of our erstwhile ally. We would, incidentally, never find out whether the Japanese got anywhere with their strike.

The Soviet officer's home was a simple one-storey build and consisted of just a few rooms on the ground floor, with a thatched type of roof built with rushes. I couldn't but wonder for whom the new dwellings along the street, which stretched far into the steppe and were still standing empty, were intended.

Once I was inside the living room, a cosy warm atmosphere enveloped me. While the master of the house showed me to the

---

* The Soviets took more than half a million Japanese as prisoners during and after their brief participation in the Pacific War. They were treated at least as harshly as German prisoners and were held for many years; at least 50,000 died. Many more were not able to return to Japan.

wall where he had envisioned the Waxenstein mountains, I was fully determined that I would remain here as long as possible. Outside, I could see the Russian lieutenant already getting into his car when I quickly pretended that I would need a pencil and asked for one, seeing as the officer's wife seemed extremely approachable.

'*Karandasch jest, pajalsta? Jest pajalsta?*' 'Do you have a pencil for me? Please?'

A moment later I tucked into my pocket a most valuable object of bartering: a pencil stub. It wasn't difficult to find some excuse for the wife, should she ask for it back; I would simply explain that I had used it down to the end; back at camp I knew that it would buy me a portion of soup.

I certainly took my time to create the commissioned Waxenstein mountains, placing them centrally between the two windows of the lounge, and meanwhile I had a fun time following what was going on behind my back. Softly, the mistress of the house sang to her three-year-old son to divert and prevent him from joining me in my work. Staring at me with his two large eyes and closely observing how I was mixing colours in the empty tin containers, he begged his mother to let him have a go. There came a point when the mother gave up trying to hold the toddler back and simply left the room, taking him with her, and allowing me to enjoy some peace and quiet in the warm lounge.

She had, I assumed, gone to her kitchen where she had briefly shown me the kitchen window she wanted surrounded by sunflowers and other greenery. 'Just like in camp – in sick bay,' she tried to explain.

Recalling the comments made by the doctor from Rosenheim, my hopes were pinned on an extra portion of food. And wouldn't you know it, come lunch time, there I was sitting at the kitchen table together with the mistress and her chirpy little fellow, and it required quite a bit of self-control not to gobble up like a pig the delicious Russian cabbage soup the lady had prepared for us.

I was somehow able to draw out my assignment at the Russian lieutenant's home for the next most agreeable three days. With the cut on my finger now fully healed, the commander's next order was, however, not long in coming. 'Herrmann, you're assigned to our construction squad with immediate effect. We're building houses along the street – nothing you don't already know!'

'In these temperatures? Really? We're speaking about minus 40 degrees!'

'Quite, but a few amongst our inventive chaps have come up with a system which the lieutenant feels works brilliantly.'

During my first shift, lasting from 0600 to 1400 hours, I got to know Rudi, the plasterer who was apparently at the heart of this innovative set-up. He had gathered a few large pieces of stone, covered them with a sheet of rusted metal, and constructed a fireplace underneath, which spread intense heat rather than pleasant warmth, but if one placed oneself in the right position, the cold was certainly bearable. My task consisted of emptying sandbags, so freezing cold that they stuck to my fingers, onto the metal sheet and then chopping clumps of sand into small pieces which, because of the heat, and much to my amazement, turned out to be easy. Two comrades and I then switched to mixing sand, warm water and cement to make up small amounts of mortar, whilst three others were busy stoking the fire under the metal sheet with logs of wood. In one part of our workspace it was too hot, in the other we were shivering it was so icy, but we got through it.

To this day I still cannot quite understand how Rudi, a plasterer from the Sudetenland equipped with nothing more than a thick pair of mittens and a simple trowel, knew how to spread the mortar deftly between the bricks just seconds before it turned rock hard from the cold. Still before my eyes are the expressions of sheer amazement written on the face of the Russian foreman who, with his spirit-level to hand, confirmed that the wall emerging in front of us was dead straight.

After a few days of us working on these shifts the Russians conceded that it in fact made no sense to try and build good, solid constructions in frost conditions such as we were experiencing at the time. Nevertheless, we believed a miracle had happened when one day a few trucks appeared in front of our camp delivering bundles of winter clothing. It was, so it was rumoured, thanks to the reports our woman doctor had filed, recording the numerous deaths due to the freezing temperatures. We were each handed a pair of felt boots, a cap with ear flaps and a coat, all of them lined with sheepskin. As I slipped into my boots, I heard my neighbour make an interesting comment. 'Looks like our work out here in the steppe makes a difference to the Russians, seeing as they are so careful to preserve our energy!' Whilst I didn't comment, I certainly felt that the changes recently implemented at the camp did much to improve our chances of survival.

For the remainder of the harsh winter of 1946/47 Rudi and I managed to secure for ourselves positions in the well-heated camp kitchen, and it goes without saying that our bribing the kitchen honcho with promises to decorate his space based on his wishes and during our spare time played a not insignificant part. Rudi was certainly my equal when it came to skill and craftsmanship.

The moment one of the openings of the large coal-heated ovens showed any signs of rusting, it required the attention of the Russian inspector, as the Soviets maintained high hygiene standards, above all in the kitchen where soup was being prepared – it was the one staple which kept us alive. Here too we were called on to help by scraping down the rusty areas and then painting over them. We didn't rush it, very much enjoying the pleasant smells, the warmth and the additional food rations.

Meanwhile, the work gangs forced to toil away outside in temperatures of minus thirty degrees were paving a road for future use, and only when temperatures sunk well below that were they permitted to continue their shifts inside the camp.

To our own amazement the look of our camp improved greatly during that winter, and though we kept wondering who might one day be the ones to benefit from this whole exercise, we didn't much care as we knew deep down that it wasn't us, particularly since we stubbornly believed in the rumour making the rounds once again that we would be liberated this year, which meant before Christmas.

Three days in a row, Rudi and I were driven to a construction site far away in the steppe and even we, who had seen many curious situations before, were taken aback by what we encountered when we got there. A thin layer of snow covered the steppe, allowing only a few twigs of the sparse shrubbery to peek out in defiance of the harsh climate. An icy wind swept across the plain, tearing at our new clothes, without which we would no doubt have frozen to death. Our assignment was to flatten a round area of about one kilometre in diameter lying within the softly undulating landscape, and we set to work once we were given picks and shovels. We had been given the official reason that this would allow some drilling for water to create an artificial lake; however, we thought that this was a really odd explanation with an even odder and unlikelier outcome. But what did we care? We had no interest in any of the Russians' future projects and in what use they might be put to. After three days, prisoners from a different camp arrived to take our place, and we never found out what tasks had been assigned to them.

Our worst fear, of not being released to return back home by the end of 1946, came true. Thus, the winter passed monotonously, one day after the other filled with the same routine, the same rations and the same longings and deprivations. At some point, though, spring arrived.

The summer of 1947, with an average temperature of forty degrees in that part of the world, turned out to be as scorching hot as the winter before it had been freezing cold. In the meantime, I had been nominated as official painter for the construction gang, and sometimes filled in as assistant for the plasterers. Food rations remained as sparse as ever, with none of us ever gaining even an extra ounce of fat that could have helped us pad our ribcages. During that time, Rudi and I became inseparable friends.

One afternoon, following a very tiring shift, I sat by a table busily cutting out flower stencils from thin cardboard remnants with a rusty razor blade. It was for our cook, who had asked me a few days earlier whether I might decorate some more of the bare walls in his workspace. 'Sure thing,' I replied, 'but I'd need Rudi's help as he's really good at mixing paints and cleaning the brushes so I can get on with my work much more quickly.'

'Fine, but I'd first need to get permission to go ahead with such embellishments.' The cook was very much looking forward to this venture.

Whilst completing my templates, I'd often have stars dancing before my eyes, obviously from sheer hunger, and had to force myself to focus on my work and ignore my grumbling tummy. I was quite out of it when all of a sudden I heard my name being called. 'Lothar!' shouted the cook standing at the threshold of the pleasingly cool room. 'You and Rudi can start straight away and make my walls beautiful. I received permission.' With that, the kitchen honcho entered and secretly, without any of the dozing comrades noticing, slipped me a tiny gherkin. Only Rudi had noticed, and he shot up as if he had had an electric shock and stood right behind me, hoping for his cut.

A quarter of an hour later, Rudi and I had embarked on our project, as Rudi had been able to convince cook that he too was adept at painting and would be instrumental in ensuring a good outcome. 'Boy, oh boy, Rudi! Let's take our time with this work. The longer we can stay here, the more nutritious it'll turn out for us.'

'Sure thing, mate! Take a look, this brush made out of sheepskin is falling apart. Should I manufacture a new one? Cook has given us all the necessary stuff we can put to good use.'

I pretended to inspect the brush critically and, nodding vigorously, I agreed with Rudi. Slowly, somewhat reluctantly, I started painting the scene on the wall between two windows. It was to be a colourful bouquet of flowers. Cook was a hard-to-please sort of a fellow and kept requesting changes and extras and I was only too willing to oblige.

Night began to fall as we returned to our bunkers, our stomachs full of good food. We had assured cook that we would return in our spare time between shifts the following day to continue our work in his domain, knowing full well that he was sympathetic towards us, but more than that, that he was keen to see the work finished.

Over the next day, a rather magnificent landscape appeared above the middle of the three large kitchen stoves, in which Easter bunnies were crouching in nests filled with colourful Easter eggs, and to which I added with a great flourish a clutch of yellow chicks, Easter candles, and ribbons all in cheerful bright colours. Cook was delighted. He gleefully clapped his hands, then patted us both on our shoulders to reinforce how pleased he was with our efforts, and hastened to reward these efforts with an extra portion of soup.

Not one of us had taken into account, or indeed suspected that the inspector whose remit included the kitchen and who was faithful to a fault to the communist party line would become involved. But he did. Legs spread apart, he plunked himself straight in front of my Easter landscape and began to spew venom. We didn't understand much, but we understood enough. 'That will not remain for another instant! Get if off! A neutral picture needs to take its place and immediately. All gone!'

The man, an ideological atheist, had obviously been offended by the Easter theme behind which he suspected Christian propaganda. My fingers started itching, as I could hardly wait for my beloved Waxenstein to take pride of place in what would soon again be an empty 'canvas'. There was plenty of space.

Towards evening of the following day, the *natchalnik*, also responsible for the kitchen, examined the mountain scene with a broad grin while grunting his approval with satisfaction. My work had admittedly turned out really well. Camp chef Nicolaus, called Nico by everyone, was also pleased, whilst Rudi softly whispered to me: 'Lothar, do you know who the Russians are building the houses in this steppe for?' He wouldn't let it go.

'No,' I answered, 'and to be honest, why should we care who'll be living here one day. What's much more important now is that we'll be allowed home soon. This bunch of Soviet crap carries no meaning for the likes of us.'

'Couldn't and won't disagree with you. I can't wait for us to be released; I'm dying to get out of here.'

CHAPTER 11

Shattered Hopes

——∙——

The summer had ended and a harsh and cruel winter followed. We were neither released to return to our homeland and nor did our living conditions much improve.

It was a spring day in 1948 when we were, yet again, taken to the station – and yet again, none of us knew where the train would take us. Yes, looking back, we had been treated somewhat better when it came down to work, or shall we say, less severely, but this did little to console us. Perhaps, on some small level, we realised that we had obviously become more valuable to the Russians and had acquired some sort of status, seeing as the dead whom we had left behind in Jezkasgan hadn't just been carted away to unmarked pits, but had been diligently registered by name and date. This filled a few of us with a measure of hope.

'Why, look, we're headed towards the west! Boys, believe me, we're on our way home. One of the guards has confirmed this to me!' I too got caught up in the excitement, hovering between optimism and anxiety.

But it seemed like we were hardly on our way – under the usual conditions I've described before – than the train stopped in the middle of some vast fields, right outside a city unknown to us. Rumours began to circulate almost immediately, flitting from one wagon to the next. 'The city ahead of us is Karaganda! We're now in the Soviet Union's second-largest coal district!'

'If that's the case, we couldn't have travelled more than eight or nine hundred kilometres.'

'Who gives a shit! Nothing will change for us, whatever the distance!'

As for myself, I felt uneasy, and feared bad news when I stepped down from the train. A tedious march of about an hour followed, with us prisoners forming the now familiar characterless column of glum and faceless men headed towards a camp. Several times, looking around, I searched for dead bodies. Has nobody been trampled on? Have no shots been fired? Does that mean we're the hardcore ones, the healthy and surviving remainder? Silently I said my prayers, thanking the dear Lord that neither during my childhood nor during my youth I had been mollycoddled or spoiled – something that so far had truly held me in good stead.

The obligatory frisking took place. Nobody was surprised, and cynical remarks abounded. 'Do the Russians fear we'd pocket coal from their crumbling pits and carry it with us?'

Or 'Might our senile captain in Jezkasgan have reported his old Nagant rifle missing?'

After we were allocated to barracks, Rudi suddenly popped up beside me as if it was the most natural thing in the world. 'One of the veterans here told me how much more sophisticated things are in this camp. Apparently there's a German commander in place who has a Russian superior who seems to oversee a number of camps. Everything around here supposedly is really well organised. There's a clothing store . . .'

Before Rudi could continue, he was interrupted by a boyish-sounding voice: 'Swell, Rudi. Why don't I get myself over there tomorrow and get myself a dinner jacket!'

Only a few of us laughed, but one man wanted to know more. 'What else did you learn?'

'There's a cobbler's workshop, a lumber yard and in the sick bay a former German medical officer is said to work alongside a female Russian doctor. I was told there's much more medication available than in Jezkasgan, and in the kitchen they only employ Germans.'

'Excellent!' said Oskar, who hailed from the Ruhr area. 'I expect that with this *Deutsche Gründlichkeit** in place, our stomachs will

---

* German thoroughness.

soon be attended to. I'm dizzy with hunger and stars flicker before my eyes.'

'Dream on Oskar!' somebody shouted over to him, adding: 'What I've heard baffles me much more. Looks like our new comrades here even receive a couple of roubles salary for their work in the colliery, if they meet their quotas. But apparently it's not enough to buy anything much. My hunch is that we'll not receive a lot more between our ribs than is strictly necessary to sustain our manpower.'

At the sight of our barracks, we were startled to see them not simply standing on bare soil, but atop posts some half a metre high made from tree trunks that had been rammed into the ground. Two solid wooden steps, no railings, led to the entrance door, and the flooring inside consisted of strong wooden beams. Nobody had an explanation for this type of construction, but we were certainly cheered by the rather unusual and much better camp conditions which seemed to exist in this part of the world. 'Wouldn't you agree, this is practically luxurious!' exclaimed Rudi, who once again chose to set up his bed right next to mine.

'Rudi, let me tell you, when people say the word "luxury" it usually refers to something different. Who knows whether we'll ever experience the real thing!'

Another hot discussion ensued between the two of us, with me finally changing the topic: 'I dread the *banja* ahead of us.'

'Yes, this is and remains a totally disrespectful procedure, with or without soap!'

The thin soup that was ladled out that evening did nothing to settle our grumbling stomachs. 'The stuff is as poor around here as it was before! One can practically drink it! Nobody'll get full on this crap!' That was our youngster whining.

The following morning, news that they were looking for decorators, plasterers, electricians and other skilled craftsmen came as a great relief to me. Once again this saved me from being carted off to one of the collieries, which everyone had told us were dilapidated and dangerous. Rudi, grinning as usual, elbowed me with a friendly nudge: 'If you get another job painting pictures on the walls in return for extra rations, don't forget about me, understood?!'

'Not a problem. But that goes both ways.'

'Tell me, are you capable of more than just plain painting?' asked Manfred Schulz, a master decorator from Berlin whom I would work alongside during the following days.

Rudi answered in my stead: 'Watch out, pal, there are some bits and pieces you could pick up from my Silesian friend from Upper Bavaria. He may well have been too young to become a master at the beginning of this god-awful mess of a war, but he jolly well knows a thing or two. Make sure to get on his good side even though he's young, because otherwise, mark my words, the guy will enjoy his extra rations without sharing them with you.'

On our first day of work, two guards took us to a construction site not far away from the camp entrance. Two large wood cabins were to be erected, with walls made of large round timber beams. Joiners assembled partitions, supporting and external walls based on drawings by Russian architects whilst we, functioning as assistants, transported the logs one by one from the trucks marked with the red Soviet stars to the future dwelling places, which quite literally grew out of the ground right in front of us. Eyes wide open, I stared in amazement at how precisely the openings for windows and doors had been calculated and accounted for, how they had done away with cellars, and how prefabricated floor and ceiling cladding magically appeared from some kind of timber mill. With ease and speed the staircases to the upper floors were installed by professional builders.

Then it was our turn to get working on the interior, under constant guidance and supervision from the Russian labourers who showed us how to affix wooden trimmings to the walls. That's when Rudi and his mates were called to help. Plasterers were instructed to render both the inside and outside walls, whereupon the electricians, plumbers and painters went into action and nobody made a secret of being mightily relieved not to have to work in some pit underground and in the dark. One of the men, he was somewhat older than most and apparently already had his own family back in Mecklenburg-Vorpommern, had quite a bit to report back to us from the colliery.

'Down there, it's not only literally the pits, they're also increasing the quotas, as apparently the more you produce, the more shiny roubles you can accrue.'

'Yes,' agreed someone else who was working alongside us, 'That's what I've also heard. Looks like now that we're in slightly better shape, the Germans are meeting these quotas. But around here it's different, just watch it. Here we're working with Russian Komsomol members,* they're something like apprentices. And they'll be pissed off if we up our quota. They'll think we're fools. And if we counter them by saying that this is what Moscow has ordered us to do, they'll have nothing but contempt: "Moscow is far away from here," they'll sniff.'

The plaster dried quickly. Now it was our, the decorators' turn. No longer questioning the Russian penchant for shades of red, we stood atop two high ladders and applied dark red paint to the outside wall of one of the houses whilst enjoying the spring rays of sun warming our backs.

'Lothar!' shouted Rudi across to me. 'I couldn't care less if they deliver us black or brown paint. All I want is our *natchalnik* grunting his "*charasho*" and occasionally supplying us with extra rations of cabbage soup!' We had long ago got used to never being given extra rations of bread, seeing as this staple, hugely valued by the Russians, was obviously in short supply for them as well.

The minute we had completed the paint job on the inside to the utmost satisfaction of a Russian inspector, Manfred and I were called away to attend to a cluster of nearly complete office buildings, a few kilometres away on the city outskirts of Karaganda. 'Lothar,' commented Manfred approvingly on viewing the new site, 'lots seems to be happening around here.'

---

* The Komsomol was the youth wing of the Soviet Communist Party.

I responded in the same vein: 'Well, of course, and I can't but agree with the Russians. Why wouldn't they have us clear up the pigsty we've turned their country into.'

Once again, we had been spared being sent underground to heave coal. And other changes came our way as well that helped ease our stay and made life more bearable. During times in between shifts, we even had a club room made available to us where we could read the German newspaper *Neues Deutschland*,* kindling our hope. There was also an undercurrent message that seemed to be gaining ground: 'Boys, we'll be home before Christmas 1948 – you can bet your life on it. Russian grandma chief medical officer here registers more and more of us seriously ill so that they might be released sooner.'

Enlivened by such news, Manfred and I doubled up on our efforts, earning huge praise from our German-speaking commander in the meantime. We even tried out our so-called coiling technique on the corridor walls of the first floor, which entailed not allowing the first coat of paint to dry but immediately treating it by taking a clean, scrunched up cloth and wiping it over the entire surface and thereby creating a marble effect.

Whilst we were busy getting the right colour mix ready for the window wall in the room at the far end of the corridor for its future occupant, the manager of the building entered, accompanied by our *natchalnik*. The manager was looking around, quite obviously happy with what he saw. I addressed him in my broken Russian: 'I'd be pleased to paint some colourful flowers and greenery around the window frame. I could indeed do the same on the upper half of the wall opposite, or I could create a mountain scene for you in whichever space you chose.'

In near perfect German the officer replied: 'Are you able to do something like that?'

'Most definitely, sir. For you, I would happily do so.'

'That would be nice. Over there, you paint mountains. With colours!'

---

* Published in what would soon become East Germany.

But other than a '*charasho*' and the habitual 'the Germans can do anything', I received nothing in return.

When the future manager left, our *natchalnik* explained: 'That was the future boss of the building. You'll get nothing from him. No extra ration. You guys are *woina plenis*. Your job is to work and to obey.'

Looking at me for a few seconds, somewhat pleadingly I felt, he asked: 'Would you be good enough to paint my flat in the first building you completed last week? In your spare time? I'll be able to offer you some flatbread and a bit of butter from my mother-in-law.' Without a moment's hesitation I agreed, whilst Manfred, with a slight tinge of admiration mixed with what I detected as a bit of envy, stated: 'Lothar, looks like you've got a stranglehold on that stuff called luck!'

'Hardly,' I replied, 'as otherwise I'd already be back home with my mountains. Looks like we'll be released by Christmas 1949, at least that's what I've heard.'

'Who cares. Not many have survived this period looking as healthy as you. Us both – we'll manage the rest of this stretch, don't you worry. I feel quite convinced of that.'

I responded: 'But before that, I'll make sure that the mountains of my homeland will look down on the boss of this building and, as seems to be the practice around here, check up on him. But Manfred, don't you agree, do you also feel that these months leading up to our release seem to be getting longer by the day? I can hardly wait.'

'Stupid question. Of course, I'd rather see my wife today than tomorrow.'

This time round I used my regular shift to paint the walls, while Manfred started with his paint job on the floor above me. But I was pleased to get the occasional visit from our *natchalnik,* who'd always leave by letting me know he was well satisfied. '*Charasho!* Very beautiful! This is nice, this is good!' On my last day working on the scene he added: 'Tomorrow, I'll show it to my Natasha. She'll probably want this in our living room.'

Just as in the many months before, I was constantly plagued by hunger, but had also got used to compensating for this by concentrating on my work, which also reduced my feelings of homesickness.

For a good long while something like a democratic system had been established in our camp. But it still took me by surprise when I, along with Rudi from the Sudetenland, another master plasterer, a joiner and two other fellows were selected as the top workers and given some title to go along with our new post. Quietly chuckling to myself, I thought this was the typical situation of receiving 'a title on paper, with no return now nor later'* and because of that I couldn't get too excited about this so-called honour.

In contrast, my election to the social committee where I would have a small say in matters of work and welfare meant much more to me. One of the issues I had to deal with was, for example, that several comrades felt hard done to by the cook because they believed that he doled out smaller portions of food to them than to others. It was decided that one of the committee members would, forthwith, attend to the distribution by standing next to the pots and supervising the cook. When it happened, however, that the German camp commander had his bowl filled more generously than others, I tended to ignore it deliberately. I sure didn't want to fall out with that guy.

As for the responsibility itself, I felt it was nothing but a nuisance with no advantage to me, as several of my ever-hungry comrades were only too happy to put the blame for allegedly having been treated unfairly on my shoulders. 'Why not take over from me,' was my usual response to them on such occasions, and I was promptly left alone.

Only once did I contribute to the wall-newspaper of our club room, as I didn't much like its clearly socialist leanings.

Stalin quite obviously tried to indoctrinate his German prisoners of war with the Soviet ideology in order to gain agitators,

---

* From the German saying '*ein Titel ohne Mittel*', literally 'a title without benefits'.

who'd then disseminate the Marxist-Leninist beliefs in Germany. Wasn't it Lenin who recognised early on that 'Whoever controls Germany, controls Europe'?

Towards the end of August 1948 our female Russian camp doctor registered those comrades who could only perform light camp duties as permanently sick, rendering 100 of them not fit for work. The deprivations and hardships we had suffered in the past had invariably left deep scars on many of us, and quite a few did not survive them. It thus didn't make any sense for the Russians to keep feeding patients who were obviously no longer of any use until they died, so instead they were soon released.

We were still taken by surprise, however, when one day at the end of roll-call the Russian major read out the names of some hundred men who were ordered to march to the station, from where they would be allowed to travel home. One after another, dragging their feet, exhausted and depleted, but their faces lit up with joy, they shuffled towards the entrance gate.

Then all of a sudden, the following words were spoken: 'And the six *charasho robotniks,* our best workers in this camp, may travel with them.' I couldn't believe my ears. Certain that I must have misunderstood, I paused for a second. But no, indeed, my name had been amongst them. I literally stormed towards the camp gate and positioned myself at the very end of the line of men, right next to Rudi, Manfred and the three others.

The frisking in front of us was in full swing and seemed to be carried out more thoroughly than usual. Meanwhile, we could see from the corners of our eyes the sad, ragged faces of a work shift struggling to keep in line and moving sluggishly towards the colliery. It didn't prevent us from blabbering enthusiastically about our hopes, and excitedly imagining what might lie in wait for us at home. Suddenly Rudi shouted:' Boys, surely we'll want to take our quilted jackets along and our bowls. Believe me, it will be quite some time until it's our turn.'

All six of us sprinted to our lodgings, with Manfred and myself being the first to rejoin the men slowly filing past the guards. The queue progressed only very gradually, and only one step at a time, did we approach the camp entrance, when Rudi all of a sudden became quite distressed.

'I'm not sure the Czechs will allow me back into my home town of Eger – it's what I've read in the *Neues Deutschland*. My only hope is that I will get to see my wife and children in West Germany. I've noted Munich as my native town, but I'm worried sick that it won't work out.'

Rudi, though, was really as happy as the rest of us. As for Manfred, he was truly beside himself: 'You guys, I can't get my head round it! My wife, well, her eyes will be popping out when she sees me plunked there in front of her, totally unexpected. Haven't seen her since just before Stalingrad!'

At long last it was our turn to stand in front of the guards, when we heard the young lieutenant shout: '*Nitschewvo! Niet damoi!* Not going home! The top workers are to remain here and will only be released later!'

'You're out of your mind!' The words escaped me before I knew it. But quickly gathering myself, I yelled out my home address in Garmisch to one of the last prisoners walking through the camp exit at that same moment. I knew the man well, as I had spent several weeks with him painting and furnishing the club room. We had grown close and I had got to know some of his story and his past. He was an ethnic German from Latvia who had joined the Wehrmacht.

'You'll make sure to let them know, won't you?!' I called after him.

Without even turning around he repeated the address of the Maier family, living at Danielstrasse 20, loud and clear, adding: 'Rest easy, Lothar, I will of course do this for you, gladly!'

Meanwhile Manfred turned towards the Russian with tears in his eyes. 'But the comrade major read out our names!'

'Comrade major has to retract! I'm in command here!' He waved some piece of paper in front of our eyes and with outstretched hand he ordered us back to the camp.

Our disappointment was as profound and devastating as our joy had been intense and exuberant. We were left dumbfounded, and once more I found myself having to bow to the powers that were. Without another word, I departed. Instead of returning to work, however, I entered the office of our German camp commander without even so much as knocking.

'Have they all gone crazy here?' I asked furiously. 'First we're allowed home and then this? I ask you to get this changed!'

'Look here now, Herrmann, calm down. I don't have so much power. If it were up to me, I wouldn't just release you, I would most definitely travel with you and get home myself.'

'I couldn't give a shit. I demand to speak to the major!'

The German commander, a mere adjunct to the Russians, put my name down to have a word with his Russian superior, then took me to his office and held the door open. In the meantime, my frustration and disappointment had given way to a raging fury, which was hard for me to put in words. I had to get a firm grip on myself and refrain from screaming something unwise which I would only come to regret. The major simply glanced up at me, unconcerned and not displaying any visible emotion.

'*Schotakoi?*' 'What's the matter?'

'Why, I might be the one asking you as to what all this means. First you read out my name and announce to all the world that I and five other top workers will be allowed to return home, and then you come to the gate and refuse our journey!'

'But Herrmann! *Nitschewo! Skorasze damoi!* It doesn't matter! All of you will go home in no time! Now leave.' His hand gesturing towards the door could hardly be misinterpreted. The last glimmer of hope had been extinguished.

'That wasn't an error,' I thought, but once again rallied. 'Garmisch and the Waxenstein will keep waiting for you,' I consoled myself. 'All you can do is try and remain healthy! Let's hope I can rely on the assurance that soon we'll all be allowed home.'

Back in the barracks I met Manfred and Rudi, both sitting on their planks and staring in front of them with dull eyes.

Rudi was the first to lift his head. 'How did it go with our major?'

'No hope.'

'Lothar! The only way forward is to keep our chins above water, continue to work for extra rations. I certainly don't want to be released like these other fellows today, broken and sick, barely standing on their last legs.'

'Me neither. But constantly suffering and being homesick, with this awful food and damned insecurity – I'm not sure I can take it any longer.'

'Cheer up chaps. Surely, they can't get us down so easily. Let's prove them wrong. They can lick our . . .'

Once again, one bleak day followed the next. And once again, we drowned our homesickness by working and finding opportunities to stock up on extra rations. Rudi and I prevailed, thanks to my good reputation as a painter and decorator and his outstanding talent as an excellent builder.

CHAPTER 12

Contact with the Homeland

The late autumn of 1948 saw us standing tightly squeezed together on the cargo beds of several trucks on our way to camp 7099/III, situated somewhere on the outskirts of Karaganda.* In appearance, the camp was hardly different from any of the others, with an equally harsh and bitter winter about to plague its prisoners. Temperatures of often minus forty degrees turned the top layer of the snow covering into a thin sheet of ice, making movement pretty much impossible.

However, and most fortunately, we – Rudi, Manfred and myself – were once again spared the descent into the collieries and their black coal faces and gooey sludge of coal dust. One day, when Manfred and I were busy doing our coiling technique in a heated new-build, we weren't just praised but we crucially also received extra rations of soup and bread.

My fur cap had gone missing, and having only a threadbare head-covering for meagre protection, I decided to ask the camp tailor, a fellow prisoner, whether he might trade the two extra slices of bread I had earned for a cap. He happily accepted, and my new hat was exactly what I needed to keep my head and ears well protected from the biting cold.

One evening, we were told that there had been a new development and that we had permission to write home. After years of being totally cut off, this change appeared to be near enough a

---

* The Soviet state operated a vast system of prison camps for its own citizens as well as POW around Karaganda. Between 1931 and 1959, over one million prisoners are estimated to have been sent to these camps. Many did not survive to be released.

miracle. Each of us received a postcard on which the sender's camp address had been printed. At long last, we were able to write to our dear ones and give them a sign we were alive. While writing my name on the card, my thoughts wandered to the sick comrade to whom I had entrusted my home address a while ago, and I wondered whether my compatriot had remembered it, as I had never heard back from him.

As we had now officially been allowed to get in contact with our relatives, I was also desperately waiting for some news from Garmisch. Nothing of the sort happened.

But our living conditions from then on improved significantly. It wasn't just that our barracks were now well heated and we no longer suffered from the cold, we also had an agreement with our miners, tacitly tolerated by our superiors, to bring each occupant a daily clump of coal. Those not busy on their shift broke them apart to heat the small iron stove. The guards posted at the entrance certainly didn't forbid us from going ahead with our routine, and in return also got a cut of the coal. Here too the saying 'one hand washes the other' applied.

I was sorely put to the test, what with being relegated to waiting for days and weeks for mail to arrive from Garmisch. Even though only a few of us had received news from their loved ones – and even then those in receipt of a letter would oftentimes see many lines blacked out by the Russian censors – I felt abandoned. Manfred was in some ways one of the lucky ones. After weeks of writing, he finally received a response from his beloved wife. It was, however, devastating news. She wrote that, thinking he was dead after such a long time of having no word from or about him, she had now married a successful businessman and given birth to two sons.

I must admit that I admired Manfred for his composure. He didn't stop working just as hard as he had done before and remained as reliable as always. The only change I could observe was that his movements had become more stilted, more automatic, he walked like a robot, but never complained; just once, he softly confided in me: 'Lothar, count yourself lucky never to have married. But I'm also trying to understand my ex-wife. Nobody can stay alone for such a long time.'

'I think you are spot-on there,' I responded, but didn't say anything more. My comrades and I knew full well that he didn't want any pity.

In the meantime, I suspected that my postcard had never arrived in Garmisch. So many weeks had gone by and it was December 1948 already. One day I decided to send one of those pre-printed postcards to Niederviehbach, near Landshut, to Lotte, my first great love. Young, blonde, fresh and cheerful, that's how I remembered her. Of course, I couldn't dare hope that she would still remember me after such an age, or indeed would have waited for me, even though we had sworn to each other to be faithful forever.

A few days before Christmas, a letter from her arrived, and she wrote that her parents had passed away, that she had taken over the farm and bought out her two siblings. She, too, had married in the meantime, unsurprisingly, but she let it shine through that her husband wasn't a great help to her on the farm. She worked seven days a week, from early morning to late at night, and had no time for anything else, as this was their livelihood.

Lotte's letter made me think, and I briefly imagined how things would have turned out had we not been abruptly separated. Nevertheless, the question why my dear ones from Garmisch hadn't dropped me a line really worried me. Had something happened to them?

Work was what kept my homesickness at bay. This was the reason that here in this camp I also contributed to the decoration of our clubroom, and just generally helped wherever I could to make our surroundings as warm and as habitable as possible, while discussing with my comrades behind closed doors how remarkably well the Russians were treating us now. We could hardly believe the freedom we enjoyed in this camp, compared to where we had been before, and after the currency reform (which happened throughout the Soviet Union) our food had become a lot tastier and more nutritious, and there was more variety and choice.

Our comrades labouring in the collieries were now able to purchase some additional food with their new roubles in the designated outlets and sometimes we'd even be allowed by the still omnipresent guards to gather some scrap metal, from which those skilled in handicrafts would fabricate some ornamental tin boxes and then artfully decorate them.

Was it the Russians' intention that we leave for our homeland having gained a more favourable impression of the Soviet Union? But the minute one of our lads enquired with a Soviet officer who was seemingly happy to chat with us, asking him when we might be released, he'd always receive the same old response: '*Skoro!*' 'Soon!' While this uncertainty of course sapped our energy, none of us lost hope.

Amongst other things, Lotte had told me in her long letter that the Allied bombers hadn't only dumped their lethal charges on larger cities, but had also destroyed many little towns. But she didn't mention Garmisch or its surroundings even in a single word. My second postcard to Garmisch had not been acknowledged either, and I grew increasingly concerned. What on earth had happened to my loved ones? The fact that my comrades had similar disappointing experiences were of little comfort to me.

Finally! When the mail was distributed on 24 December, my name was at long last amongst those called out. Even before opening the envelope with its Garmisch postmark, I suspected that perhaps the camp administration had kept it back and made it out to be a Christmas present, as I had noticed that on that particular day many more letters were being handed out.

Garmisch had not been touched by the Allies; they had only occupied the military barracks. The Maiers were doing well, and so were many other friends, and together with my comrades who had similarly been blessed with good news, I spent Christmas evening in the comfortable clubroom enjoying a special serving of *tchai* – tea. Some may find it curious, but with that envelope in my hand, I truly felt as happy as a child receiving their presents, firmly convinced that this had been my best Christmas ever.

Even though we had hoped to be released before Christmas 1948, as several officers from the Red Army had assured us that this was the date set, and in spite of being deeply disappointed that it hadn't come to pass, we all believed that we were better off now than before, when we hadn't been allowed to write home. Our clubroom looked quite reasonable, and we'd often ask ourselves what the Russians would use the space for after we left.

As for now, and much to our astonishment, we were allowed to organise plays in our clubroom. Not only that, but would you believe it, the Russian officers and their wives would reserve the front seats at these productions.

'They're really keen on our performances!' stated our 'representative for arts and culture' and his words rang with considerable pride. He was a slightly older man who had worked in the Semper Opera House in Dresden before the war, and had now organised a concert which I eagerly attended, taking a seat in the back row. That same evening, the camp choir performed excerpts from operettas, arias and popular songs, and this was followed by the representative's announcement that a soloist from Düsseldorf, whose name was vaguely familiar to me, would offer a selection of his repertoire as a final highlight. There he was, standing in front of us on the stage singing *'Ich bin nur ein armer Wandergesell . . .'**
His tenor voice filled the entire clubroom to the furthest corner. For a split second I could literally see Lotte before my eyes and felt my throat clogging up. A melody from the operetta *The Tsarevich* tore me out of my reveries: *'Es steht ein Soldat am Wolgastrand . . .'*†

Rousing applause and a standing ovation by the Russian officers in the front rows was offset by our restrained clapping in the back seats; men were sunk in memories, lost in thought and with tears

---

* The song 'I am but a poor journeyman' is from the operetta *Der Vetter aus Dingsda*, 'Cousin from Nowhere', by Eduard Künneke.

† The operetta *The Tsarevich* by Franz Lehár features the song 'A soldier stands on the bank of the Volga'.

in their eyes. Nearly all the comrades we had known from previous camps had by now disappeared in all four directions across the vast country, some into one labour camp, some into another. We hardly knew anyone any more when we looked around, which only intensified our feelings of loneliness and our desire to return home.

During the following months our feelings of being homesick were somewhat alleviated by the frequent and entertaining routines, which had in part been written and performed in the clubroom by my comrade; we were all much comforted by these evenings, and it was truly astounding how much undiscovered talent had lain dormant in the camp.

That particular winter certainly turned out the most tolerable of all I had so far endured as a prisoner of war. I was practically always working in near finished and well-heated new-builds in the city, supported by a team of painters, and not infrequently I was allowed to carry out special commissions, which gave me much joy whilst of course offering welcome variety.

Towards the last days of April 1949, the Russians had another sort of variety in store for us. Daddy Frost seemed to have taken his leave earlier than usual. In pleasant temperatures and with the sun warming our backs, we were asked to sweep the streets for the May parade. Along the road, tribunes had been erected and they got us to stick placards onto billboards, though we couldn't make out what they said as they were written in Russian.

At the beginning of summer we were told that the Russians were recruiting prisoners who were prepared to receive political education along with classes in Russian and German history. A few comrades crowded around the information board in the clubroom where they could see the notice for themselves. A heated discussion ensued: 'They just want to indoctrinate us and drum communism into us!'

'This would only be of interest to me if it meant being released from work, even if it's only part-time! Just as they promise on the leaflet, here.'

'There are also notices in the *Neues Deutschland,* which have obviously been put in by the Russians.'

'What I think is that they can kiss my arse. I'll have to stay on longer if I join. You guys will already be on your way home!'

I decided to take up the offer of the three-month training course, as I couldn't quite see a reason not to. The suspicions voiced by my comrade that it might extend the duration of our imprisonment seemed absurd to me. Hardly, I thought. Surely the opposite would be true and any participation would hold us in good stead. If anything, it would speed up our release. As for being brain-washed, well, I could always pretend.

After finishing my shift the following day, I put my name down with the camp commander, and not two days had gone by when I left the camp in a truck along with twenty other course participants on our way to the venue in the city.

Sitting next to me in the cargo area during the journey was a theology student from Esslingen near Stuttgart who had been plucked from university when the Prussian Glory[*] called him to enlist. His name was Walter Roller, and we exchanged home addresses. He kept the reason why he had volunteered for this course private, whereas I had no qualms openly admitting that I simply wanted to be surprised at what they would come up with.

Participants from other camps joined as well, and not a single chair remained empty, though hard as I tried, I couldn't recognise a familiar face. Finally a man, his dark hair at the temples greying a bit, approached the lectern and introduced himself. Werner Frik from Frankfurt was to be our course leader. Walter Roller leaned over to me whispering into my ear: 'He sure hides the fact that he's been trained up in Moscow.'

'I have no problem asking him afterwards what his home address is,' I grinned.

'He'll definitely not give you the correct one.'

---

[*] A reference to one of the most famous German military march tunes 'Preußens Gloria'.

I must admit that the history lectures we attended during the following weeks generally made total sense to me. When, however, I would ask the opinion of my failed theologian, he just shrugged his shoulders and didn't say much. Truth be told, I never could get my head around the communist goals, and when it came to this topic I simply closed my ears whilst outwardly feigning interest. I couldn't bring myself to believe what they'd broadcast to all and sundry.

For some time, prisoners had been receiving mail from unknown senders, and we all knew that the authors of these letters were living in the occupation zone. But when, towards the end of the training course, I received a letter from a sixteen-year-old girl, it was certainly a highlight for me. She lived in Chemnitz and described herself as a committed Free German Youth member who was convinced that the goals of communism were justified and noble, and that she considered me a like-minded comrade, albeit one she didn't know. She had, she continued, received my address from the State Security Ministry, and would look forward to hearing from me by return mail.

This entire experience took me aback, and I felt that the socialist message drums were working just a bit too efficiently for my taste, but then again, why not answer the young girl? She had added a photograph of herself to her second letter, and as I happened to find her exceedingly pretty, I immediately decided to take the picture home with me once I was finally released. Who knew what would happen then . . .

The course had finished, but I remained as homesick as ever and the days dragged on much as before. And just as in the months past, I did all I could to push away my sorrow and sadness through work, driving every day with five colleagues in a lorry to the theatre where we had been entrusted with the decoration work. The exterior of the building seemed to be of an oriental design, whilst the inside was totally modern, though admittedly, I had never really seen a theatre building properly. A rather elderly man, the building manager, always greeted us with a friendly hello, but remained reserved and matter of fact. He spoke German fluently and when he allocated work to us, he had the annoying habit of nervously running his hands through his grey beard which reached down to his chest.

Quietly whispering in my ear, my companion from Berlin-Tegel thought that this guy was perhaps Jewish. 'Quite possibly,' I responded equally softly, 'but that shouldn't bother us.'

It took us fourteen days to restore the rooms to their new glory, during which time the old man paid us several visits in his capacity of supervising us, always sticking to practical issues and what was important. But we were still able to tease a bit of information out of him, for example that practically the entire electrics, as well as some other things, had been installed by *woina plenis.*

When, on the last day of our work, we were about to climb onto the cargo area of our lorry, he held out his hand to each of us, and, stony-faced, waited for us to shake hands. 'See you around!' he said. 'Hopefully not,' our cocky Berlin boy retorted. The Russian didn't react, or if he did, we didn't see even so much as a twitch.

Three days later we would find out what he actually meant when he said: 'See you around!' The 'arts and culture representative' from our camp, a position created by the Russians, handed each of us an invitation to the opening of the new theatre building. 'Real classy!' exclaimed our cheeky one. 'I wonder whether they'll send along rented tuxedos for us?'

'Actually no!' The representative seemed as surprised as us. We, in turn, were taken aback when we realised that we had been especially selected to attend. 'If one of you doesn't wish to make use of this invitation,' he said modestly, 'I'd sure be happy to go in his stead. They're putting on *Swan Lake*, and I hear the girls of the Russian ballet are supposed to be absolutely charming dancers.'

Because of his remarks and his obviously expert opinion, we all broke out in laughter. I wouldn't know today who it was, but one of us came up with a curious thought: 'Do you think the Russians want to sweeten our departure, otherwise I really can't figure out why they have become so incredibly friendly!'

'Who cares!'

'You can bet your life that nobody will want to remain here in Russia just because of that.'

'No matter, the evening promises to be one of the most delightful we'll ever have experienced in this part of the world.'

And this is exactly how it turned out to be. Each one of us had swiftly ensured that the camp laundry handed him the smartest shirt and pair of trousers they could come up with, first come, first served. Thus attired, we drove with our lorry taxi to the theatre and arrived well in time. The old Russian manager was expecting us, standing at the entrance and, just as reserved but friendly in that understated way of his, he led us to the back row in the brightly lit auditorium.

'This row here is reserved for the *woina plenis* who worked on this building. There are a few more coming. I myself have to leave now, but would like to wish you gentlemen an enjoyable evening.'

The soft murmuring filling the auditorium, as well as the elegant ladies sweeping past on the arm of officers or gentlemen dressed in dark suits showing them to their seats, was enough of an experience for us simple folks to entertain us even before the start of the evening. 'This too is Russia,' I thought. 'Here I am, turning twenty-nine this September, and I get to hear and experience *Swan Lake*. I would never have dared dream that such a beautiful leaving gesture would have been granted to us.'

Gradually the lights dimmed and the last gong to announce the start of the show sounded through the vast hall whilst my eyes still roamed around, watching my neighbours as they fidgeted in their seats, nervous with both expectation and impatience, anxiously leaning forward to catch the best view of the stage.

I had hardly had any occasion to go to the theatre prior to being drafted by the Wehrmacht. Thus the hours that followed were all the more enchanting, opening a world unknown to me beforehand. Even today I think back fondly to this unique ballet performance, which surpassed all my expectations. When rousing applause filled the auditorium at the end of the show, I felt I had been woken from a beautiful dream and, glancing at my comrades, saw that they obviously felt similarly.

Later, when we *woina plenis* clambered onto the truck, people stared at us. Being the last one to get myself onto the cargo area, I could hear one of my comrades shouting to the Russians curiously ogling us. 'Haven't you ever seen *woina plenis* before? Without us, your theatre wouldn't have turned out so beautiful, and certainly wouldn't have been ready on time.'

The following day saw the return of the routine. The current edition of *Neues Deutschland,* which was kept on display in the clubroom, had an article announcing that the last prisoners of war still in Russia would be released before Christmas.* Reading these lines, my heart jumped. Never before had such a concrete date for our release been reported. The dates announced previously had always proved to be nothing but rumours. This time, things seemed to be serious at last. I'd finally be allowed home, back to my beloved Loisach valley, back to my Waxenstein mountains and all my dear ones.

In the meantime, though, I and six other painters had been ordered to sort out the walls of several halls in a paper factory on the outskirts of the city. The entire week the job lasted, we could only talk about what each one of us would do first once he got home.

On one of the evenings during this assignment, returning back to camp, we managed to take with us a few sheets of the high-quality paper they were producing there. The days of the thorough body searches had long become a thing of the past.

But Daddy Frost returned to us in the first days of October 1949 in his old guise: it had turned cold and damp. Still, things were different. In years past we certainly hadn't owned any warm winter clothing, and we did so now; with deep sadness I'd think back to the poor chaps who hadn't survived those earlier winters.

---

* In fact the last prisoners were not released until 1956.

CHAPTER 13

Returning Home

———•—•———

Even though, by October 1949, the days had indeed become shorter, it felt like quite the opposite. All of us kept wondering when they'd finally take us to the station. Two or three times, a group of our comrades had been summoned to report for their final medical examination, but my name was never on the list. At long last I was called up: 'Lothar Herrmann'. I literally had to hold tight so as not to burst out shouting with joy.

Half an hour later I stood, together with fifty other camp inmates, with my bare chest in front of a female Russian doctor and an army officer. The check-up was only superficial, but every one of us had to lift his arms up high; even though many years had passed, they were still hunting for ex-SS men. But not a single one of us had his blood group tattooed on the inside of his upper arm, which could have identified them as such. 'Surely they've found all of them by now,' mumbled my neighbour. 'Why all this fuss?'

A few minutes later we heard somebody cry out: 'No, no, this scar came from chopping wood. The wound got infected, but couldn't be treated at the time. I was a private in a tank division! Surely you know that!'

We all pitied the poor guy as a Red Army man led him brusquely away. As for us, we were allowed to slip into our quilted jackets, but not before undergoing another frisking. That small amount of paper I had smuggled from the factory was immediately taken off me, but I was at least allowed to keep the picture of the pretty girl from Chemnitz, as well as her letters.

When I was handing over the pile, a comrade standing next to me couldn't hold himself back, commenting loudly: 'Do they really think you covered these sheets of paper with invisible ink? Lothar, don't worry about losing the stuff. I saw how quickly that guy snatched them away from you . . . bet you he'll keep them for himself. I can't see them anywhere.'

Before we filed past the camp entrance, a Russian officer addressed us to wish us a good trip home and all the best for the future. But not one of us believed him, or even paid much attention to his obviously well-rehearsed words.

A little while later we stood tightly squeezed together on top of an army truck. We all wore our fur caps with the earflaps down to protect us from the icy wind blowing hard across the open space, but not one of us was cold. All of us, me included, were warmed by joyous anticipation. But there was no train waiting for us at the station. Instead, we were led to a storage shed, where we were to spend the night on thin beds of straw.

We had been the first lot to arrive, and once again our patience would be sorely tested by a further waiting game. Gradually other groups from different camps around the region filtered in, some larger and some smaller ones, and only after a week of waiting around, when our crowd had swelled to some 300 POWs, was our departure announced, with a lieutenant of the Red Army leading us across the tracks to a freight train.

Steam was rising from the engine, and groups of twenty men climbed up into each wagon as fast as their legs could carry them. Briefly, I recognised in the carriage in front of me the face of my theologian student from Esslingen with whom I had attended the training course and, having obviously spotted me too, he nodded in my direction.

For just a moment I feared that the two of us who had participated in the training would be required to convince our co-passengers on our return trip of the advantages that communism had to offer our society and, silently, I prepared my excuse: 'Dear comrades, I'll have to disappoint you. You can't expect me to do anything which is against my inner convictions. You've harassed me long enough.'

With the engine rumbling, we left the station. Due to the cold airflow penetrating the inside, we rammed shut the doors on both sides of the wagon and noted with relief that they hadn't been bolted from the outside. 'Boys! These are the first signs that we're free!' shouted someone in exultation.

'They've made us wait for a damn long time!' Voices, exclamations, shouts, all the clamouring excitement filled the carriage but you couldn't make out a word.

Later on, we tried to guess how long our trip home might take. Everything seemed to have been well planned and organised, and at several stations our train had obviously been scheduled to bunker coal and water whilst we, contrary to the past, were kept well fed throughout and allowed to disembark for a brief stroll on the platforms.

Now that so many years have passed, I can't remember precisely at which station we were ordered to descend from the Russian train and switch to a train equipped to use standard-gauge tracks, but I do recall the words spoken by our two officers who accompanied us: 'Please stay in the groups you've been in until now as you board the trains which have been prepared for you.'

Those words, spoken politely and respectfully made several of us snigger, one of my mates observing cynically: 'Well, look who's talking . . . Up until now we were pure shit to you.'

'Too late, Ivan! You can get stuffed, as far as I'm concerned.'

'Don't make me laugh – you can kiss my arse!'

'Fritz, what do I care! Main thing is that we're home soon.'

We travelled through Poland and the temperatures were much more pleasant and warm. Standing close together at the wagon's side doors, we saw our train slowly rolling into the freight station of a small town. When our train came to a stop, our carriage stood on tracks running along a bridge when, all of a sudden, we felt stones being pelted at us. 'Shut the doors!'

Looking at each other terrified as the hail of stones hitting our roof intensified, we heard screeching female voices drowning out men who were also screaming and shouting, but though we couldn't understand anything, we certainly gathered that they were hostile. The sharp sound of a pistol quietened the raucous affray.

Once the train started to move and began gathering speed, we opened the side doors again and stared out at the evening sun which, blood-red, fast disappeared behind the horizon. When day broke, the landscape outside appeared enveloped by a faint mist. 'Lads, I know this area, though I haven't been here in ages! We're not far from the Oder!' shouted one of our guys, barely able to contain his excitement.

In the early morning of the sixth day of our journey, the wheels of the train made a hollow sound: 'This is it! We're crossing the bridge in Frankfurt an der Oder!' someone declared most theatrically. Three or four men had scrambled to the front of our train and climbed up to the German locomotive driver and his boilermen. They called back to us, waving their hands: 'Welcome home! We've made it!'

We all had a different reaction. Some threw themselves into each other's arms, crying, others were laughing, others still wiped tears of joy from their faces.

When, on 19 October 1949, a Russian officer shoved my release papers into my hand in the station hall of Frankfurt an der Oder and waved me to move past him – not in an unfriendly way I might add – I quickly calculated how many years I had spent in the Soviet Union as a POW. Swallowing hard and painfully, I tried not to choke. And then, only when I found myself alone, I too couldn't help but shed tears of joy that slowly rolled down my cheeks. I could hardly believe that soon I would once again see my beloved Loisach valley, and Garmisch, which had long ago become my home town, and the Waxenstein, and all the other mountains.

Once again, everyone seemed to be looking out only for himself. Clutching my release papers and train ticket in my left hand, I briefly shook hands with some mates. That was it. We dispersed into all corners of the country: some had their homes in the

German Democratic Republic (DDR, East Germany), those from the northern parts of West Germany were to return via Friedland and we, who hailed from southern Germany, received train tickets to Moschendorf/Hof.*

Behind me I could overhear a conversation between two returnees: 'Karl, I just heard somebody from the Security Ministry offering Richard the chance to remain here in the DDR as a lieutenant in the People's Army. His wife has married an American and moved to the USA. Don't you remember him, he was part of our training in the camp. But I'm not sure what he'll decide.'

That same moment I noticed that other than my train ticket to Moschendorf, I also held in my hand one to Chemnitz, and, wrapped in an envelope, some East German bank notes. Feeling somewhat apprehensive, I wondered whether we returnees were being watched, and whether they had set me up with that pretty girl from Chemnitz whose picture I was carrying to entice me to join their army. I am not sure how long I stood there lost in thought and wavering, but my curiosity prevailed and in the end I resolved to board the train to Chemnitz.

'Why,' I said to myself, 'You haven't been home for a very long time, so, taking a quick look at the so-called DDR perhaps for one day, maximum two, can't do you any harm. Surely, when you meet Anneliese you'll know if she's a decent person or if her intentions are to turn you into a DDR communist. I'm not sure who put that idea into your head, but who cares. After a brief visit, you'll go home and that's that.'

Eagerly peering out of the window of the train now travelling south-west, I could see for myself that the signs of war, even though it had ended four years ago, had not disappeared, not by a long shot. And what about the west part of the now divided Germany? Patience! I admonished myself. I'd see it the day after tomorrow at the very latest.

---

* There were major resettlement camps for 'displaced persons' at Friedland and Moschendorf, run by the Allied military authorities and the new German government.

Surprisingly, Anneliese, who stood in front of a miserable-looking grey apartment block, didn't seem surprised to see me in the least, and held out her hand to greet me warmly, as well as giving me a quick peck on the cheek.

'Lothar! How nice you made it. Wouldn't it have been a pity if you hadn't come to visit me. In truth, I should be sitting in a two-hour training course at my socialist centre, but I was given time off to see you!' She seemed to be genuinely pleased to see me, and suggested we take a boat ride on a nearby lake.

The young girl who was beaming at me with her large and shiny blue eyes was even lovelier than her picture had led me to believe, and in some ways she seemed more mature than I expected. When she held me by my arm just like an old acquaintance and drew me away from the entrance, I had to muster up all my willpower not to embrace her. But good sense prevailed. However, it was quite obvious that we took an immediate liking to each other.

'Anneliese, tell me, of whom or of what do you think you need to convince me?' I asked her, whilst steering the boat out against the cool breeze. Giving voice to what was weighing on my chest, I launched into further questions.

'Didn't you write and tell me that you intended to demonstrate how awful life was in the west part of Germany? Tell me, have you been there recently? I must stress that I want to and will return to my beloved mountains. You are most welcome to visit me and see for yourself what life is like over there. But believe me, I spent a long time becoming acquainted with the kind of socialism they've drummed into you! The education I received in Siberia couldn't have been a better case in point, but I haven't lost my good sense, nor my views.'

Looking at me silently with oddly hazy eyes and what I took as some sadness, she whispered: 'Lothar, what I wrote to you was what they expected me to write.' She didn't make any further attempt to instil in me enthusiasm for a socialist lifestyle.

I, of course, had also done my homework back at the education centre where I learned that Lenin had managed to return to Russia from his Swiss exile with the help of the German government, who had organised a sealed train to take him back to the Tsarist empire during the First World War. Of course, the Germans jumped at the opportunity to get him back to his country and instigate the revolution.

When it came to Chemnitz, I agreed with Anneliese that capitalism does not always offer advantages, and that socialist principles might actually have some benefits of their own. When she suggested, however, that I remain with her in the DDR, I declined and shook my head emphatically. She seemed saddened more than disappointed, and some minutes later we bade each other farewell, promising to write to each other.

I was reminded that several years ago I too had mindlessly repeated the Nazi slogans about the humiliation suffered because of the Treaty of Versailles, and had accepted them unquestioningly. In good faith, trusting in Hitler, we had embarked on the war. How could I blame today's youth? It was only now after bitter experience that I had come to realise how utterly gullible young people are, and how easily they're convinced of some artificially constructed ideals that have been knocked into them.

I spent the night in simple accommodation in Chemnitz, but couldn't sleep properly and so moved to a modest hostel near the train station in Leipzig with a shared shower and toilet located in the corridor. It had only been my curiosity to see for myself how people were living in the Russian-occupied zone which had kept me from travelling home immediately, but seeing as I was here already, I wished to explore further. So I took the bus to the Völkerschlachtdenkmal the next day, as I simply had to see it.[*]

Having taken in as much of the monument as I wanted to, I finally felt ready to go home, indeed by now I was itching to return. Like many of my comrades, I had sent a telegram home the moment I arrived in Frankfurt an der Oder. For me, home

---

[*] The monument to the 1813 Battle of Leipzig, also known as the Battle of the Nations, in which Napoleon was heavily defeated.

was Garmisch, and the Maiers were my family. All I could hope for was that they'd be thrilled to get word from me and welcome me back.

Travelling towards Hof-Moschendorf, it was hard to overlook the devastation this dreadful war had visited upon our land. But what could I expect? The cease-fire and capitulation had only been declared four and a half years ago. 'Of course,' I had to admit to myself, 'the ruins left behind by the Allied bombers and our ground troops couldn't possibly have been removed in such a short time span. And the wounds afflicted on the civilian population couldn't possibly have healed. Scars will remain for many years to come.'

Preoccupied with these thoughts, I kept myself to myself and ignored my fellow passengers' barrage of questions and attempts to involve me in conversations that in fact only annoyed me, as they seemed meaningless and ignorant.

In the transit camp at Hof-Moschendorf, an elderly Red Cross worker pointed me and some others to the financial aid office. 'Boys, listen up! Even though you're entitled to free train tickets, the authorities didn't leave it at that. You must of course have a bit of cash on you, and so please accept this small token – just ninety marks – you've more than earned it!'

The good nurse received a prompt reaction. 'Sure, mummy dear! The promise of our Fatherland's gratitude will chase us like a shadow, always at our backs but never quite reaching us.' The rest of the response was thin laughter, which sounded more like scoffing.

Silently I joined the queue. Once I stood in front of the chubby cashier, I saw him peering at me over his glasses, remarking somewhat amused: 'Well son, you sure weren't in a hurry, seeing as you've just come here today. Where have you been lounging about?'

'I've visited some friends and had a look around in the DDR.'

My answer must have sounded somewhat curt, as the man continued in a placating tone: 'Certainly! None of my business.

I didn't mean to sound gruff. In any case, I wish you a pleasant trip home – you've been gone long enough!'

Glancing at the unfamiliar bank notes, I softly replied: 'Thank you. I didn't mean to sound gruff either.'

Once again, I boarded a train, this time heading south, towards the Werdenfelser Land. Even though along here, and above all in Nuremberg, Munich and other larger cities, I could still see heaps of rubble and the remains of war all around me, I got the impression that more had been cleaned up and restored in the West than in the DDR. Munich soon lay behind me, and I could make out the outline of the mountains.

I got up from my seat and with my heart thumping I looked out the window. It is hard to describe the emotions which overwhelmed me after all those years I had spent in captivity.

Finally, the white peaks of the Waxenstein, sparkling in the light of the late autumn sun, came into view, and those of Mutter Alpspitze seemed to wink down at me. I had to admit that when I painted them in the mud huts of the steppe, I hadn't really been able to capture their true beauty. I felt reborn.

Churned up and dazed, I left the Garmisch train and strolled down the Bahnhofstrasse as if in a dream. I gawked like a child at the window displays, which were heralding the forthcoming Christmas season, and marvelled at the already plentiful selection of goods available. I myself wished for nothing, having at long last been given the most precious gift of all: my freedom.

The Red Cross at Hof-Moschendorf had supplied me with what I thought was quite a luxurious winter coat, a new shirt and a set of underwear. I had taken off my fur-lined leather cap and preferred to carry it in my hand, as with the warm sun shining down on me, I felt too hot. It still felt like a dream when I approached the small family house that belonged to the Maiers.

Not taking any notice of the curious looks passers-by threw in my direction, I kept walking with the light powder snow crunching underneath my feet. The quiet surroundings calmed my nerves and I felt at peace.

When I knocked, Frau Maier opened the door and threw her arms around me, shouting with joy – like a mother. I was home at last.

CHAPTER 14

A Difficult Beginning

———•:•———

During that first evening back, Frau Maier, her daughter Kathi, Kathi's husband, and I chatted until the wee hours of the morning. The moment I had entered, Frau Maier wanted me to know that they had all been expecting me eagerly.

'Lothar, I've always kept your room free for when you'd come. We never had to rely on those few marks rent. Why I have no idea but I always firmly believed that you'd return home.'

'Mother,' added Kathi quickly, 'You weren't the only one so confident. All of us knew how tenacious our Lothar is. And here he stands before us – living proof.' Then, turning towards me, she said with a smile that confirmed my innermost hopes that the Maiers really were my family: 'Lothar! Your skis are up in our loft. They've been waiting for you, along with the suitcase containing your civilian clothes.'

That same evening, the three of them desperately wanted to find out everything that had befallen me. When they noticed, however, that I became deeply disturbed when I tried to get the words out, they didn't press me further and instead told me everything that they had lived through during the turbulent years, during which I had been 'missing'. They also handed me a letter one of my comrades, who had been released before me and had meanwhile settled in Thüringia, had mailed to them in Garmisch.

Pößneck, 3 May 1948

Dear Family Mayer! [sic]

I returned from Central Asia and Russian war imprisonment with a transport on 2 May and am pleased to inform you that I was imprisoned together with your dear Lothar.

Your dear Lothar asked me to send you many good wishes and embraces you. He is healthy, always in good spirits, and doesn't allow himself to be defeated.

I got to know Lothar in the summer of 1947 and we worked together as painters.

Lothar always supported me as the human being and good friend he was. May God grant him continued good health so that he may soon return.

Today, having spent four years in imprisonment, I am enjoying my birthday cake with my family.

Do not worry yourself too much about your dear Lothar, he'll also come home soon.

Dear Family Mayer, I wish you all the very best and good health.

Yours,
Samblowsky

'So he did remember your address!' I burst out loudly, deeply moved after reading his note.

'I'll write and let him know that I'm back home. The man has a curious past. Being an ethnic German he had to join the Wehrmacht and feared becoming a POW more than any of us. Along with many of his sort, he escaped to Sweden where he was interned. But would you believe it, the Swedes then handed him over to the Russians. And the Russians then sent him and his comrades to the Asian steppes.

'Because of my attempt to escape, I haven't told you about that yet, they carted me off to the same god-forsaken place. My crime was the escape. The crime of others might have been as petty as having "organised" Russian food items. We formed a curious lot, we did.'

Frau Maier brought me up to my room just as any mother would have done. I had always considered her as such. Before comfortably stretching out on my bed, which had been the stuff of so many of my dreams when I was far away, I could still hear her giving me motherly advice.

'Lothar, first thing tomorrow you'll go to the town hall, report back as an old citizen and register with the municipality as a new citizen. And by the way, your previous master often popped in and enquired after you. Maybe you can start off with him?'

The following day I was quite the sight at the town hall, which made me feel a bit uncomfortable. I received a payout of 50 Deutsche Marks and I never could find out whether that money came from the community, from the social welfare office, or from another charitable organisation. Other than that, I returned back home with another set of underwear and a shirt.

That same day the owner of the Wolf painting and decoration company warmly shook my hand to welcome me back.

'Of course you'll be working for me again, Lothar. I sure could do with somebody as hard-working and competent as you. I'm really upset that you didn't follow my advice and register as "exempt" at the time. But that's water under the bridge – they'd probably have come and got you anyway. Towards the end of the war I too became a soldier.'*

My aim was to sit for the master craftsman diploma as soon as possible and start up my own business. But I made sure to keep my plans close to my chest.

Back home, I was notified by the municipality that I had been summoned by an American lieutenant from the CIA to report to my previous barracks the following day. I was there on time, and when I knocked at the door, somewhat apprehensive though not exactly frightened, I kept wondering why I had been asked to go there.

'Come in!' I heard somebody shouting loudly in English.

---

* Over-age for standard military service, he was presumably conscripted into the Volkssturm.

Dressed in his elegant officer's uniform, the man rose from his desk and casually walked across to me. Offering to shake my hand, he never let go of my face, scrutinising me with x-ray eyes, and I wasn't quite sure what to think of him. Was the man intending to be friendly or was he just pretending?

'Well, hello there, Mister Herrmann! And why, might I ask, didn't you immediately continue your travels from Frankfurt/Oder to Moschendorf/Hof? What were you up to in the DDR? I'm aware that back in Russia you, along with some of your other friends, attended a re-education training course.'

'Ahem,' I thought, 'so that's where the wind is blowing from. They think I'm a communist agent. So it's the same story here in the west as it is in the east.'

'Two questions all at once!' I responded frankly, facing the officer: 'I'm happy to answer them for you. Firstly, I had received mail back where I was in camp and a picture of a very pretty young East German woman, whom I was hoping to meet upon my return. She actually wanted to convince me to remain in the Soviet-occupied zone with her. But nothing came of that, as you can see.

'Secondly, I am by nature a curious sort of a fellow and simply wanted to have a look around, seeing as circumstances had put me there in the first place. So I took myself to look at the Monument to the Battle of the Nations near Leipzig.

'Would that be all you wanted to know about me? I have been questioned more than I care to remember during these past few years – these were interrogations by the other side, it has to be said.'

He spent a few moments more checking me out from top to bottom, firmly fixing his penetrating steel-blue eyes on me and not saying a word. A look of questioning surprise rather than dislike appeared in his face. 'But why did you participate in that training?' he continued.

'Just because I was curious. I must admit that I learned a lot about Russian history. But you might not be able to imagine how much better it was for me to run with the pack. Surely you must be aware of how many of us kicked the bucket back there in the Russian collieries!'

'How long did you have to slave away?'

'No time at all. In the various camps I was interned in, I always managed to keep my head above water in my profession as a painter. You have no idea what hunger means and what an extra portion of soup can do for you. So what did I do? During my free time in between shifts I decorated Russian apartments and made them look more beautiful. I rarely received bread in return as that was worth pure gold – for the Russians as well!'

'Fine, that'll be enough. And how do you intend to make your livelihood back here? Are you being supported by the DDR for any reason?'

'What a stupid question,' I couldn't help blurting out, but fortunately noticed something of a smile crossing my questioner's face just before I was able to mumble 'I do apologise,' and quickly added by way of an explanation: 'Before I served in the RAD and after that the army, I worked here as an assistant to a master decorator. As of next week, I'll be working there again. But at some point, I want to set myself up with my own business. I will most certainly not die of hunger!' I couldn't quite tell whether my answers had satisfied the American, but, in the end, he shook my hand goodbye.

'OK, you can leave now.' He showed me the door.

At home, Frau Maier listened to my summary with interest and felt that it had gone well overall. 'Lothar, you're a lucky man to be able to start with Master Wolf again. From what I know of him, he is pretty selective when it comes to choosing his employees.'

'That's not news to me, it was always like that with him. Always pleased with my work, he was, yes. Looks like I've been his best assistant up to date.'

Everything seemed to be turning out in my favour, and I could hardly remember another time when I had been so happy. There was just one thing niggling at me: in order to attend the master craftsman classes in Munich, I needed money that I didn't have. Funding by government organisations specifically supporting former prisoners of war or other organisations didn't exist at the time, in the winter of 1949/50. So when the master then offered me a foreman's position in the renovation works of the Post Hotel in Walchensee, a commission his firm had just received, I jumped at the opportunity.

At the time, not a single one of us assistants owned a car, and even the firm didn't have its own company vehicle. Neither companies nor workshops were run as they are today, and provisions like expense accounts or severance pay weren't yet in place. We thus set off early on Monday mornings by the postbus, which took us to Walchensee and returned late Saturday afternoons to Garmisch; thus we were only able to spend the weekends in Garmisch.

Closely familiar with hard work, I used my winter evenings to study for the exams, sitting on my bed (under which I had tucked the paint pots for the job) and memorising the material till late at night, with only a single light bulb keeping me company. Though I kept to the deadlines of the decoration and refurbishment job at hand, I never wanted to lose sight of my goal. I had to do all I could to become knowledgeable in accounting, colour theory and materials science, and I doggedly pursued my studies.

I had put my name down to sit for the master craftsman exams in the autumn. They were held in Munich, would last a week and luckily, with the help of some friends, I had managed to secure a reasonably priced room. The practical part of the exams was followed by four days of theory exams comprising written and oral tests, and at long last, after a gruelling week, I was the proud owner of a master craftsman diploma. Fortune, it seemed, had seen fit to show me favour in my new life. A quick look at my meagre wallet wasn't exactly encouraging, but I decided that I had sufficient cash to buy a bottle of Danziger Goldwasser liqueur in order to celebrate in style with my dear ones at home.

The beginning of my new career had promised to start with a bang, but after only a few days I was to experience a heavy blow in the form of a hepatitis virus that condemned me to bed for a long time. I probably contracted this insidious bunkmate back in Siberia, and now hovered between life and death for several weeks. Thanks to the wonderful care of the good Dr Neureuther from the Partenkirch hospital, and thanks also to my unswerving determination to stay alive, but also not least thanks to my new love, a girl from Garmisch, I again escaped the scythe of the grim reaper. Recovery was, of course, largely due to me very strictly adhering to a prescribed diet, and renouncing alcohol from then on.

I continued to remain focused on doing everything I could to achieve my goal and set up my own business. The girl who was at my bedside throughout my illness, faithful and supportive, became my wife. After searching for a very long time, we found a flat with a working bathroom, a windowless kitchen, and two rooms on an upper floor that I set about turning into my workshop and stockroom.

I never stopped admiring my wife, who by the time we moved in was already expecting our child, and who, bless her, was intent on always looking at things on the bright side. 'Lothar, looks like we'll never have to say: easy come, easy go . . .' she said with a mischievous smile on her face.

I held her tight in my arms, laughing. 'Therese, if I didn't have you, I wouldn't know what to do. You give me even more strength now than the Waxenstein tried to time and again back in Russia.'

My first deed in our new home was to offer a good neighbour a return favour for kindly having improved my diet by giving us fresh milk and curd cheese. I popped round to her place with paint brush and paints and decorated her rooms. Whilst I didn't yet have a reputation in the neighbourhood as a master decorator, 2 May 1953 was finally the day I opened up shop. We didn't have our own phone in those days, so another neighbour gave me the message for my first, albeit modest, commission. I knew that my work for the woman farmer had made the rounds, and in my mind there was no better advertisement than word of mouth.

I was working entirely on my own during the first years of running my own business. Additionally, I had no capital, seeing as no business loans nor government funding were available for a '*Russland Heimkehrer*'* who had a history of ill health and no guarantors. I didn't give up, though, and tenaciously working hard, I managed to build up a home for me and my family on the banks of the Loisach River, which had everything that an independent master decorator would require for his loved ones and his business.

Somehow, my success didn't sit well with the tax authorities and made them suspicious, as one fine day a rather sceptical-looking official knocked on my door and asked to go through my accounts. Only after studying my papers, receipts and expenses in minute detail for a whole three days was he convinced that, yes, indeed, a man who works day and night, seven days a week, and doesn't take a holiday can accumulate, if not exactly great riches, at least a decent income without anybody's help, nor having to resort to illegal acts.

Despite my professional responsibilities, I always found the time to keep writing to Anneliese, as we had promised each other. Sadly, however, she eventually let it be known that her being in contact with a capitalist who lived in the West was frowned upon by her Free German Youth comrades, and that she even ran the risk of arousing the suspicions of the Stasi secret police. It would, she wrote, be preferable to end the correspondence.

On top of that, my letter to my old comrade from Russia, Fred Samblowsky in Pößneck, was returned to me unopened, mailed back by the local municipality who noted that he couldn't be located, not even through trawling the archives. It couldn't have been made much clearer to me than that: the ruling powers in East Germany did not want their citizens to have any contact with West Germans.

In the late fifties, we, like so many others, owned a rather clumsy black-and-white television set. Suspicion between the two

---

* *Russland Heimkehrer* – Russia returnee/homecomer.

world powers, Russia and USA, had grown from one year to the next, and the Cold War was about to reach its climax. I remember the night when my wife, my daughter and I were looking forward to watching a popular entertainment show, but before that had switched on the news report showing the launch of the Russian spacecraft, the first to carry a living animal, a dog. This followed the launch of Sputnik 1 and was the second triumph of the Russians, triggering the space race. To all intents and purposes it convinced everybody around the globe that Russian technology was in the lead.

When the cameras beamed not only to the launch site but also scanned its surroundings, it all of a sudden hit me like a bolt of lightning, and I screamed into the living room: 'Look everybody, that's the steppe where we worked as prisoners of war. What were we told at the time? They were looking to drill for water, is what they'd have us believe, and that they'd put in an artificial lake. Of course, I now realise who we built these comfortable houses for in such an inhospitable area. I bet you, over there in the USA, our compatriot Wernher von Braun and his team[*] have been treated precisely the same.'

Pushing me back down into my armchair, my wife tried to calm me down.

'Lothar! You're here with us at home, in your living room. Just take it easy. Don't let the past rob you of your sleep! Enjoy the present, together with us!'

'Yes, Therese, I'll do that. But the years I spent in Siberia, I'll never forget them as long as I live. I'll always have one or the other camp appear in my dreams, and the gloomy landscape of the steppe. The saying goes that time heals all wounds. I cannot agree. My memories of the war and being imprisoned will forever remain with me.'

---

[*] The Nazi rocket pioneer Wernher von Braun and some of his colleagues were taken to the USA after the war and became leading figures in the NASA space programme.